Dear Reader:

The book you are [ ] Martin's True Crime Library, the imprint *The New York Times* calls "the leader in true crime!" Each month, we offer you a fascinating account of the latest, most sensational crime that has captured the national attention. St. Martin's is the publisher of Tina Dirmann's VANISHED AT SEA, the story of a former child actor who posed as a yacht buyer in order to lure an older couple out to sea, then robbed them and threw them overboard to their deaths. John Glatt's riveting and horrifying SECRETS IN THE CELLAR shines a light on the man who shocked the world when it was revealed that he had kept his daughter locked in his hidden basement for 24 years. In the Edgar-nominated WRITTEN IN BLOOD, Diane Fanning looks at Michael Petersen, a Marine-turned-novelist found guilty of beating his wife to death and pushing her down the stairs of their home—only to reveal another similar death from his past. In the book you now hold, LOST AND FOUND, John Glatt takes a look at one of the most incredible cases of abduction to make national headlines in recent years.

St. Martin's True Crime Library gives you the stories behind the headlines. Our authors take you right to the scene of the crime and into the minds of the most notorious murderers to show you what really makes them tick. St. Martin's True Crime Library paperbacks are better than the most terrifying thriller, because it's all true! The next time you want a crackling good read, make sure it's got the St. Martin's True Crime Library logo on the spine—you'll be up all night!

Charles E. Spicer

Charles E. Spicer, Jr.
Executive Editor, St. Martin's True Crime Library

Lost and Found

JOHN GLATT

St. Martin's Paperbacks

LOST AND FOUND

Copyright © 2010 by John Glatt.

Cover photo of schoolgirl by Adam Crowley / Getty Images; photo of tent by Jamie Kripke / Getty Images.

All rights reserved.

For information address St. Martin's Press, 175 Fifth Avenue, New York, NY 10010.

EAN: 978-0-312-38827-0

Printed in the United States of America

St. Martin's Paperbacks edition / October 2010

St. Martin's Paperbacks are published by St. Martin's Press, 175 Fifth Avenue, New York, NY 10010.

10 9 8 7 6 5 4 3 2 1

For Audrey and Mavis Hirschberg

Acknowledgments

After Jaycee Lee Dugard's allegedly heartless kidnapper Phillip Garrido was unmasked as a twenty-first-century Charles Manson, many questioned how a human being could commit such unspeakable crimes. But Garrido's arrest came as no surprise to Katie Callaway Hall, who had been his first victim in 1976, when he had forcibly taken her across the California/Nevada border to rape her.

As a result, Garrido was sent to prison for half a century. But after only serving 11 years, he had cunningly managed to beat the system to be freed back into society.

Soon after getting out, he tracked Katie down to the casino where she was working and threatened her. Terrified, she warned his parole officer that it was only a matter of time before he struck again, but was told nothing could be done.

If only law enforcement had heeded Katie's desperate pleas, little Jaycee might have been spared her terrible eighteen-year ordeal.

Over the years, while Jaycee and her daughters Starlit and Angel lived in squalor hidden away in his backyard, the authorities missed many opportunities to catch the sexual predators and free their captives. And they would almost certainly still be there if the increasingly delusional Garrido had not virtually given himself up, seeking a world stage to preach his bizarre religious beliefs.

Perhaps the only precedent for this strange case is Austria's

Josef Fritzl, who imprisoned his own daughter Elizabeth for almost a quarter of a century, fathering her seven children. In 2008 I wrote a book about the case, *Secrets in the Cellar*, but in many ways the Jaycee Lee Dugard tragedy is even more disturbing and heartbreaking, as it should never have happened in the first place.

Lost and Found is the result of ten months of exhaustive research and countless interviews. In it I have attempted to explore what went wrong with the system, allowing such a dangerous sexual predator back on the streets to commit the outrageous crimes with which he has been charged.

In September 2009, I visited Antioch and spoke to many people with first-hand knowledge of Phillip and Nancy Garrido, some of whom wished to remain anonymous.

I would like to thank: Tim Allen, Deepal Karunaratne, Lorenzo Love, Christine Mecham, Maria Christenson, Murray Sexton and Tony Garcia of the Bridgehead Café, Lt. Jim Lardieri, Michael Cardoza, Phillip Sherlwell, retired detective Dan DeMaranville, Janice Dietrick, Janice Gomes, Marc Lister, Victor Acosta, Eddie Loebs, Tommy Wilson-O'Brien, Jim and Cheyvonne Molino, Wayne Thompson, Betty Upingco, Polly White and Carol Lloyd of the Washoe County Library System.

As always, I would also like to thank my editors at St. Martin's Paperbacks, Charles Spicer and Yaniv Soha, for their unstinting support and the superb job they always do.

Gratitude also to Gail, Jerome and Emily Freund, Debbie, Douglas and Taylor Baldwin, Trudy Gerstner, Henry Kaufman, Charlie Chen, Danny and Allie Tractenberg, Cari Pokrassa, Milda Koueder, Providence Juca, Alex Hitchens, Virginia Randall, Ena Bissell and Annette Witheridge.

Prologue

June 1991

Phillip and Nancy Garrido had spent months preparing. Behind the white picket fence that surrounded the middle-aged couple's three-bedroom cinder block home, less than an hour's drive from San Francisco, there was anticipation and excitement.

Always obsessive, Phillip had worked hard on his most ambitious project to date. He had divided the acre of land behind his house into two parts, creating a backyard within a backyard. At the front he had planted shrubbery, trees, and built an eight-foot fence to conceal the rear half from his neighbors. This he had transformed into a kind of concentration camp, installing an escape-proof shed.

The onetime rock musician had carefully soundproofed it with foam insulation, to muffle any sounds. Alongside it he'd constructed a primitive outhouse and shower, laying green high-voltage electricity cables all the way from his house for power.

It was in this shed that the Garridos would hold their captive. For they intended to kidnap a young girl to act as both their sex slave and the bearer of their children.

This wouldn't be the first time the six-foot, four-inch Phillip Garrido had snatched an innocent young girl off the streets to satisfy his uncontrollable appetite for sex. But fifteen years earlier, in Reno, Nevada, it had ended badly. High on LSD, he'd been raping and sodomizing his unfortunate victim for five hours when a policeman arrived at his mini-warehouse and caught him red-handed. Even hardened detectives were shocked by the extraordinary lengths he had taken to prepare that early version of his prison, equipping it with flashing stage lights, a bed, sex toys, explicit magazines and copious quantities of wine and drugs.

"It looked like a scene from a porno flick," recalled retired detective Dan DeMaranville. "He actually used a pair of scissors to shave off her pubic hair."

After federal and state trials, Garrido had been sentenced to fifty years to life in prison. But the master manipulator had managed to beat the system, getting out after only eleven years.

It was while caged inside the tough Leavenworth Federal Prison that he'd first met Nancy Bocanegra, a devout Jehovah's Witness there visiting her uncle. From his cell he had courted her with letters, and they eventually fell in love. In 1981 they were married in a jailhouse ceremony by a nondenominational pastor.

Several years later, the wily Garrido persuaded a parole board he had found God behind bars, and he was freed on parole. Heading west with his new wife to Antioch, California, they had moved into his mother's house. But when Nancy discovered she could not have children, Phillip persuaded her to help him kidnap a young girl to bear their children.

It was God's will, he explained, that they start a family.

One afternoon in early June 1991, the Garridos set off in their old gray two-door sedan, driving three hours east to South Lake Tahoe, California, where Phillip once lived. They were searching for a prepubescent female, who would be easier to handle than an older one. But just in case she put up a fight, they had brought a stun gun.

By the time they arrived at the picturesque ski resort 6,200 feet high in the Sierras, the schools were letting out for the day. Phillip drove through town until he spotted a pretty elementary school pupil getting off the school bus, and drew up behind her.

Amelia Edwards still remembers the sound of the tires pulling onto the dirt road behind her.

"[It] turned my stomach and sent chills down my spine," said Amelia, who was then eleven years old. "I remember walking faster, hearing the tires go faster. So I ran home."

But she did manage to get a good look at the battered old car and its occupants—an "Arab-looking woman" with dark hair and a man—before they drove off at high speed.

After returning to Antioch to regroup, the Garridos returned the following Sunday to hunt for new prey. It was late afternoon when they arrived in Meyers, California—five miles outside South Lake Tahoe.

Before long Phillip Garrido saw her for the first time, skipping along a street with a couple of school friends. He immediately knew he had to have her.

"She's perfect," he told his wife, Nancy.

Jaycee Lee Dugard was the sort of little girl Garrido had always lusted over. The blue-eyed, blonde-pigtailed child had the innocent smile of an angel and was just a month past her eleventh birthday.

The predators then followed as Jaycee went into an arts fair, getting out of the car and going inside to watch her from a distance. Then they followed her out of the fair, watching her wave goodbye to her friends and walk up Washoan Boulevard to her home and go inside.

They then drove off up the hill to wait until the next morning, when she would be alone and vulnerable.

Monday, June 10, was the beginning of the last week of the school year. It was a typical morning in Jaycee's household. Jaycee's mother Terry was running late, so she left for work in a hurry, without kissing her eldest daughter goodbye. It would haunt her for years.

Jaycee got ready for school. She showered and put on her favorite pink sweater and stretch pants, white blouse and white sneakers. Then after looking in on her baby sister Shayna, who was sleeping soundly, the fifth-grader checked the clock on the microwave oven, which read 8:05 A.M.

Jaycee's stepfather, Carl Probyn, was working in the garage when he saw her come out of the house. After saying goodbye he watched from his window as she walked out of the driveway, skipping up the steep pine-studded hill toward the school bus stop, three blocks away on Pioneer Trail.

It was a beautiful sunny morning without a cloud in the sky. There was just a dusting of snow on the dreamy Sierra mountains, rising above the town.

While he watched Jaycee go up the hill, Probyn was suddenly aware of a two-tone silver Ford, slowly driving by and making a U-turn below his driveway. Then it headed back up the winding hill toward Jaycee. As it passed by his house, Probyn got a good look at the female passenger—an olive-skinned woman with straight black hair. His initial thoughts were that they were probably lost and needed directions.

Then he watched as the car reached the top of the hill, drawing alongside Jaycee. Suddenly, it turned sharply and screeched to a halt to cut her off. He heard Jaycee scream, as the passenger door was flung open. Then to his horror, he saw the woman grab Jaycee and drag her into the car, which sped off up the hill, disappearing in a cloud of dust.

Part One

1

"THE BABY OF THE FAMILY"

Phillip Craig Garrido was born in Pittsburg, California, on April 5, 1951, to Manuel and Pat Garrido. His brother Ron was seven years older and the two brothers would never be close. The Garridos were a lower-middle-class family. Manuel worked as a forklift operator and Patricia as a secretary.

In the early 1950s, Pittsburg was a largely middle-class rural town, forty miles northeast of San Francisco. Originally known as Black Diamond for its rich coal deposits, the town lay on the busy State Route 4 highway, carrying commuters to Oakland and San Francisco.

"I had been raised in the country and lived in a very clean house," Phillip wrote in 1978. "I was the baby of the family and spoiled in the long run."

When Phillip was small, Manuel moved his family fifteen miles east on Route 4 to Brentwood. There they lived in a tiny house at the end of a dirt road, with Phillip sharing a room with Ron.

"Phillip and his brother Ron were good boys when growing up," said their mother Pat. "But I always wished I could have had a daughter."

Manuel Garrido was a strict father who often disciplined his youngest son, while his doting mother let him do whatever he wanted. Phillip was her favorite child and in her eyes he could do nothing wrong.

"I was more strict than his mother," explained Manuel in

2009. "She gave him everything. Anything he wanted growing up, he got."

Years later, Phillip told a psychiatrist that his parents had caused him "considerable emotional conflict" during his formative years.

Manuel Garrido remembered his younger son as a sweet, gentle, well-behaved child, who loved making people laugh.

"He was never any trouble," he said. "He was bright, intelligent and polite."

With his dark good looks and inscrutable smile, little Phillip Garrido could have been a choirboy. And from the very beginning he was a charmer, easily manipulating his parents and teachers to get exactly what he wanted.

He also had a natural sense of humor that the other kids liked.

"[He was] very popular with a lot of friends," said his father. "They loved his jokes."

By the time he entered Liberty High School at fourteen, his father had high hopes for his future.

"He was clever and good with his hands," Manuel remembered. "He could do complex electronics."

But he was a mediocre student, with little interest in his studies or school activities. Although he was now over six feet tall and athletic, Phillip disliked sports and did not belong to any school societies. But he loved rock music, spending hours in his bedroom, listening to his favorite British invasion bands, instead of doing his homework.

In 1967, San Francisco was ground zero of the Summer of Love, but according to his father, sixteen-year-old Phillip hated the flower children and what they represented.

"He'd see hippies with long hair," said Manuel, "and laugh at them."

But according to Manuel Garrido, everything changed when his son had a motorcycle accident, sustaining serious head injuries.

"They had to do surgery," Manuel recalled. "He would talk funny and do funny things. After that, he was a different boy. Entirely different. That's when he started to change."

Janice Gomes grew up near Brentwood and knew many of Phillip's Liberty High School friends.

"He got a very severe head injury," said Gomes. "And after that they say he wasn't really the same."

When he finally came out of hospital, Phillip grew his hair long, started smoking marijuana and taking LSD. He rarely attended classes and his grades plummeted.

Girls liked his new outlaw image, tall and devastatingly handsome with long flowing hair, and flocked to him.

He was now missing school, smoking grass every day and taking LSD at weekends, and to finance this he started dealing drugs.

"Then he got onto that LSD crap and he was gone," said his father. "It ruined his life. He stopped going to school. He fell in with a bad crowd of Mexicans. He went nuts."

After someone gave him an electric bass guitar, Phillip learned a few lines and formed a band, playing covers of Jefferson Airplane and Credence Clearwater Revival at local dances.

His 1968 junior year class photo had shown a clean-cut seventeen-year-old, his jet black hair smartly slicked back surfer-style. But the following year when Phillip Garrido graduated, there was no photograph for him in the Liberty High Yearbook.

In his last year at Liberty High, Phillip Garrido devoted himself to getting high and writing songs. He spoke about grandiose schemes to make millions of dollars, telling his father he could now talk to God.

"I thought he was weird, but not that weird," recalled his classmate Steve Lucchesi. "I'm not sure if he was high all the time or saw things differently. But something went haywire."

Phillip had converted an old shed at the bottom of his parents' garden into his private den and rehearsal space. He painted it black and soundproofed it with mattresses, covering the walls with psychedelic posters. No one else was allowed inside, and he would spend hours in there getting high, playing guitar and masturbating to his growing collection of pornographic magazines.

"He was a sex addict," explained his father. "He started going crazy. We tried to get him help, but what could a doctor do? The LSD had killed his brain."

Lois Freitas, whose son Bill was in Phillip's class, remembers him as an outsider who never participated in any school activities.

"He was a lone wolf," she recalled. "Not a lot of friends. A misfit. My niece knew him as well [and] said some of the girls were frightened of him."

It was rumored that Phillip Garrido enticed innocent young girls into his shed in his parents' garden with the promise of free drugs before taking advantage of them.

"He would drug girls and rape them," said Janice Gomes, "and then they couldn't really go home and tell their parents, because they were under the influence of drugs. They didn't tell their parents or the police, and to this day a lot of them don't want to discuss it."

Manuel Garrido now says his son was obsessed with deflowering young virgins, and made no secret of it.

"I lost count of the times my wife would tell me he brought another virgin back to the house," said his father. "It was dozens. It was kind of like a trophy."

Although Irene Thompson, who was in his English class, knew nothing of it, she still remembers the long-haired rebel well.

"He was sort of strange," she said. "I just thought he was eccentric, not evil."

But Carol Harris, who took the school bus with Phillip every day, says he made her uncomfortable.

"He gave me the creeps," she recalled. "The way he looked at me. I just got a really bad feeling about him. You know when the hairs on the back of your neck stand up for no reason."

So Harris always did her best to avoid him.

"I have a really good sense about people," she said. "And with him I sensed danger."

But not all Phillip Garrido's female classmates felt the same way. Christine Marie Perreira, a pretty brunette two years his junior, became his high school sweetheart. The pretty teen with a fashionable beehive hairdo faithfully followed him everywhere, although he treated her badly and would later beat her.

Soon after they started dating, Garrido was accused of raping a young girl. He talked his way out of trouble, insisting she was lying. And as it was just her word against his, it never went any further.

"He could talk you pretty much into anything," said Christine.

Phillip had little interest in graduating high school, but as his father wanted his son to go to college, he offered to buy him a new blue Oldsmobile to graduate.

"We had a hell of a time getting him to graduate," recalled his father. "He didn't want to go to school."

In 1969, Phillip Garrido graduated from Liberty High School with a diploma, finishing the twelfth grade with B's, C's and D's. But his mediocre grades hardly mattered, as he had set his sights on becoming a rich rock star.

A few months later, Phillip Garrido was arrested in Contra Costa County for possession of marijuana and LSD. He was sent to the minimum-security Clayton Farm Facility. After serving his time, he moved back in with his parents, got a succession of odd jobs and resumed dealing drugs.

He was now part of the Antioch music scene, playing pick-up bass guitar with local musicians, wherever he could find a gig. And he had also started channeling his sick sexual fantasies about young girls into the lyrics of his derivative songs, influenced by his progressive rock idols—Emerson Lake & Palmer, the Moody Blues and Yes.

Sex now dominated his life. Where once he had satisfied his urges by masturbating to pornographic movies and magazines in his parents' shed, he was now pleasuring himself in public.

Several years later, he would admit to masturbating in restaurants, amusement arcades and bars. He was also a Peeping Tom, peering through windows at women as they undressed.

He loved to get high and park his blue Oldsmobile outside schools, masturbating as he watched young girls as young as seven. Then he would open the car door and expose himself to them, with his pants down to his knees.

Later he would testify about his unusual practices at the local drive-in movie theater.

"I would take my automobile," he said, "and I would put up on the side windows two towels . . . to keep anybody from seeing me. And I would sit in the back seat [and masturbate]."

Garrido's taste in pornography was also getting harder, and *Playboy*, *Penthouse* and *Oui* magazines no longer satisfied him.

"Well, I always looked at women that are naked," he explained, "but there has been a type of bondage picture. Women in handcuffs, chained. There is [a certain] position that the women are in the magazines."

Garrido now took large doses of LSD and masturbated for hours, believing the hallucinogenic drug increased his sexual pleasure by quantum leaps.

"I just increased it into a realm," he explained, "that I didn't even realize."

On May 28, 1970, nineteen-year-old Phillip Garrido had his second run-in with the law, being arrested for marijuana and put on probation. Eight months later his parents divorced, with his mother Pat moving out of the family house.

"We separated in 1971," said Manuel Garrido. "And I haven't talked to her since. I had nothing to do with her. Then [Phillip] left home at nineteen."

According to his brother Ron, Phillip fled town in a big hurry, after discovering local drug dealers had taken out a contract on his life.

2

INSANITY

One step in front of the drug dealers, Phillip Garrido headed to South Lake Tahoe. His high school sweetheart Chris Perreira soon followed and they married, moving into a small house together in the sleepy ski resort town.

To pay the rent, Chris found a job as a blackjack dealer in Harrah's Casino in downtown Reno, while Phillip devoted himself to music and getting high. Without complaining, she bankrolled his increasingly lavish lifestyle.

"I was in love with him," she later explained.

With one of her first wage checks, Chris bought him a gleaming new Rickenbacker bass guitar, like the one his hero Chris Squire of Yes played. She also bought him an expensive PA system and a vintage set of Marshall stack amplifiers.

And with his long dark flowing hair and mustache, sharp cowboy shirts, white fedora and cowboy boots, Phillip Garrido looked every inch a rock 'n' roll star.

He immediately began playing at local bars, soon becoming part of the lively local music scene. And his charm, enthusiasm and easy humor won him acceptance by the other musicians.

Guitarist Eddie Loebs first met Phillip Garrido when he was sixteen years old, after they were introduced by a mutual friend.

"He was a lot of fun to be around," remembered Loebs. "He

sang, played bass, wrote songs and seemed like a pretty nice guy."

The two musicians started playing together, and Garrido talked for hours about his musical heroes—the Moody Blues, Pink Floyd and Lynyrd Skynyrd. He often whistled his favorite song of the time—Emerson Lake & Palmer's big hit, "Lucky Man"—saying the lyrics could have been about him.

Soon Eddie Loebs's brother Steve joined the as yet un-named band on drums, and they played their first gigs with a revolving door of other musicians.

"Early on we played in a Mexican restaurant called El Pavo that had a stage," Eddie recalled. "But mostly it was parties."

Phillip Garrido drove a green Monte Carlo sports car through South Lake Tahoe, as well as a white Ford van, which he used to roadie the band's equipment to gigs.

Before going on stage, the band members would get stoned, and Garrido always had large quantities of marijuana and other drugs available.

"He smoked pot a lot," said Loebs, "but then he started getting cocaine and stuff like that."

At the beginning, they mainly went on stage and just jammed, playing covers of the Allman Brothers Band and Chuck Berry.

Over the first few months they worked hard to become more professional and find their own sound, rehearsing every day at the back of Eddie Loebs's father's plumbing shop. They would run through their new set of songs, and Phillip Garrido's pre-tentious singing style was a constant source of amusement.

"He sang like some kind of opera singer," recalled Eddie Loebs. "I never liked his voice and we always made fun of it. Imitated him and stuff like that."

One day Garrido turned up at rehearsal with several new songs he had written, which he wanted to add to the set.

"He wrote a song called 'Insanity,'" said Loebs, "in which he sang, 'Yes, I know that I'm going insane.' And then he screams, 'Insanity! Insanity! Insanity!' and then a guitar solo. I think there were two or three other ones, including one called 'Gipsy Lady.'"

"Insanity" eventually became the climax of the band's set, with Garrido yelling, "I'm going insane," over and over again into the microphone.

But the sheer intensity of his performance scared some of his fellow band members, who thought he was taking it a little too seriously.

When Eddie Loebs first met Chris Garrido, he was amazed at her total subservience to him.

"She was kind of quiet," he remembered, "and you knew that there was controlling going on. She was under his thumb."

Years later, Chris would describe how her marriage had soon turned into a nightmare.

"He started hitting me," she said. "He smacked me, he told me to grow up."

And she claimed that Phillip wanted her to participate in his sexually deviant lifestyle, and flew into a rage when she refused.

"Multiple partners is what he wanted," she explained. "I wouldn't go for that."

Eddie Loebs says Garrido was so obsessed with young girls that the other band members nicknamed him "Filthy Phil."

"Phil was a big womanizer," he recalled. "He wasn't a bad-looking guy and women liked him. But when a good-looking girl walked by, Phil would almost salivate, saying things like 'Wow, look at that! Oh man, I'd love to jump on her.'"

The bassist also freely indulged in the South Lake Tahoe groupie scene, picking up young girls in the audience and bringing them home for sex. Then he would order Christine to move next door into the spare room, so he could have sex in their bed.

"Nothing slowed him down," said Loebs. "His wife just had to put up with it. I didn't like that because I liked Chris, but she's quiet and never complained."

In April 1972, Phillip Garrido drove to Antioch to celebrate his twenty-first birthday. A month earlier he had been put on probation, after yet another arrest for drugs. Garrido and a friend had arranged to meet a girl at the West 18th Street library to get high together. And she had then invited a fourteen-year-old girlfriend to join them.

It was late afternoon when Phillip Garrido and his friend pulled up outside the library to meet the girls. Although the men were far older than they had expected, the two girls got into the backseat of the car.

As they drove around Antioch, Garrido gave the girls barbiturates, a popular recreational sedative at that time. At one point the police began chasing their car, but Garrido sped away, managing to lose them.

Eventually they all ended up at the seedy twenty-three-room Riverview Motel on East 18th Street, on the edge of the town. Garrido and the fourteen-year-old then checked into a room, where he gave her more barbiturates until she passed out.

The next thing she remembered—she later told police—was waking up sometime the next day, in bed with Phillip Garrido.

"She remembers being repeatedly raped," said Lieutenant Leonard Orman of the Antioch Police Department. "Sexually assaulted, by him."

Later that day, the girl's worried parents tracked her down to the motel and found her in bed with Garrido. They then called the police.

Phillip Garrido was arrested and charged with rape, contributing to the delinquency of a minor, and providing dangerous drugs to a minor. The Contra Costa District Attorney's Office believed it had a solid case against him.

But at the preliminary hearing, the traumatized girl suddenly refused to testify against him. Later it would emerge that Phillip Garrido's defense attorney had threatened to portray her as a "slut" and a "whore" if she took the stand against his client.

So the Antioch Police Department had no alternative but to dismiss the case for "furtherance of justice," letting him go free.

When Eddie Loebs learned his bassist had been arrested for raping a fourteen-year-old girl, he asked him about it. Garrido said he was completely innocent, and police had dropped the charges as the sex had been consensual.

"He was pretty much saying he didn't do it," said Loebs. "I believed his side of the story."

In summer 1972, the band recruited an aging hippie keyboard player and a new female singer. But when they turned up for their first gig at the El Pavo restaurant, their bassist decided she was too ugly to play with him.

"She sang real good but she was a little bit plump," remembered Loebs. "Phil didn't like that she wasn't good-looking."

So after Garrido told her she was fat and should loose some weight, the singer quit the band in disgust.

A few weeks later, Eddie Loebs and his girlfriend went to Phillip Garrido's house to collect some equipment. But when they arrived they were disgusted to see Garrido had attached a rubber pipe to his van's exhaust. It then led straight into a box with a litter of puppies his dog had just given birth to.

"They were newborn puppies," recalled Loebs, "and he's killing them by exhaust fumes. We asked him what he was doing and he said, 'I've got to get rid of these dogs.'"

3

ROCK CREEK

In early 1974, the band recruited a new drummer after Steve Loebs abruptly quit. Tommy Wilson-O'Brien, who was twenty-eight and lived in Los Angeles, was in South Lake Tahoe for a weekend of skiing when he went to a local club to hear some music.

"Phil came over," remembered Wilson-O'Brien. "He said he had this band he was putting together, and some gigs lined up. I wasn't playing with anybody at the time, so it was kind of a no-brainer."

Two weeks later, Wilson-O'Brien packed his stuff and relocated to South Lake Tahoe, moving in with Phillip and Chris Garrido until he could find his own place.

"I lived in his house," said Wilson-O'Brien. "But it got so crazy very quickly."

Wilson-O'Brien soon became curious about the huge amounts of the best quality cocaine, marijuana and LSD Garrido always seemed to have, although he never appeared to work.

"There were times he'd pull out a bag of cocaine that looked like a sack of feed," said Wilson-O'Brien. "And back in the seventies cocaine was very expensive. It was like a hundred dollars a gram."

When the drummer asked him how he could afford so many high quality drugs, Garrido claimed his wife had some kind of scam at the casino, without providing any evidence to support this.

"Phil implied she was embezzling it," said Wilson-O'Brien. "But I never knew if he was just blowing smoke or what the deal was. But he always had money to buy drugs and the newest musical equipment. I never knew him not to have any money."

Soon after he started rehearsing at Eddie Loebs' father's shop, Wilson-O'Brien named the band "Rock Creek." And the three-piece band started playing the local clubs and ski areas around Lake Tahoe, becoming the house band for the popular Kirkwood Ski Resort.

Although they still reluctantly played Garrido's "Insanity" song, the band now concentrated on developing a more progressive rock approach to their music. And Garrido became angry when the other members started vetoing his new songs.

"Phil was always putting together songs," recalled Wilson-O'Brien, "but we didn't do many of them."

Over the brief time he lived at the Garrido house, Wilson-O'Brien got to know Phillip, finding that all the cocaine he was now taking often made him impossible to deal with.

"He was always kind of manic and really high energy," explained the drummer. "He looked like he had ADD, because he was all over the map. It was hard to keep him focused on one thing. You'd be talking about something and within five minutes you'd have five different subjects going.

"You never knew what the hell was going to happen. One night at about eleven or twelve o'clock, I was in my room sleeping and he came busting into the room with a whole pile of drugs and a bunch of beer and whisky and stuff. 'Get up! Get up! It's time to party!' So naturally I got up."

Another night, Wilson-O'Brien came home to find thirty hard-core pornographic magazines carefully laid out on the living room floor. They were all open to different pages and Garrido insisted on critiquing each one, explaining like a connoisseur how each particular pose aroused him.

"He was heavily into porno," said Wilson-O'Brien. "All

kinds of porno magazines. He had a projector and a bunch of other shit."

On one occasion he arrived home to find the front door locked, and no way to get in. Phillip was obviously inside as the lights were on, but the drummer left, not wanting any part of his friend's "kinky" activities.

For Phillip Garrido had made no secret of his obsessive craving for very young girls.

"He always had a thing for young chicks," said Wilson-O'Brien, "Some of the ones that I knew he was running after were borderline. I never [paid] attention to their exact age, but he would tell me these stories about young girls."

He also wondered about Phillip's somewhat unusual relationship with his wife Chris, who acted more like his servant.

"Except for the fact that she wasn't turning tricks," he said, "their relationship was like a hooker and a pimp. He was very controlling. He always had things for her to do and she did [them] very willingly."

One night, according to Wilson-O'Brien, Phillip invited him to join him and Chris in a threesome. But he declined the offer, saying he did not feel well.

Although Phillip Garrido spent most of his time under the influence of one drug or another, on the rare occasions he was sober he could be perfectly rational.

"Early in the morning before he was all coked up," said Wilson-O'Brien, "and we were just sitting around having coffee and waking up, he was a pretty level-headed, really nice guy."

Tommy Wilson-O'Brien also walked into the front room on several occasions, finding Phillip Garrido studying the Bible.

"He started reading Bible scriptures to me," recalled Wilson-O'Brien. "He goes, 'I got into reading the Bible. This is a great book.' I was just like, 'Whatever, fella.'"

One time, Garrido began telling him about a black box he had invented, allowing him to hear people's thoughts.

"I kind of blew him off like he was either joking or in a

cocaine psychosis," said Wilson-O'Brien. "He referred to it as his box where he could put his thoughts in it, and people would be able to hear them coming out the other end."

After a month living with Phillip Garrido, Wilson-O'Brien decided he had to "get the hell out of there," moving in with Eddie Loebs and his girlfriend.

By the summer of 1974, Rock Creek was one of the most popular bands in the Lake Tahoe area. They were practicing hard and improving rapidly, and for a short time even Phillip Garrido seemed focused on the music.

"We were getting more and more serious, and starting to push harder," recalled guitarist Eddie Loebs. "We played a lot, and we were getting better and better and getting gigs."

And Garrido always kept the band supplied with *the* best drugs and *the* best musical equipment.

"We had good equipment," remembered Tommy Wilson-O'Brien. "He had a couple of really nice Rickenbacker basses . . . and they were pretty pricey. And we also used Marshall amplifiers."

Phillip Garrido was now acting like a rock star, cruising around South Lake Tahoe in his sleek two-door green Monte Carlo.

"He fancied himself as a rock star," recalled Wilson-O'Brien. "And he looked the part. He was very tall and had pretty long hair down past his shoulders."

And the Rock Creek bassist usually had an entourage of very young girls, which he started bringing to rehearsals. One night, after arriving with two girls who looked like they were still in high school, his two bandmates asked him to stop.

"Eddie and I thought it was very disrupting for rehearsal," explained the drummer, "to have him bring these young girls over the house. He's just trying to show off. 'Come on over and watch the band.' He was a total egomaniac."

Garrido was now taking a lot of LSD, disappearing for two or three days at a time into his house and refusing to answer the door.

"Sometimes him and Chris would lock themselves in their house," recalled Wilson-O'Brien, who once dropped acid with them. "And I'd know he'd be in there and he wouldn't answer the door."

According to Wilson-O'Brien, Garrido often boasted how his wife brought him girls home from her casino.

"Chris was like a puppet," said Wilson-O'Brien. "She would be doing something and if he said, 'Go here and get this!' she would snap to it—boom, boom, boom. In fact Eddie and I used to talk about it—she's like a freaking puppet."

Years later, Chris would reveal her nightmarish married life, and her attempts to get away from his clutches.

"I was always looking for a way to . . . get away," she told *Inside Edition* in 2009. "He'd always told me he'd find me wherever."

On one occasion Phillip Garrido flew into a violent rage when he thought another man was flirting with her.

"He took a safety pin and went after my eyes," she said. "He left a scar on my face. He tried to gouge my eyes out with it."

When she ran away soon afterward, Garrido tracked her down.

"He pulled up in front of me and we got in an argument," she remembered, "and he grabbed me and threw me in the car. He's a monster."

Phillip Garrido's sexual fantasies were now becoming increasingly violent. His latest one was to kidnap a young girl and turn her into a sex slave. He dreamed of being a Roman emperor like Caligula, with unlimited sexual powers over his beautiful slaves.

And he started driving around South Lake Tahoe, looking for beautiful girls to kidnap and rape, to fulfill his fantasy. One year later, he would admit to abducting a girl from the Bay Area and another from around Las Vegas, proudly boasting that he had never hurt either of them.

By 1975, Phillip Garrido was veering out of control, powered by huge amounts of cocaine and any other drugs he could lay his hands on. And over the next few months, his two band-mates became increasing concerned about his sanity.

"He got weirder and weirder," explained Eddie Loebs. "More and more into pornography and womanizing, putting less energy towards the music."

Then their troubled bassist stopped turning up for paying gigs.

"He got really unreliable," said Tommy Wilson-O'Brien. "One time I hunted him down for two days, because I was going to kick his ass."

Garrido would now disappear for weeks at a time, suddenly reappearing as if nothing had happened.

"He'd say, 'Oh, I'm really sorry, guys,'" said Wilson-O'Brien, "'I'm not doing drugs right now. Blah, blah, blah. Let's play some music.' And we'd go, 'Okay.'"

But the final straw came in late 1975, when he missed an important Saturday night show at the Squaw Valley Ski Resort.

"We were all set ready to play," recalled Loebs, "and there's a house full of people ready to party and drink and dance. We set his equipment up and he doesn't show."

It was a disaster and they were forced to play the set as a guitar and drums duo. Afterward they went round to Garrido's house, demanding an explanation.

"We were really pissed off," said Loebs. "We pounded on his door, but he wouldn't answer it. So we threw him out of the band."

After being kicked out of Rock Creek, Phillip Garrido went solo, buying himself a smoke machine and lighting equipment. He attached a fuzzbox to his bass and started playing his own songs at maximum volume.

Eddie Loebs saw his new solo act in a small bar in South Lake Tahoe.

"It was lame," he remembered. "Probably not too many people would hire him with an act like that."

A few days later, an excited Phillip Garrido turned up at Eddie Loebs's apartment with a movie projector. He then started to screen *Deep Throat*, Linda Lovelace's infamous porn movie, for Loebs and his new fiancé.

"It had just come out," said Loebs. "He was turning into a pervert and was really turned on by it."

After watching the first half-hour of the movie, Loebs and his fiancé asked him to leave.

Over the next few months, Phillip Garrido's behavior became even more disturbing. One day Tommy Wilson-O'Brien arrived home to find his bedroom door ajar. And when he walked in it was obvious somebody had been inside.

"I'd been burglarized," he recalled. "Except there was a twenty-dollar bill I had left on my dresser that was still there."

He then noticed that a little metal can, where he kept his marijuana stash, had been moved from the dresser to his bed. Although it was open, the bag of weed remained untouched. Then he realized his treasured collection of 35 millimeter slides were missing.

"I had boxes and boxes of slides and they were all gone," he said. "Just a bunch of personal pictures of all the other rock 'n' roll bands I had played with earlier in the sixties."

When he asked neighbors if they had seen anything suspicious, one mentioned a green Monte Carlo car parked outside his house.

"That's what Phil was driving at the time," said Wilson-O'Brien. "I went over to his house and I was livid."

When he confronted him, Garrido readily admitted going to the house, saying he'd knocked on the door but no one was home. But he vehemently denied taking the slides.

"But I know he did it," said Wilson-O'Brien. "I just thought he was doing it to hurt me. That's so perverted, to look through somebody's pictures and take them. And that's when I wrote him out of my life."

4

RENO

In early 1976, Phillip and Chris Garrido moved to Reno, Nevada, sixty-two miles north of South Lake Tahoe. They took out a lease on a house at 1855 Market Street, and Chris found a dealer job at Harrah's casino.

Soon after arriving, Phillip rented out a mini-warehouse at 3245 Mill Street, a few blocks away from their new home. He told the owner he was a musician and needed Unit 39, a small ten-foot-by-ten-foot space, to rehearse his music.

But he had a far more sinister purpose in mind. Over the next few months he would transform it into his den of pornographic pleasure, in readiness for the sex slave he had now decided to kidnap and imprison.

Garrido started spending most of his time at the warehouse, buying alcohol at Shep's Discount Liquor on South Wells Avenue. And he soon became friends with the store owner's son Gregory Sheppard, also an aspiring musician.

"We played a lot together," recalled Sheppard. "I would see him about once every two weeks."

Sheppard later testified that he witnessed Garrido taking various drugs, including LSD, cocaine, pot, uppers and downers. He would often take two or three doses of strong blotter-type LSD at a time.

"It just depended on what mood he was in," explained Sheppard.

Garrido also befriended William Emery, a twenty-five-year-old taxi driver, who lived two doors down in Unit 36.

"He seemed open and friendly at first," Emery later told Reno police. "He was a good natural musician doing only his original music."

Initially, Emery was much impressed by the "oily long-haired musician," who was now "hard at work" getting a new band together to make it in the music business. They often hung out together that summer, smoking dope and sniffing cocaine.

"He was most usually stoned or in the process of being that way," said Emery. "When he was stoned he was more involved and extreme in everything he did."

Emery bonded with Garrido, as they discussed philosophy, religion and the "ultimate truth."

One day, Garrido asked his new friend to keep an eye on all his valuable musical equipment, as he was living there full time. He gave the taxi driver a list of vehicles allowed to park in front of his shed, with a phone number to call if necessary.

In June 1976, Phillip Garrido drove to South Lake Tahoe and kidnapped a nineteen-year-old girl. According to El Dorado Superior Court papers, Garrido sweet-talked his victim into his car before handcuffing and brutally raping her. Somehow she managed to escape and apparently never pressed charges.

Three months later, Eddie Loebs visited Reno to buy a new guitar, and his old Rock Creek bandmate invited him to a party in a local hotel room. Loebs walked in to find Garrido had unscrewed the mirror from the back of the door and placed it on the dresser. On it were several carefully laid out three-foot lines of cocaine, leading to a huge rock.

"He goes, 'Help yourself,'" recalled Loebs. "I think the pile was as big as my hand. And it was really good stuff. It was really strong."

After snorting a huge line, Garrido produced a stack of pornographic magazines, spreading them out over the floor.

"He was flipping through them with a sick-sounding giggle,"

recalled Loebs. "He was saying, 'OK, look at this, Eddie.' And showing me these chicks saying, 'Isn't that amazing?' "

Loebs was so "sickened" by Phillip Garrido's behavior that he never saw him again.

"He's a sick guy," said Loebs. "His sexual demons had taken over."

Phillip Garrido had started organizing blue movie stag shows and hard-core orgies in his new warehouse retreat. He had equipped it with a large mattress with gaudy red bedding, several heavy rugs and other furnishings. And there was also a movie projector, colored lights and handcuffs, as well as restraints and various sexual devices.

One day, he invited William Emery over to see some "dirty films." Emery agreed and as Garrido set up his movie projector, he explained how he bought his blue movies through a mail-order catalogue. Also there was a young man, whom Garrido introduced as a lighting director, explaining he was eager to see pornography for the first time.

Then Garrido turned down the lights, projecting a hardcore lesbian movie on his warehouse wall.

"He became very excited," remembered Emery, "and started making verbal statements [about] their practices."

Garrido gave a running commentary on the action, becoming particularly excited when lesbians used "large synthetic dildos and vibrators" on each other.

"It was of extreme nature," Emery later told police, "manual, oral and anal action."

After the film, Garrido invited Emery to "one of their parties" in his warehouse. He promised that there would be many beautiful women, supplied by his wife Chris from Harrah's Casino where she worked.

"He said his wife fully accepted the idea," Emery later told detectives, "and kept him in a constant supply of companions."

When Garrido began explaining how it all worked, Emery told him he did not want to know, as it was not "his trip." Eventually Emery did agree to go to one of his warehouse sex parties, arriving to find three "attractive women," as well as a "young negro boy."

An enthusiastic Garrido told his neighbor he was in a for a treat, and to be prepared for some "extreme" sex. Then the party started, with Garrido getting everyone high.

"There was the usual paraphernalia," explained Emery. "Strong pot, chemically treated pot, PCP crystals and wine with LSD in it." The women began drinking the LSD-laced wine and everyone was smoking the "heavily saturated pot."

Then a beautiful woman arrived, and Garrido made a big fuss over her.

"She's a lady's lady," he announced, "for all of you who understand."

Not knowing quite how to respond to that statement, Emery remained silent. And then a few minutes later, with the party in full swing, he quietly slipped out.

It would be some weeks before he saw his neighbor again, who appeared angry he had left early.

"He seemed more distant then ever," said Emery, "and was standoffish. I feel that this is because I failed to acknowledge his statement about the woman and . . . didn't go to the extremes that they did."

During the few months he knew Phillip Garrido, Emery watched him become stranger and stranger. And after the orgy, he did his best to avoid him.

"Right in front of my eyes," said Emery, "he seemed to be changing. More extreme in everything he was doing."

In their last ever conversation, Garrido tried to persuade him and a group of other musicians to play a gig in a brothel. They thought it a bad idea and refused. But Garrido refused to take no for an answer, asking them to imagine all the fun they could have with the prostitutes.

"They said they couldn't play their music in a whorehouse," said Emery.

By mid-November, Phillip Garrido had finished preparing Unit 39 for his long-awaited sex slave. He had stacked the front of the small storage area high with boxes of china and other items. Directly behind he had hung three heavy rugs from the ceiling, about a foot apart one behind the other, effectively soundproofing the warehouse. At the end of each was an opening for access, creating an overall maze effect.

The final rug then opened out onto his inner sanctum, resembling a stage with gray, blue and gold carpets hanging on each of the three walls.

Inside was a large dirty mattress, covered by an old ripped red satin sheet and a dirty imitation fur blanket. On a table nearby lay handcuffs, dildos, Vaseline, a large pair of scissors and several bottles of wine. A stack of pornographic magazines were piled against a wall.

In one corner was a movie projector and he'd hooked up multicolored stage lights. Like the director of an elaborate theatrical production, Phillip Garrido had spent weeks painstakingly setting up his warehouse. He'd written the script in his head, and now all that was needed was his leading lady.

5

"ALL I WANT IS A PIECE OF ASS"

On Monday afternoon, November 22, Phillip Garrido drove to South Lake Tahoe, California, to kidnap a young woman and realize his long-anticipated sexual fantasy. It was the week of Thanksgiving and there was heavy snow on the ground.

Dusk had just fallen and it was below zero when the predator entered a supermarket, searching for a young woman to snatch. He was now running on pure adrenaline, nervously stroking a pair of silver handcuffs in his trouser pocket.

Anxious not to scare off possible victims, Garrido had adopted a collegiate look. His long brown hair was tied into a neat ponytail and he wore a blue denim suit, a fashionable brown turtleneck sweater and engraved brown cowboy boots.

Before long he spotted an attractive woman shopping. After she paid the cashier, he followed her out into the parking lot, waiting as she got into her car, and started the engine. Then he walked over, tapped on the window and asked for a ride, explaining his battery had frozen and his car would not start.

She took pity on the well-dressed young man, unlocking the front passenger door for him to get in. After politely thanking her, Garrido asked to be taken to a street nearby. But a few minutes later when they arrived, he suddenly grabbed her, slipping a handcuff around one of her wrists and locking it.

Terrified, she slammed on the brakes and hit the horn as she jumped out of the still-moving car. Then with Garrido still in the passenger seat, gripping the other end of the handcuffs, she ran alongside her car still tethered to him.

"Let me go! Let me go!" she yelled. "I won't tell anyone."

Finally, after making her promise not to go to the police, he unlocked the handcuffs and freed her. But amazingly, he tried to entice her back in her car. When she refused he jumped out, running away into the freezing dark night.

A few blocks away, beautiful casino blackjack dealer Katie Callaway was preparing for a romantic night with her boyfriend, David Wade. The twenty-five-year-old blonde with a then fashionable Farrah Fawcett haircut had spent the afternoon preparing a crock pot dinner to take over to his house in nearby Stateline, California.

At 6:45 P.M. Wade called, asking her to pick up some coffee, oil and rice on her drive over. The young mother of a seven-year-old boy then took a shower, dressing in a green and blue ski jacket, with a striped hooded T-shirt and Britannia Levi jeans.

At 7:15 P.M., she left her house and five minutes later was parking her blue Ford Pinto in front of Ink's Al Tahoe Market, on the corner of Talac and Highway 50. As she was running late, she dashed inside to get the items she needed. It was then, out of the corner of her eye, that she first noticed a tall, well-dressed man with a ponytail standing in an aisle. But she paid little attention to him.

After paying for the groceries, Katie walked out to her car and started the engine. She was about to back out of the parking space, when she heard a light tap on her window.

"I rolled down the window," she would later testify, "and a young man was standing there. He said, 'Excuse me, I didn't mean to frighten you, but which way are you going?'"

Katie replied that she was going toward Stateline and the tall, slim man with a ponytail and oddly spaced teeth politely asked for a ride. He pointed at the Mercedes-Benz convertible parked down the street, joking it did not like the cold and refused to start. Could he possibly get a lift to his friends, he asked, so they could come back and help him to start it.

Katie said he could, as long as he would hold the plastic containers containing the hot meal she had prepared, occupying the passenger's side floor and front seat.

"Okay," he said, as he got into her car and sat down, loading the containers onto his lap.

She then asked where he was going.

"A little ways," he replied, as he pointed down Highway 50 toward Stateline.

They sat in silence, before the stranger asked if she lived and worked in South Lake Tahoe and skied. Katie had no interest in making small talk, so she just replied yes or no to all his questions.

A few minutes later, she took a right into Ski Run Boulevard, informing him that her turn to Stateside was coming up soon. The man nodded, replying that that they were almost there. She asked what exact street he wanted. He said he could not remember the name but would know it by sight.

Katie turned left on Willow Avenue until she reached Birch Street, saying this was where she turned off for her boyfriend's house. That was fine, said the man, pointing to the Slalom Inn Motel neon sign a couple of blocks ahead.

When they got to the motel, Katie asked where he wanted to be dropped off. The man then pointed toward the end of the street at a set of duplexes with a yellow porch light on. The house he needed was on the other side of them, he said.

"As I pulled in," she later remembered, "there was no house. There was an empty lot, and I looked at him to say, 'Are you sure this is the place?'"

The man then casually took the salad off his lap and placed it on the back seat. Then without warning he suddenly lunged at her, grabbing the ignition key and throwing it on the ground.

"I thought he was going to try and kiss me," she said. "Then he got me and just started grabbing."

He seized her hands, smashing her head down hard into the steering wheel.

"All I want is a piece of ass!" he declared. "If you do everything I say, you won't get hurt. I'm dead serious. I'll hurt you if you make me."

Katie tried to raise her head, but he forced it down below the dashboard. Terrified, she asked what he wanted, saying she would do anything.

His only reply was to produce handcuffs from his pocket, tightly cuffing her hands behind her back.

"Okay," he told her, "we're going to go for a little ride. Now we're going to change places."

Then he stood up, easily lifting the 105-pound woman across into the passenger's seat. He then maneuvered himself into the driver's side, forcing her head down hard into the seat.

"All right," he told her. "I am going to strap your head down . . . until we get out of town."

He then pulled a leather strap out of his long hair, placing it around her neck and under her knees, forcing her face down below the dashboard to conceal her from view. Then he threw a coat over her head and drove off.

Petrified, Katie asked where he was taking her.

"Somewhere far away," he replied calmly. "Don't worry, I've got it all planned."

Phillip Garrido adjusted the driver's seat and mirrors before heading north on Ski Run Boulevard. So far everything was going to plan, and he would have her inside his Reno warehouse in a couple of hours.

Trembling beneath the coat on the passenger-side floor, Katie Callaway could smell the beer batter which had splashed onto her pants in the struggle. She knew her boyfriend was expecting her soon and would worry if she was late.

She then asked her abductor when he was bringing her back, and whether it would be very long.

"Maybe I will bring you back tomorrow," came Garrido's cold reply.

Now Katie became really scared, thinking he was going to kill her. But her survival instincts kicked in and she told him to stop the car, so they could have sex in the bushes there and then.

"I told him I would do anything he wanted," she later testified, "if he would not hurt me. I figured we were going off on some dark road, and I just wanted to get it over with. And I said, 'Why can't we stay right here?' "

Garrido told her that that was not what he wanted and she should not argue, as he had everything planned.

"You might as well understand that you're going to be with me," he told her, as they drove on into the night.

A few minutes later he broke the silence, saying he'd gone to South Lake Tahoe to abduct a girl. He said they should wait until they reached a shed he had rented in the desert. Then if she did everything to please him sexually, he promised not to hurt her unless he had to.

"He kept saying he wasn't going to hurt me," recalled Katie. "He said he would not kill me, he would only go to the extent of knocking me out if I tried to scream."

Garrido then boasted of abducting two other girls recently, saying that he had not hurt either of them.

"I realized that he had plans of taking me to somewhere he had all fixed up that was far away," she said, "and I wasn't coming back. I had to cope with the situation."

Then Katie pointed out her car was almost out of gas, and he wasn't going to get very far. Garrido told her not to worry, as he knew a self-service gas station nearby, where he was going to stop for gas because it did not have an attendant.

"I automatically thought about gas stations around the area," she said, "that are self-service and would be open that late at night. I tried to be aware . . . even though I couldn't see."

When Garrido asked if she was expected anywhere, Katie said her boyfriend was waiting for her to come over with the dinner.

"That is where I was going," she told him.

"Is anyone going to miss you tomorrow?" he asked.

"Well," she said. "I have to get my son off for school at seven in the morning and I have to be at work at nine."

"If you're real good," he told her, "I will try and have you back by dawn."

* * *

A little while later, Katie, who was still lying handcuffed under the coat on the passenger floor, realized that they were now driving through Stateline into Nevada. She recognized the three stoplights in quick succession, and the noise of the casinos. Soon afterward, he pulled off the road and took the coat off her. Then he announced he had to tape her mouth and blindfold her, to stop her crying out for help at the gas station.

Katie begged him not to blindfold her, explaining she wore contact lenses, and could not stand tape being placed over her face and eyes. Garrido told her to take her contacts out first, but Katie said she was unable to unless he unlocked her handcuffs. He refused and then he taped her mouth shut, placing the coat back over her without bothering with the blindfolding.

A few minutes later, Garrido pulled into a gas station, stopping in front of a pump. Lying on the floor by the front passenger's seat completely bound and gagged, Katie was terrified. Before getting out of the car to fill up at the pump, Garrido warned her not to scream for help, or he'd come back and hurt her.

Then he attempted to fill the Ford Pinto with regular gas, but when the nozzle would not fit, as it only took unleaded, he threw a fit.

"He jumped back in the car very nervous and upset," Katie recalled. "He started up the car and demanded to know why the gas nozzle wouldn't fit my car. He just started yelling at me . . . that I had done it on purpose so he couldn't put gas in the car."

Now Katie was terrified he was really going to hurt her. She desperately tried to speak, but was unable to make a sound with her mouth taped shut.

"You're trying to tell me something—right?" asked Garrido.

Katie nodded her head.

"Okay," he said. "I am going to take the tape off a tiny little bit. If you try to scream, you are going to get hurt."

Garrido then pulled back the tape a little, and Katie managed to say, "Unleaded."

He then put the tape back over her mouth, pumped un-leaded gas into the car and drove away.

Five minutes later, he pulled over to the side of the road. He had calmed down, saying he knew she was uncomfortable and removed the tape from her mouth. He also took off the strap that bound her neck to her knees, loosening the handcuffs a little.

He then lifted Katie over the front seats, laying her face-down on the back seat, and throwing his coat back over her.

Then he headed east on Highway 50, back toward the Nevada border.

"He seemed very nervous," she later said, "very uptight . . . and scared."

As the coat was slightly open, Katie could just see out of the back window, and she now tried to see where he was tak-ing her. At one point, just over the Nevada border, she recog-nized a distinctive brick house, a few miles past Zephyr Cove.

As Garrido had told her it would be a long drive to their destination, she now tried to strike up some kind of rapport with her kidnapper in order to survive.

"I was terrified," she later testified. "I tried to engage him in some normal conversation to try and figure out what kind of person had abducted me, what was going through his mind, how best to cope with the situation that I was in to get myself out of it alive. I was trying to keep myself alive."

When she asked his name she took him by surprise.

"Phil," he replied, but immediately realizing his mistake, said it was actually "Bill."

Then she asked why he had selected her. Garrido then re-plied it was her fault, because she was so attractive. She asked what turned him on about raping young women. Garrido thought for a second, replying that it wasn't the pain. He said it was just a fantasy that he had to live out, and he had no real control over it.

Trying to relate to her attacker, Katie pretended she too fan-tasized about being raped. She said maybe it wouldn't be too bad if he didn't hurt her, and only wanted to give her pleasure.

She then asked if he was married. Garrido said he was and

that he and his wife shared a "very heavy" and "happy" sex life. She was aware of what he did and understood his needs, he said, even buying the handcuffs from a pawn shop store.

"He was happily married," Katie recalled. "And that the main reason he was doing this was because of a sexual urge. That he just really enjoyed it, and he had done it twice before."

Phillip Garrido said none of his friends knew what he was really like, and would never believe him capable of something like this.

Soon afterward, Katie Callaway recognized they were passing through Carson City, when they hit a stoplight outside a casino and she saw a billboard. Her abductor then headed north on U.S. 395 toward Reno, as she lay helplessly bound in the backseat of the car.

Phillip Garrido now began talking about religion.

"He talked a lot about Jesus on our ride," she later told police. "Telling me how he was going to turn himself over to God next year, because Jesus was the way. And on and on . . . did I understand what he was saying about God?"

He then started talking about his wife again, slipping up saying, "My wife said Phil the other day." This mistake was not lost on Katie, who kept calling him "Bill," so he wouldn't realize she now knew his real name.

When she mentioned being a 21 dealer in a casino, Garrido chuckled, saying so was his wife. When Katie asked if he was from Reno, he then became evasive, saying just because his wife did casino work they could be from Las Vegas or many other places.

He then asked if she had ever taken LSD.

"I said yes," she recalled. "I said yes to everything. 'Oh, yes, I have done this. Oh, yes, I have done that.'"

At one point, when she mentioned wanting a marijuana joint to relax her, Garrido said the stuff he had waiting for her where they were going was so good it would blow her head off.

At around 9:00 P.M., Phillip Garrido stopped the car and turned off the engine.

"Okay, we're here," he announced, as he got out of the car to open his shed. Katie Callaway was certain they were in Reno, as she had heard planes and recognized the treetops of the Reno Valley, through the back window.

A couple of minutes later, he returned in an agitated state.

"I lost the key," he snapped. "I can't get in. I knew I heard it drop at the lake. I should have picked it up."

He then announced they were driving to his car, so he could get a crowbar and pry open the lock of his shed door. They then drove along a dirt road for five minutes, finally stopping at a white building, before getting out. Katie could hear him hunting around in another car for a tire iron.

He then came back, complaining he couldn't find one and asking if she had one. Katie told him there was one in her trunk and where the key was.

"I was thinking," she later explained, "if I just let him go on with his own fantasy . . . I'd be safe until I had a better chance to change the plans."

Garrido soon found her crowbar and drove back to the shed. He then spent the next fifteen minutes trying to force open the lock. As she lay handcuffed on the back seat under the coat, Callaway could hear the sound of a rock band playing so she thought they must be outside a discothèque.

Finally, her abductor managed to break the lock and returned, putting the crowbar back in the trunk.

"He told me he was going to have to blindfold me," recalled Katie. "Then he lifted me out of the back seat, and he led me into the shed, as he called it."

Back in Stateline, David Wade began to worry when there was no sign of Katie Callaway. She should have arrived around 7:30 P.M., and when she didn't he kept looking out of the window and watching the clock.

At around 8:00 P.M. he called Forrest Dougherty, who worked with Katie at the Harveys Lake Tahoe casino, asking if she'd seen her. Dougherty said that she had seen her earlier, pulling out of a parking spot in front of Ink's Al Tahoe Market.

She had been with a dark-haired man, and she'd watched them drive east on Highway 50.

Wade then called South Lake Tahoe police to report Katie missing. But he was told that a person had to be missing for forty-eight hours before he could file a report.

6

"JUST IMAGINE THAT YOU WERE IN ROMAN TIMES"

Phillip Garrido led his terrified captive into his warehouse in handcuffs, closing the rolling aluminum door behind them.

"Here we are," he told her. "You can open your eyes."

He then left, saying he was going to park her car around the side of the building. He promised to unlock her handcuffs when he returned, warning her not to try to escape, as he would be watching.

After he left and rolled down the door, Katie Callaway took a deep breath and opened her eyes. She saw a stack of half-opened storage boxes by the door, with china and other items visible.

Directly in front of her was a wall of Visqueen plastic sheeting, obscuring the rest of the warehouse.

"It was freezing in there," she recalled. "I didn't know where I was. I thought I was out in the middle of the desert."

A few minutes later he returned, locking the door from the inside. As he released the handcuffs he warned Katie there was no escape for her.

He then led her through a succession of three heavy rugs suspended from the ceiling, making her feel disoriented, like being inside a maze.

"I couldn't see," she said, "because there were several partitions in the front of the door. I didn't even know the size of the room, because of the way it was set up."

Behind the final rugged partition was a room, which he'd carefully prepared like a stage set. Then he turned on the colored spotlights and ordered her to undress.

"I saw a dirty mattress on the floor," she later remembered, "with a red holey satin sheet and a filthy fake fur blanket. He had colored stage lights focused on the mattress and a projector on the floor with some film in it. I asked him if they were porno films, he said yes. There were also stacks of pornographic magazines.

"And then I saw the three solid walls were covered in carpet, which really scared me because I'm thinking, 'Oh God, he's tried to soundproof this room.'"

At one end of the shed, she could hear the muffled sounds of a band practicing, assuming they came from another part of the warehouse and were made by her abductor's friends.

When Katie said she needed the bathroom, he found a little red jar for her to urinate in. Then as she undressed she noticed a gleaming new silver trash can full of water, with an electric heater on the outside, which he used to wash her with warm water. There were also two bottles of cheap wine, a jar of Vaseline, some disposable douches and a vibrator with three attachments, lying by the mattress.

"I took my clothes off," she later testified, "and it was freezing in there. I got under this filthy, furry, fake fur blanket that he had on this old mattress. It was filthy, but I was freezing. He sat on the mattress and I was shaking so badly.

"I was terrified. I think that he felt sorry for me, and he told me I was the only person that ever made him feel bad for doing this."

Then Garrido opened a bottle of cheap wine and offered her a glass, saying it would stop her shaking and relax her. She accepted half a glass, but he then started drinking the wine heavily. Later, he would claim to have taken four doses of LSD, to increase his sexual pleasure.

"He was a lot calmer," said Callaway. "But he would get very distant looks, like he was kind of spaced off. And all of a sudden he would come back to me."

For the first half-hour, Phillip Garrido sat on the bed fully clothed, chatting to Katie, who was shivering under the covers. He turned on a radio, tuning it to a local Reno rock station.

"He told me I was making him feel bad because I was terrified," she said. "And that if I fought him it would turn him on more and make him more aggressive."

He spoke of renting the warehouse under an alias, and preparing it for several weeks. He said he also used it for his band to practice in but expected to be evicted soon.

Garrido then began to explain why he had kidnapped her, and the more he talked the more sexually excited he became.

"He was trying to put me at ease," said Katie, "by trying to assure me that he wasn't going to hurt me. It was a sexual fantasy that he had planned. He said things to me like, 'Just imagine if you were in Roman times and you had to do everything the man said if you were a slave.'"

Finally, Garrido stopped talking. Then he began taking his clothes off, neatly placing them on an old battered brown chair. She noticed an ugly burn-type scar on his left shoulder.

He then got into the bed and started rubbing himself against her, before entering her with his erect penis. Katie just lay there very still, praying her nightmare would soon come to an end.

"He pulled out," she later told detectives, "and ejaculated on my stomach the first time."

Garrido then ordered Katie to stand over him on the bed and rub her vagina and breasts and keep repeating the words "fuck me, fuck me," while he masturbated to climax.

"Then he told me to lie on the bed," said Katie, "and he took a handful of Vaseline, rubbed it on my vagina and his penis and then entered me again."

He then forced her to have anal sex, but did not ejaculate. He also made her stand by the wall with her hands above her head, moving her hips around as he masturbated. Then he ordered her to sit on a large speaker with her legs up, roughly penetrating her with a clitoral vibrator.

"He was hurting me," she recalled. "I tried to push his hands away and he knocked my hands away. [He] told me to knock that shit off."

Next Garrido ordered her down on her hands and knees, entering her from the rear.

"Then he made me masturbate him," she said. "He made me stimulate his penis with my hand, and if I would slow down at any time because I was exhausted or sore, he would very threateningly say, 'Come on, come on,' like if I didn't I was in trouble. Just do what I say."

Over a five-and-a-half-hour period, Phillip Garrido repeatedly assaulted and raped Katie Callaway at least a dozen times. Periodically, he would stop to drink wine or smoke hash or marijuana. And the higher he got, the more frenzied and priapic he became.

"He got almost to the point of intoxication," Katie later told investigators. "He got giggly and saying, 'Oh, I hardly ever drink.' He kept insisting that I take a few drinks, because I was shaking so terribly."

At one point he took some hash from a glass vial and filled his pipe. After taking a large hit, he handed it to Katie, who inhaled.

"[It was] very strong," she later testified. "It intensified all my paranoid feelings extremely. And I didn't smoke any more, because I wanted to be fully competent, fully aware and fully alert because of the situation I was in."

Just after midnight, William Emery arrived home to his warehouse in Mill Street, after a long shift driving his taxi. There was a strange blue Ford Pinto with California plates parked outside Phillip Garrido's unit next door, and he remembered how his neighbor had asked him to keep an eye on it.

Emery went inside his unit and changed, coming out again to walk his dogs. He noticed Garrido's Unit 39 was unlocked, so he knocked on the door a couple of times.

"There was no response," he later told police. "Nobody came out and there wasn't any noise. But the hasp was down so I knew somebody was in there."

After writing down the Ford Pinto license plate number, he walked to a nearby gas station, calling the number Garrido had once given for emergencies. When he got no response, he got on his bicycle and pedaled to the Garrido house on Market Street.

"There was nobody at home," said Emery, "so I turned around and went back to the shed."

The strange car was still parked outside, but Emery decided there was nothing more he could do, going back inside his unit to sleep.

After hearing the loud bangs on his warehouse door, Phillip Garrido put on his jeans and boots and went to investigate. A few minutes later he returned giggling, saying it was only the guy next door, asking about a tune on the radio. Then he started laughing, saying his neighbor probably knew exactly what he was doing.

He poured himself another glass of wine, ordering Katie Callaway to lie down on the mattress. Then he took a large pair of orange-colored sewing scissors and cut off her pubic hair, saying it was making him sore.

He then left again for a few minutes, saying he needed some marijuana rolling papers.

"He said he was going to his friends to get papers," Katie said. "I don't know whether he meant the band, or the guy that had come by and banged on the door."

Hour after hour, Katie Callaway focused on the radio and the periodic time checks, which punctuated her nightmare. Phillip Garrido seemed insatiable, as he repeatedly raped her in every way possible. And whenever she tried to resist, he just became more aggressive.

"The more I resisted," she said, "the more force he used. He just kept doing the same things over and over."

Katie considered grabbing the scissors he had cut off her pubic hair with and stabbing him to death. But she never got the chance.

7

"PLEASE HELP ME!"

At around 2:20 A.M. on Tuesday, November 23, Reno Police officer Clifford Conrad was on patrol in Mill Street when he saw an out-of-state Ford Pinto parked in front of storage unit 39. He was immediately suspicious, as there was hardly any frost on the windows like all the other cars.

He took a closer look at the warehouse, observing that the door lock had been torn off. As there had been a spate of recent warehouse robberies in the area, he called police headquarters, requesting a plates check on the suspicious vehicle.

While he was waiting for an answer, he walked over to Unit 39 and tried the door. It opened about four inches and when it would not go any higher, he started knocking on the door.

Hearing the loud bangs on the door, Phillip Garrido jumped off the bed and went over to see who it was. Then he came back, telling his prisoner it was the police.

"Are you going to maintain?" he asked Katie. "Are you going to be quiet?"

At first she thought it was a setup, so she promised to stay silent. Then Garrido put on his jeans and disappeared behind the rugs. Katie could then hear him opening the door and being asked his name and a few other questions. She listened carefully to see if it was really a policeman or just a friend of her attacker. Then she heard her abductor coolly explain that he had lost the key and had had to force open the lock.

Then Katie decided to escape. Although she was still naked,

she tentatively got off the mattress, venturing out through the hanging rugs toward the sound of the voices. Then she peeked out from behind the vinyl sheet by the entrance and saw her attacker was talking to a policeman.

Suddenly she burst out of the warehouse into the street screaming, "Help me! Help me!"

Stunned by the sudden appearance of a hysterical naked woman, Officer Conrad demanded to know what the hell was going on.

Without missing a beat, Phillip Garrido calmly replied: "This is my girlfriend. We're having a good time."

"No, I'm not," screamed Katie.

Then Officer Conrad asked who the blue Pinto belonged to, and Katie said it was hers.

"Who drove it here?" asked the officer.

"He did," she replied.

"May I see your license, please?" asked Conrad.

"I don't have a license," replied Garrido. "I didn't drive the car. She drove it."

When Katie desperately protested that she had not driven her car here, the officer told her to go and dress, while he questioned Garrido further. After she went back inside, the wily Garrido conspiratorially told the officer that he was a married man and lived down the street. He said the naked woman he called "Kathy" was really his girlfriend.

He then asked permission to go back inside and fetch his jacket. And Officer Conrad allowed him to do so, as he called his dispatcher for backup.

Katie Callaway was dressing at the back of the warehouse, when to her horror her abductor suddenly reappeared.

"He let the guy go back in there with me," she later told police. "I was terrified he was going to take me as a hostage."

But Phillip Garrido took another tack, pleading with her to tell the policeman they were "sweethearts having a good time." And he warned that if she gave him up, he would fight her all the way in court. She would never win, he said, as it would only be her word against his.

"My abductor was begging me not to tell on him," she later testified. "That it would be terribly embarrassing."

Katie now really felt her life was in danger, as he had nothing to lose.

"It was just he and I," she said. "He could have done anything to me at the time. His life was in jeopardy. He knew he was caught . . . unless he could convince me not to tell on him."

As he pleaded with her not to turn him in, Katie suddenly ran outside again half-naked.

"I just wanted to get out of the warehouse," she said, "and back to the police officer before he tried anything rash."

She rushed up to Officer Conrad, repeating she had been raped. A few seconds later, Garrido followed her out, and Officer Conrad continued questioning them both in his cruiser's spotlights, as he waited for more officers to arrive.

Finally, an emotional Katie Callaway asked Officer Conrad to just let her abductor go home, saying she had had enough. She made sure the officer stayed between her and Garrido, matching him step by step.

"My nerves were shot," she said. "I was almost at the snapping point. It had been a long ordeal. A horrible ordeal. And I wanted the officer to take me."

Eventually, Officer Conrad realized how terrified she was, telling her to go and warm up in the back of his squad car.

As Katie Callaway waited in his cruiser, Officer Conrad continued questioning Phillip Garrido as to why the warehouse lock was broken. Garrido said he and a friend used the warehouse to play music and store their instruments. He had lost the key and had broken off the lock to get inside.

At 2:51 A.M., Reno Police officer Erick Soderblom arrived, after getting a call over the police radio, to find Officer Conrad interviewing Garrido.

And after consulting with Conrad, Officer Soderblom walked over to the police cruiser to speak to Katie Callaway.

"She appeared to be upset," Officer Soderblom later testified. "Miss Callaway told me that she was a victim of rape and kidnap."

When Soderblom asked how she had been taken to Reno against her will, Katie said she had been handcuffed, holding out her wrists for him to see. The experienced officer shone his flashlight on her wrists, immediately recognizing the distinctive red parallel chafes that can only be caused by handcuffs.

Katie Callaway then signed a criminal complaint against Phillip Garrido, as Officer Conrad called his supervisor, Sergeant Saunier, to the scene.

While they were waiting for Sergeant Saunier to arrive, Conrad escorted Garrido back into the warehouse to get his shirt and jacket. Inside the officer noticed a large pair of scissors, as well as drug paraphernalia and a vial containing what looked like hashish.

He started asking specific questions about his alleged victim's accusations. Up to then Garrido had been "calm" and "rational," but he suddenly went on the defensive, saying he did not have to answer.

At 3:00 A.M., after Garrido was read his Miranda rights, Sergeant Saunier arrested Phillip Garrido for the kidnap and rape of Katie Callaway. Another officer then found the key to the handcuffs in Garrido's pants pocket, as well as a set of keys in a black plastic Harrah's Casino club case, where his wife Christine worked.

Phillip Garrido was handcuffed and taken to Washoe Medical Center to be tested for alcohol and drugs, as well as to have a sample of his pubic hair taken.

At 5:10 A.M. he was moved to Reno City Jail and booked on charges of kidnap, rape and infamous crimes.

"I guess that I should learn to grow up," he told Officer Soderblom.

8

"IT LOOKED LIKE A SCENE FROM A PORNO FLICK"

At 3:30 A.M. Tuesday morning, Reno Police detective Dan DeMaranville was assigned the Phillip Garrido kidnap/rape investigation. The experienced forty-year-old robbery/homicide detective had been sleeping when he'd received the call. He immediately drove to Reno Police headquarters to be briefed by Officer Clifford Conrad.

"I was called out in the middle of the night," recalled DeMaranville, "and asked to lead the investigation."

A few blocks away at Washoe Medical Center, Katie Callaway was undergoing forensic rape tests by Dr. Boss of the Reno CSI unit.

Her wrists were carefully photographed, as well as the numerous scratches and bruises all over her body. And a cutting of what remained of her pubic hair was taken.

After the forensic testing was completed, Sergeant Saunier drove her to Reno Police Headquarters. At 5:40 A.M. she was interviewed by Detective DeMaranville and his assistant, Officer Carolyn Jean Carlon. And over the next two hours Phillip Garrido's victim described her terrible ordeal at his hands in graphic detail.

She told the investigators how she had unwittingly given him a ride the previous evening in South Lake Tahoe, after he'd said his car had broken down. Frequently bursting into tears, she described how he had lured her to an empty lot before taking her prisoner.

"He told me all he wanted was a piece of ass," she said. "And if I did all that he asked I wouldn't get hurt. He said that he had come to Lake Tahoe specifically for the purpose of abducting a girl."

She then detailed her long, terrifying ride to Garrido's warehouse in Reno, and how he had boasted of spending weeks preparing for her arrival. The detectives took notes as she described the six hours of almost nonstop violent acts of rape she had endured.

"It was a sexual fantasy that he had planned," she told them. "He held my arms down to the bed with the weight of his body."

She said Phillip Garrido had raped her both vaginally and anally, as well as using his fingers and a vibrator to penetrate her.

"He just kept doing the same things over and over," she sobbed. "He drank quite a bit of wine and he became somewhat intoxicated, and when he became intoxicated he became more forceful and mean."

And she told investigators she was certain that Officer Conrad's timely intervention at the warehouse had saved her life.

Toward the end of the interview, Detective DeMaranville asked her if Garrido had ever mentioned doing anything like this previously, or taking girls to his warehouse. Katie said he had admitted doing something similar to two other girls, saying he had not harmed either one.

"He said he was very happily married," she told them, "and that he was a musician and that only his wife knew where he was, and that if she had to come bail him out of jail in the morning, she would know why."

At 7:30 A.M., Detective DeMaranville turned off the tape recorder and concluded the interview. The still distraught Katie Callaway was then taken to the office of Washoe County deputy district attorney Mike Malloy, where she gave an affidavit statement to support a search warrant. Then finally she was released to her parents.

But just a few hours later, she had to relive her ordeal, when Reno FBI agents reinterviewed her. As the alleged crime crossed state lines, the case would also be going to a federal grand jury.

Meanwhile Katie Callaway's blue Ford Pinto had been towed to the Reno Police Department Crime Laboratory. After being first processed for fingerprints, the vehicle was thoroughly searched and photographed.

On the floor behind the driver's seat, investigators found the key to the Master padlock of Phillip Garrido's unit 39 warehouse. This supported Callaway's evidence that her attacker had broken into his warehouse after losing his key.

Investigators also found the strap Garrido had used to tie up his victim on the passenger front seat. And there were beer batter stains on the seat that had spilled from Katie's crock pot during the attack. Other traces of the batter were later found on both her and Garrido's clothing.

Later that morning, Washoe County Superior Court Judge Beemer signed a search warrant for Phillip Garrido's mini-warehouse.

"There is probable cause to believe," read the warrant, "that certain evidence of the crimes of forcible rape, the infamous crime against nature, kidnapping, and possession of a controlled substance, are locked and hidden within a certain mini-warehouse storage unit located at 3245 Mill Street, Reno, Washoe County, Nevada; you are therefor [sic] directed to search the said mini-warehouse unit for the following items." The list of items included:

a torn red satin sheet,

a grey fur or fake fur cover or bedspread,

an electric vibrator with three attachments and a package for it,

disposable women's douche materials,

a jar of Vaseline,

two bottles of wine and glasses,

a pair of scissors,

a pair of women's beige panties,

a silver colored trash can and an electric heater,

a movie projector,

movie film,

colored stage lights,

a red container, appearing to be part of a kerosene-type lantern,

handcuffs,

a piece of white tape,

a women's earring, described roughly as a gold ball with a post,

a dark coat or blanket,

a belt or strap,

a women's size 6 right foot brown sandal,

a multi-colored knee sock,

a long sleeved tee shirt with a hood, navy blue and black,

samples of pubic hair,

samples of possible semen stains,

and a glass vial, approximately 2" high, containing a substance believed to be hashish.

At 2:30 P.M., Detective DeMaranville and three other Reno investigators arrived at 3245 Mill Street, where they met FBI agent Riggs and members of the Reno CSI Unit to conduct the search.

"I went to his mini-warehouse," recalled DeMaranville. "It was all planned and he had it all set up. It looked like a scene from a porno flick. He had stage lights, and I'm not talking about bright lights, I'm talking about different colored lights— red, green, yellow. On and off. There was a bed. Marital sex toys. He actually used a pair of scissors to shave her pubic hair with. He's one sick puppy."

The CSI technicians carefully photographed the outside of Unit 39, before moving inside to look for evidence to support Katie Callaway's allegations.

"I found the handcuffs," lead detective DeMaranville later testified. "A piece of tape, the tape was silver in color. And found some small baggies, containing a substance believed to be marijuana. And a pill bottle containing a substance believed to be hashish."

The investigators also found a hash pipe, a roach clip and burnt cigarette rolling papers, and seized samples of pubic hair and semen stains found on the mattress.

A few blocks away, another team of Reno police officers were searching Phillip and Christine Garrido's Market Street house. Earlier, Sergeant C. Nearpass and Detective Penegor had interviewed Chris Garrido at Harrah's Casino, where she had given written permission for her home to be searched.

She claimed no knowledge of her husband's activities the night before, as she'd been working the swing shift. But she believed he had driven her car to South Lake Tahoe.

When asked if Phillip owned handcuffs, she admitted once

buying him a pair at a Reno pawn shop, saying she had not seen them for a while.

Chris then accompanied the officers to 1855 Market Street, Reno, taking them on a tour of the residence.

"There were numerous pornographic books and magazines . . . on the bookshelf," Sergeant Nearpass later wrote in his official report.

But when the officer discovered a scrapbook hidden inside a clothing drawer in the bedroom, she asked him not to open it, as it contained explicit Polaroid photographs her husband had taken of her vaginal area. She asked the officer to respect her privacy.

"Sgt. Nearpass did not look in the scrapbook," read his report, "as she stated that all the pictures were of just her."

A few hours later, Phillip Garrido was arraigned on charges of "kidnapping, rape and infamous crimes against nature." A Washoe County Superior Court judge set bail for $50,000, until a federal grand jury could be convened and decide if he should stand trial.

9

"HE'S A SICK PUPPY"

On Wednesday, November 24, the *Nevada State Journal* reported Phillip Garrido's dramatic arrest. Under the headline "Victim Freed: Man Arrested in Kidnap," the four-paragraph story said Garrido was under investigation for kidnapping, rape and infamous crimes against nature. It reported that the FBI was also investigating Garrido, as the crime crossed the California-Nevada border.

At 9:50 A.M., Phillip Garrido was brought into an interview room at Reno Police Department. A few minutes later, Detective Dan DeMaranville and Officer Carolyn Carlon entered and advised him of his rights. After reading and signing the Miranda sheet, Garrido asked to see a lawyer before answering any questions, explaining he did not "understand legalities."

The interview was then terminated to allow him to fill out an Admonition & Waiver of Rights form. And where it asked if he wished to talk now, he wrote, "No Sir, I want to talk to a lawyer first."

But within a few hours Phillip Garrido had changed his mind and agreed to be interviewed. He was brought back to the Reno Police Department, where Detective DeMaranville was waiting in an interview room. Just before he had arrived, the detective had learned a minute quantity of LSD had been found in a vial seized at the warehouse.

"He was a nice-looking young man," recalled the detective

in 2009. "He was tall and well built, not a bad-looking guy at all."

At the start of the two-hour interview, Phillip Garrido was uncooperative, refusing to answer any questions.

"So we just talked for a while," recalled DeMaranville. "We had a conversation. I tried to relate to him and get him to like me."

Initially the detective made general conversation, asking if he was married and what he did for a living. Slowly, Garrido began to relax, enthusiastically discussing his music and his ambitions to be a rock star.

"I got him to talk to me," said DeMaranville, "and then I just told him, 'Phillip, it's time to fess up. You got caught in the mini-storage unit with a naked woman, who says you kidnapped her from Lake Tahoe. Come on. Be a man and let's talk about this. Are you ready to talk to me now?' "

After Garrido nodded his head, the detective asked why someone as handsome as him needed to resort to kidnap and rape.

"He said, 'That's the only way I can get my sexual satisfaction,' " recalled DeMaranville. "And I think he likes the power. I think he likes the control."

Garrido appeared contrite, saying he regretted what had happened. But the seasoned detective distrusted Garrido, suspecting that he was just trying to play him.

"Well, of course he appeared remorseful," explained DeMaranville. "But I think a lot of that was because he got caught. And he was trying to put the spin on me and that's fine. I let him think he was."

At one point in the interrogation, Garrido broke down in tears, saying he hadn't meant to do it but couldn't help himself.

"He was actually crying," said the detective. "I had my right arm around his shoulder and his head was on my shoulder and chest. I wanted the guy to like me. I wanted him to talk to me. So that's the name of the game. But I think a lot of it was put on."

Detective DeMaranville came away from the interview thinking Phillip Garrido was sly, devious and calculating.

"He's actually pretty intelligent too," said DeMaranville.

"He's a con artist. But the bottom line is I don't think he's crazy. He's got a problem and I think he knows it and he doesn't care."

And after spending two hours with Garrido, the lead detective was certain that Katie Callaway would never have got out of the warehouse alive if Officer Conrad hadn't intervened.

"He wouldn't have had any other choice but to get rid of her," he said. "The guy's not stupid. He's not going to turn his victim loose and have her go right to the police, which is what she would have done. She's a pretty strong girl. He picked the wrong victim."

10

SATYRIASIS

At 11:30 A.M. on Wednesday, December 1, a Washoe County grand jury was convened at the Reno Courthouse to decide if twenty-six-year-old Phillip Garrido should stand trial in Nevada. The first witness was Katie Callaway, who entered the grand jury room and was sworn in.

For the next several hours, Washoe County deputy district attorney Michael Malloy gently led Callaway through the horrific sequence of events that had brought her to Phillip Garrido's mini-warehouse in Reno. And throughout her often harrowing testimony she remained composed, vividly describing what Garrido had subjected her to.

"Do you want to take a minute to relax?" Malloy asked, before asking what had happened in Garrido's warehouse.

"He undressed," she testified, "and started to have sexual intercourse with me."

"Did he penetrate you?" asked the deputy DA.

"Yes, he did," she answered.

"Were you going along with this only because you were terrified?"

"Yes, I was lying there very still. I was tolerating it."

"It was against your will?"

"Oh, yes."

"How many times did he have sexual intercourse with you?"

"Oh, about ten."

"That many times?"

"Twelve, yes. Just continuous. I couldn't believe it."

"Okay," continued Malloy, "and then what other sexual acts did he perform?"

"He entered me from the back."

"Anally?"

"Anally and in the normal fashion."

"Was all this against your will?"

"Yes," she sobbed. "All the sexual acts were against my will, and he was just very rough and very forceful. And then he got out a vibrator and made me sit on the speaker while he just really hurt me with his vibrator, my vagina."

"How long were you in there?"

"Approximately five and a half to six hours."

Then she described running out of the warehouse naked to escape, while Garrido was talking to Officer Conrad.

"I fought my way through a couple of walls of carpet," she told the grand jurors, "and peeked my head around the corner. I saw an officer and I started yelling, 'Help me!' Help me!' and he stood there with no reaction, and so did the abductor. And so I ran out there completely naked, and then they just stood there . . . and I thought, 'My God, he is not going to help me.'"

Callaway testified how Garrido had first claimed she was his girlfriend, and they were having a good time. And her terror after Officer Conrad had ordered her back into the warehouse to dress, before allowing Garrido back inside alone.

"He let the abductor go back in with me," she said. "And I was scared that he was going to take me hostage."

She described how Garrido had then "pitifully begged" her not to turn him in, before she ran out again half-naked.

"I think [the policeman] really realized I was terrified when every time he took a step sideways, I was right beside him taking one step with him."

Then Officer Conrad had told her to sit in his patrol car, until more officers arrived.

"They asked me if I wanted to press charges," she said. "And I said 'Yes.'"

After Malloy finished his questions, a grand juror asked if she could recognize marijuana by looking at it.

"Yes," she replied. "It was in a plastic baggie, and he rolled joints out of it."

Then Katie Callaway was excused and Reno Police Department detective Dan DeMaranville entered the Grand Jury room to testify.

The detective told the grand jury about his search of Phillip Garrido's warehouse.

"I found the handcuffs," he testified. "A piece of [silver] tape . . . and some small baggies containing a substance believed to be marijuana, and a pill bottle containing a substance believed to be hashish."

The detective said he also found a roach clip on the floor, as well as a hashish pipe. There was also the burned end of a marijuana cigarette, which he informed the Grand Jury members was known as "a roach."

The next witness was Lloyd Whalen, the chief chemist of the Nevada State Department of Law Enforcement Assistance. He testified that his laboratory had been given a number of samples of suspected drugs found in Garrido's mini-warehouse.

He testified that testing had confirmed there was 1.88 grams of marijuana and 3.01 grams of hashish, as well as a "clip-type smoking device" with cannabis residue.

At the end of the chemist's testimony, a grand jury member had a question.

"Hashish, or whatever you call it," asked the grand juror, "what do they do—take it as a pill, or do they smoke it?"

"Either way," Whalen replied. "Normally it would be smoked, but it can be taken orally. The word hashish itself I believe is from the India dialect, and the word means assassin. There were hired assassins that would get high on this stuff and go out and do their work."

Then the juror asked if marijuana was an aphrodisiac.

"Neither in my search of the literature," replied the chemist, "nor in my personal experience."

Later that day, the Washoe County grand jury returned a three-count indictment against Phillip Craig Garrido for forcible rape, an infamous crime against nature and possession of a controlled substance.

And the following day—after a separate hearing of the evidence—a federal grand jury returned a one-count indictment, charging him with interstate kidnapping. From now on the federal and Washoe County cases would run in tandem, with his federal trial being held first.

On December 6, United States Magistrate Harold O. Taber appointed assistant federal public defender Willard Van Hazel, Jr., to represent Phillip Garrido. And two days later, Garrido was arraigned in the Washoe County case in the Second Judicial District Court in Reno.

Ron Bath, the deputy public defender assigned to represent Garrido in the state case, told Washoe County district judge Grant L. Bowen that he was having problems communicating with his client.

"Mr. Garrido has been under a great deal of stress," he explained. "And we would like to ask that we have two psychiatric examinations prepared."

The defender said he also wanted the reports to see if Garrido was a danger to the "health, safety and morals of the community."

Judge Bowen asked if Phillip Garrido had ever spent time in an institution, and Bath said he had not.

Washoe County deputy district attorney Donald Coppa said the state also needed to determine if Garrido knew the difference between right and wrong when the alleged kidnap and rape were committed.

Judge Bowen agreed that the defendant should be examined by two psychiatrists, one for the state and one for the defense. And he adjourned the case for a month until the results could be known.

On Friday, December 10, defense-appointed psychiatrist Dr. Charles Kuhn spent an hour examining Phillip Garrido at the Washoe County detention facility. The doctor conducted a clinical evaluation, but could not find any thinking disorder or organic impairment.

"There is no question in my mind," said Dr. Kuhn, "that Mr. Garrido has an intelligence somewhat better than average."

During the examination, Garrido became highly emotional, telling the doctor about his overpowering sexual fantasies of masturbating in public. He explained how drugs sexually aroused him, saying that he had taken four hits of LSD after kidnapping Katie Callaway. And since his arrest, he told the doctor, he had found God and spiritual sanctuary in the Bible.

The psychiatrist later observed that Garrido had displayed "strangely erratic judgment" by kidnapping a girl in South Lake Tahoe and then taking over the state line to Nevada. Going to all these lengths to fulfill his sexual fantasy did not reflect proper use of his intelligence.

"There is nothing in the sexual fantasy that has any geographical significance," wrote the doctor in his report, "and unless a person was pretty fogged up one way or another, they wouldn't incur the involvement of federal law."

On December 14, Dr. Kuhn wrote to Garrido's Washoe County attorney, Ron Bath, saying he believed the defendant had known the difference between right and wrong during the kidnap and rape. And he also found that Garrido fully understood the nature of the charges he faced, and would be able to assist in preparing his defense.

Five days later, the Federal District Court–appointed psychiatrist, Dr. Lynn Gerow, examined Phillip Garrido for an hour and forty-five minutes in Washoe County Jail. Unshaved and disheveled, Garrido frequently clasped a Bible in his hand, appearing obsessed with God and religious events.

"He talked at some length about the Bible, the Lord and God," Dr. Gerow later reported. "I felt he was preoccupied by those things."

Unlike Dr. Kuhn, the state psychiatrist did not think Phillip Garrido particularly intelligent.

"His judgment was very poor," Dr. Gerow observed. "His insight was minimal. His intelligence appeared to be average."

During the examination, Garrido became emotional as he

spoke of his childhood, saying that he had "considerable emotional conflict" with his parents.

"He worked on and off as a musician and began abusing drugs increasingly," wrote the psychiatrist. "He was married in 1972 and his wife currently works as a dealer in a local casino."

Garrido told Dr. Gerow he suffered from migraine headaches, but otherwise appeared completely rational, providing "a clear, concise statement," from when he had seized Katie Callaway until his arrest the following morning. And finding no signs of either psychosis or neurosis, the doctor diagnosed Garrido as suffering from satyriasis, or excessive sexual compulsion.

"There was nothing in what he told me," said the psychiatrist, "nothing in the mental status examination that one could say that he wasn't responsible and competent."

During the examination, the doctor asked Garrido to respond to a series of proverbs, including "Those who dance should pay the fiddler."

"He responded that he had committed a crime," said the doctor, "and that he should pay for that crime."

The next day, Dr. Gerow sent off his psychiatric report on Phillip Garrido to United States district judge Bruce Thompson, now assigned to oversee the federal trial.

"Mr. Garrido was a tall, thin white male," it began. "He appeared as an unshaved, unkempt man looking his stated age. He presented his story in a clear and logical fashion."

Garrido had appeared dejected throughout his jailhouse evaluation, breaking down in tears on several occasions.

"He looked and acted depressed," noted Dr. Gerow. "He would occasionally cry during the interview. He denied suicidal ideation."

Garrido had readily admitted abusing LSD, marijuana, cocaine and alcohol for the last six years, claiming to have taken five doses of LSD daily. And he boasted of swallowing "four hits" of the powerful hallucinogenic after abducting Katie Callaway.

"He believes strongly that LSD increases his sexual power," reported the doctor. "He was preoccupied with the idea of sex and admitted to a history of several sexual disorders. He complains of some memory and preceptual [sic] disturbances secondary to chronic LSD abuse."

Garrido also claimed to have hallucinations, which the doctor noted was common among LSD abusers.

Throughout the examination, reported Dr. Gerow, Garrido stressed his recent discovery of God and how he now wanted to turn his life around.

"He made mention of recent increasing religiosity," wrote the doctor. "There were several references to God and Jesus. He stated that he had become more religious in recent weeks. His verbal productions were not delusional in quality. He based his new religious interests more appropriately on the considerable guilt and fear he was experiencing since being incarcerated."

At the end of his three-page report, Dr. Gerow diagnosed Phillip Garrido as suffering from "a mixed sexual deviation" and "chronic drug abuse," finding the drugs may have led to his sexual abnormalities.

"In men with satyriasis," he wrote, "we usually see an excessive constant preoccupation with the desire for coitus. It is usually associated with compulsive masturbation. This aspect is clearly present in this man and is part of his multiple sexual deviation."

The doctor suggested Garrido should be neurologically tested, as his condition could be the result of brain damage caused by "temporal lobe disorders, cerebral syphilis, or excessive use of drugs."

But he agreed that Garrido was fully competent to understand the charges he faced, and able to participate in his defense.

"It is also my opinion," reported Dr. Gerow, "that at the time of the crimes charged, the defendant as a result of mental disease or defect, did not lack substantial capacity either to appreciate the wrongfulness of his conduct or to conform his conduct to the requirements of the law."

* * *

Two days before Christmas, Phillip Garrido was led into district court, where Judge Thompson declared him competent to stand trial. And after his attorney Willard Van Hazel waived the formal reading of the indictment, Garrido pleaded not guilty to all charges.

Then Van Hazel filed a motion to have his client undergo a neurological examination, as Dr. Gerow had suggested. Judge Thompson agreed, setting a trial date for February 7 and remanding the defendant in custody.

On January 6, 1977, Reno-based neurologist Dr. Albert Peterman examined Phillip Garrido for possible brain damage. He conducted an electroencephalography test (EEG), placing multiple electrodes around the scalp to measure the electrical activity in Garrido's brain.

But the thirty-minute test produced no abnormal results, showing Garrido's brain activity was normal.

"I cannot find any hard evidence of organic brain damage per se," Dr. Peterman later reported. "He can do serial 7's and retain 5 digits in forward and reverse order with considerable concentration."

During the examination, the defendant appeared distraught and contrite about what he had done, tearing up on one occasion.

"He states that he is looking forward to going to court," Dr. Peterman wrote, "has found religion and feels his life will change for the better. He shows appropriate concern for whatever crime he is charged with."

Surprisingly, when asked if he had ever suffered any serious head injuries, Garrido failed to mention the one he'd sustained as a teenager, leading to an operation and lengthy hospital stay.

"This man has a perfectly bland neurologic history," noted the doctor. "There is no history of significant head injuries, skull fracture or concussion."

But the defendant was far more forthcoming about his chronic drug abuse.

"LSD made him quite sexually aggressive which he realizes," wrote the doctor. "He had used LSD prior to his alleged offense, but remembers the details of the abduction and sexual activity quite well."

Garrido also told Dr. Peterman that he had started getting migraine headaches since his incarceration, which was his only neurological complaint.

"I see no evidence," concluded the doctor, "either by history, examination or EEG of brain damage per se, although there is considerable evidence of anxiety and depression and personality disorder."

Four days later, Phillip Garrido appeared in Washoe County Court, pleading not guilty to three charges of rape, an infamous crime against nature and possession of a controlled substance.

In late January, Garrido's defense suddenly changed strategy, when federal public defender Willard Van Hazel requested that Dr. Charles Kuhn reexamine his client to see if there was anything different since his first examination.

Dr. Kuhn carried out a second examination but found Garrido's condition remained unchanged.

Then on February 1, the same day Dr. Kuhn's second report was filed with the district court, Phillip Garrido withdrew his not guilty plea. But Judge Thompson refused to accept it.

Three days later, at 4:45 P.M. on the Friday before trial, Willard Van Hazel suddenly announced his client would now be pursuing a psychiatric defense.

11

KATIE CALLAWAY TAKES THE STAND

At 1:30 P.M. on Wednesday, February 9, 1977, Phillip Garrido was led into U.S. district court in downtown Reno in handcuffs, wearing a faded gray suit with a striped shirt and brown tie, his long hair tied back in a ponytail.

After the jury was sworn in, the clerk of the court read out the indictment, stating that the defendant was pleading not guilty.

Assistant United States Attorney Leland Lutfy made his opening statement on behalf of the prosecution, but Van Hazel reserved the privilege not to make one on behalf of his client.

Then Lutfy called Katie Callaway to the stand as his first witness. Once again the young woman bravely relived her terrible ordeal for the jury, as Phillip Garrido sat impassively staring at her from the dock.

The prosecutor asked her if the young man who kidnapped her was present in the courtroom.

"Yes, he is," replied Callaway. "He has his hair pulled back in a ponytail."

And for the next several hours, Katie Callaway calmly told the jury about her nightmare at the hands of the tall, handsome defendant. Gently led by Lutfy's questions, the articulate witness bravely gave yet another detailed account of her six hours with Garrido, and how she had survived it.

"Can you remember any of the conversation that you had during this time?" asked the prosecutor.

"Yes," she replied, as the jury hung on her every word. "I asked him, 'Why me?' And he said, 'Well, it wasn't you intentionally; could have been anyone. It just happened that you happened to be attractive, and that is a fault in your case.'

"And I asked him what aspect of this rape . . . that he got off on. And he said that he didn't get off on pain; it was just a fantasy that he had to live out. And he had his fantasies. He had a very heavy sexual life with his wife. He was very happy, but it was just something that he had to do. And that his wife was the only one that knew where he was and what he was doing."

When she began to tell the jury about how Phillip Garrido had viciously raped her in his Reno warehouse, defender Van Hazel objected, calling it irrelevant.

"The necessary elements," he told Judge Thompson, "as outlined in the government's opening statement, is an unlawful seizure and a kidnapping. [This] was consummated when she got to that gas station."

The prosecutor argued the issue was the defendant's "state of mind," and the events in the shed were why he had abducted her in the first place.

Judge Thompson overruled the objection, and Lutfy asked Katie what had happened inside the warehouse.

"Do you want me to go into the rape?" she asked.

"Your Honor," said Garrido's attorney, rising to his feet, "I object to the characterization 'rape.' I believe rape is something that the jury will conclude in this case, whether it occurred or did not occur."

"She can call it what she wants," declared Judge Thompson.

Then Katie described once again what Phillip Garrido had done to her to satisfy his perverted sexual fantasies.

"The sexual intercourse activity was constant," she told the jury. "He ejaculated maybe three times, twice inside of me, once on top."

"How long would you estimate, if you can," asked the prosecutor, "did these sexual activities take place?"

"Approximately five and a half hours," she replied. "He had a radio on and I would hear the Reno station say, 'This is Reno.' And I would hear them say the time. I heard them say twelve-something. Then I heard them say two-twenty some-thing, right before the officer came in."

There had been a loud bang on the warehouse door, she told the jury, and Garrido had put on his jeans to investigate.

"He came back in and said, 'I think it's the heat,'" she said. "'Are you going to maintain? Are you going to be good?' And I said, 'Yeah, okay, I'll be good.'"

At first she thought it was a setup, but had decided to take a chance, literally fighting her way through the series of hang-ing carpet walls and out of the warehouse naked, screaming for help.

She described her abject frustration, when the uniformed police officer standing outside with her abductor and rapist did not appear to take her seriously.

"They both looked at me like I was insane," she testified. "I just stood out there in the freezing cold, while the officer [asked] what was going on."

Then to her horror the officer ordered her back into the warehouse to dress, before allowing Garrido to follow her in-side.

She told the jury she was "terrified" Garrido would now take her hostage, but instead he began "begging" her not to tell on him, because it would be so embarrassing. Finally she had dashed out again half-naked, with the officer this time telling her to sit in his car until backup arrived and Garrido was ar-rested.

In his cross-examination, Willard Van Hazel asked Calla-way if she had been provocatively dressed at Ink's Al Tahoe Market, when Garrido had first seen her.

"Was your jacket zipped while you were in the store?" he asked.

"I don't remember," she replied.

"Were you wearing a brassiere that night?"

"No."

Then Garrido's defender asked if his client had ever threat-ened her with a weapon.

"The only weapon," she replied, "was a pair of scissors [which] he cut my pubic hairs with."

Van Hazel said he assumed that after his client overpowered and handcuffed her, she had done everything she could not to antagonize him.

"I was completely passive," replied Callaway. "I was trying to deal with the whole situation as logically as I could, without allowing terror to take over completely. I do have a son and that makes you think twice."

"All right," said the defense attorney. "Now, what were the things that put you in fear?"

"The fact of being bound," she replied. "My hands handcuffed. My head strapped to my knees and being at the complete mercy of someone I had no idea what they were going to do with me, or what was going on in their minds at the time. I could go on and on."

Van Hazel then asked if she had offered his client sex while they were still in California.

"Yes, I did," she answered. "I asked him, 'Couldn't we just pull over to the side of the road and get it over with,' because, you know, every girl has to think about rape sometime."

Later in his questioning, Van Hazel asked if Garrido had ever mentioned his wife's job.

"He said she was a [21] dealer," she replied. "I asked him why he told me that if he didn't want me to do anything about him. He also told me his name was Bill, and then he slipped up later on and he said, 'My wife said Phil the other day.' But I continued to call him Bill, so he wouldn't . . . think that I knew his real name."

Then Van Hazel wanted to know if she had discussed her own sexual fantasies, after his client mentioned his.

"I completely went along with everything," she told the jury. "I said, 'Oh yes. Oh I like that too.' I tried to completely stay on good terms with him. 'I'm all for what you're doing.' "

"And this was part of that passive role?" asked Van Hazel.

"That was it," she replied.

"In that conversation then," continued Garrido's attorney, "did you say you often wondered what it would be like to be raped?"

"Every girl thinks about that, yes."

"But did you say that to the defendant, Mr. Garrido?"

"Oh, yes," replied Callaway. "I said, 'If everything you are telling me is true, that you are not going to hurt me, that all you want to do is give me pleasure and just make me feel good, even though you have abducted me under force, I guess it is not going to be so bad.'"

The public defender then asked if his client had discussed religion on their way to Reno.

"Yes," she answered, "he talked about Jesus. He said he was going to turn himself over to Jesus next year."

After a fifteen-minute recess, Katie Callaway retook the stand, and Van Hazel asked if on the drive to Reno she had told his client she wanted a marijuana joint.

"Yes, I did," she replied. "I said, 'Gee, I sure wish I had a joint right now,' meaning it sarcastically to relax my nerves. He said, 'Oh, well, I've got some stuff back at the shed that will just blow your head away.'"

Callaway said that when they got to the warehouse she had smoked some of Garrido's hash, which had been a mistake.

"[It was] very strong," she said. "It intensified all my paranoid feelings extremely. And I didn't smoke it any more."

Late that afternoon, William Emery took the stand. Under direct questioning he told prosecutor Leland Lutfy that he had lived in an adjoining Mill Street storage shed to Phillip Garrido.

The taxi driver told the jury he had met Garrido soon after moving in, and they had become friendly.

"He asked if I would watch his shed," Emery testified, "and make sure that nobody broke in or anything, because he played music."

Garrido had then told him which vehicles were allowed in front of his shed, giving him a phone number to call if he saw anything suspicious.

The prosecutor then asked what he had been doing on the night of November 22. Emery said he had arrived back in Mill Steet and seen a blue Pinto with California plates parked in front of Garrido's mini-warehouse.

He had then gone inside his unit to change clothes, letting his dogs out for a walk.

"Then I went over to his shed," he told the jury. "I figured he was there, so I went over and knocked twice. The hasp was down so I knew somebody was in there."

When there was no reply, Emery sat outside for the next hour watching, while his dogs played outside. He then got a pen and paper from inside his shed, writing down the Pinto license plate number before going to a nearby service station to call Garrido's home.

When there was no answer, he had jumped on his bicycle and cycled to Garrido's home in Market Street, three blocks away. And when there was no answer there, he cycled back to Mill Street and went to bed.

In his cross-examination, Willard Van Hazel cryptically asked if his client would have been able to score marijuana from anyone within a five-minute range of his shed.

"You did not give Mr. Garrido any grass on that night?" asked the defender.

"No, I didn't," replied Emery.

"Have you on other occasions?"

At that point, the prosecutor objected, saying it was irrelevant, and Judge Thompson agreed.

At 4:30 P.M. Judge Thompson recessed for the day, telling the jury to return the next morning.

12

"HE IS FOLLOWING A PATTERN"

At 9:30 the next morning—February 10—Reno Police officer Clifford Conrad took the stand. Under prosecutor Leland Lutfy's questioning, he told the jury how he had been patrolling Mill Street at around 2:30 A.M. on November 23, when he saw a suspicious out-of-town vehicle parked outside Unit 39.

"The vehicle shouldn't have been there at that time of the morning," he testified. "So I checked further and found the lock on the warehouse broken off."

He then tried to open the warehouse door, but it would only rise four inches, so he started banging on it. Eventually Phillip Garrido appeared and rolled it up.

Asked if he rented the warehouse, Garrido said he rented it from a friend who lived over in Market Street.

"He said he had lost the key," said Conrad. "I asked him for his date of birth and things like that . . . just everything to check [his] story."

"Was he able to respond to each of your questions?" asked Lutfy.

"Yes, sir, he was," replied the officer.

"Did he respond coherently?"

"Yes, sir."

Then while he was questioning Garrido, Katie Callaway's head appeared from behind a plastic curtain, pleading for help. Then she ran out of the warehouse stark naked and stationed herself behind the astonished policeman, who asked her what she wanted.

"Help me!" she told Officer Conrad. "He is trying to rape me."

Officer Conrad then told the jury he had sent Callaway back into the warehouse to dress, permitting Garrido to follow her back inside.

"Why did you allow Mr. Garrido to go back into that warehouse," asked Lutfy, "when Miss Callaway was in there?"

"I was led to believe by Mr. Garrido," explained Conrad, "that he was married and lived down the street and that was his girlfriend."

"Is that what Mr. Garrido said to you?" asked the prosecutor.

"He implied that," said the officer. "He didn't come out exactly and say that."

"How did he imply that?"

"He said he did live down the street, he was married, and this was a friend of his. And he even called her 'Kathy.'"

Although up to then Garrido had answered his questions, he now became "evasive" when asked about the naked girl.

"I asked him how long he knew the victim and where he met her," the officer told the jury, "and he said, 'I don't have to answer that.'"

For the rest of the morning, the jury heard from a series of government experts, testifying that laboratory tests had proved positive for small quantities of cannabis, marijuana and LSD found in the warehouse. And samples of Katie Callaway's pubic hair were consistent with ones found on clothing in Garrido's warehouse and on a pair of his scissors, although none of her hairs were discovered in samples of the defendant's public hair.

Just after 11:00 A.M., the United States government rested its case. And after the jury was dismissed for lunch, defense attorney Willard Van Hazel raised the possibility of Phillip Garrido incriminating himself for the upcoming Washoe County trial, if he now took the stand in this one.

"Your Honor," Van Hazel told the judge, "Mr. Garrido and I have conferred about trial strategy."

The defender explained he had "cautioned" his client of the necessity for him to testify to the jury, in order to establish his psychiatric defense.

"If he takes the stand," said Van Hazel, "to sustain that defense of not knowing that what he did at the time was morally wrong, that he exposes himself to incrimination on outstanding charges in the state of Nevada . . . carrying major penalties."

Then Lutfy told Judge Thompson that if the defendant did take the stand, the jury should be told about his unsuccessful attempt to kidnap another young woman prior to Katie Callaway, in order to show a pattern of behavior.

"The defense is coming up with the insanity, or some kind of defense, based on LSD abuse, as I understand it," argued Lutfy. "That this man was in some kind of fantasy, could not differentiate between fantasy and reality. We think by pointing to and questioning the defendant about specific acts prior to this incident, we can show he is following a pattern of attempting to kidnap and attempting to, and raping, other women. And we do have . . . information of other acts by this defendant."

Pointing out that any evidence of prior acts would be "prejudicial," the judge asked why the prosecution wanted to offer it.

"I think to show the fact that he has the intent prior," said Lutfy, "and this is a consistent act."

"How does it bear on intent," asked the judge, "if he claims that he has been using LSD for four years, and that he is spaced out, or whatever they call it?"

The prosecutor replied there was no evidence that Garrido had taken LSD that night, and did not know what he was doing.

"We can show a similar pattern of behavior in a prior offense relative to the handcuffs, the whole thing is there," said Lutfy. "I think, again, it goes to intent. The jury has the right to see that and determine whether or not this man was fantasizing one time or whether or not this was a thought-out plan of kidnapping and raping women."

Judge Thompson said he would rule later on whether the jury could hear about any of the defendant's prior criminal acts.

Then he turned to Phillip Garrido, telling him that he must decide whether or not to take the stand in his own defense.

"I want to advise you that that is a decision you have to make," said the judge.

"Yes, Your Honor," replied Garrido.

"I have to tell you this, also, Mr. Garrido," said the judge, "that if you decide to take the stand and testify, any testimony that you give can be used in any criminal prosecution. You are not testifying under any form of immunity whatsoever. Do you understand that?"

"Yes, Your Honor," said the defendant.

Van Hazel then asked the judge whether he would allow his client to be cross-examined about the "unnatural act" he was charged with as well as the rape. Judge Thompson replied that as it had not been raised on direct examination, he would not allow it, admitting even he did not know what it was.

Then Judge Thompson recessed the court until 1:30 P.M., when the defense case would begin.

13

"I HAVE HAD THIS FANTASY"

At 1:30 P.M., Willard Van Hazel rose from the defense bench, announcing he was waiving his right to deliver an opening statement. He then called Phillip Garrido's friend and Reno liquor store salesman Gregory Sheppard to the stand.

The twenty-seven-year-old aspiring musician told the jury how he'd met Garrido at his mother's liquor store and they'd become friends, sharing an interest in music.

"Now, during the two years that you knew him," asked Van Hazel, "did you ever observe him using any drugs?"

"Yes, I have," replied Sheppard. "I've seen him taking LSD, pot, cocaine, downers, uppers."

Sheppard said he usually saw Garrido every couple of weeks, when they jammed together in the warehouse.

"At the time he was playing," asked the attorney, "was he also administering drugs to himself?"

"Yes," replied Sheppard.

"Do you have any idea of the type of dosage of LSD he would take?"

"I would say one or two at a time," said Sheppard. "Sometimes maybe three. It just depended on what mood he was in."

"Three what?" asked the judge.

"Three tabs of acid," said Sheppard.

Then the judge asked the witness to explain to him and the jury the different types of LSD.

"Comes in pill form," said Sheppard, "capsule form. It comes in paper, comes in sugar cubes. Those are the most common forms that LSD does come in."

In his cross-examination, Leland Lutfy asked Sheppard about the different strengths of LSD.

"When you saw the defendant taking this LSD," asked the prosecutor, "did you know the strength?"

"It was fairly strong," said Sheppard. "It was blotter-type LSD . . . on a piece of paper."

"And the blotter type of LSD," asked Lutfy, "there are different strengths in that, is there not?"

"Yes, there is," said Sheppard.

Then Willard Van Hazel called his client, Phillip Garrido, to the stand. The tall, thin defendant, wearing a blue suit and brown tie, stood up and walked across the courtroom to the stand.

"Are you married?" asked the defender.

"Yes, sir," answered Garrido.

"Happily?"

"Very happily."

"Do you find your wife attractive?"

"She is beautiful," Garrido replied emphatically.

Then Van Hazel asked how long he had been using narcotics. Garrido replied that he had started using marijuana in 1969, a month after graduating high school. His first LSD experience came just a month after that.

He told the jury he had first been arrested in 1969 for marijuana and LSD.

"What other drugs besides marijuana and LSD have you used?" asked Lutfy.

"Cocaine has been one of the more frequent drugs I have used," Garrido replied matter-of-factly. "On occasion I have taken downers and uppers, but not very often."

Then his attorney asked if he ever combined drugs with each other.

"Whenever I take LSD," he replied, "I also smoke marijuana. And whenever I have had the chance, I have snorted cocaine at the same time. It is a very expensive drug, so that the occasion is only off and on."

Van Hazel asked how frequently he had taken LSD over the previous couple of years. Garrido said he tripped out on LSD every couple of days, but if he took it too frequently, he would have to take more and more for it to work.

"What is the most you have ever taken on an occasion in the last two years?" asked Van Hazel.

"I have taken up to ten hits," replied Garrido. "All at once."

"Have you ever OD'd, or whatever the proper expression is?" asked the defense attorney.

"The only time that I have ever had bad trips is in my younger part of my experiences with LSD. As far as frightening experience."

Then his attorney asked if LSD and cocaine stimulated him sexually.

"Beyond a doubt," Garrido replied, adding LSD turned him on the most.

Van Hazel then asked him if he had taken cocaine around the time of the alleged offense. Garrido said yes, as he'd had some money available.

"I would buy quite a bit," he told the jury. "A large amount that I would put myself up on a cocaine high for two or three days. And sometime even without sleep to the manner of burning out my whole body."

But he claimed not to have taken cocaine the day he had met Katie Callaway, although he had dropped four hits of LSD purchased in South Lake Tahoe.

Then the defense attorney asked if he had sexual fantasies in the late sixties, when he had first got into drugs. Garrido said he certainly did. He would masturbate at home to pornographic magazines, or at a local drive-in. Then he described to the jury how he would arrange two towels over the side windows of his car, so he couldn't be seen, and masturbate in the backseat. But over the past two years, he said, he had begun screening pornographic movies at home on his projector.

"Did you engage in that activity in any other public places?" asked his attorney.

"You mean masturbation?" asked Garrido.

"Yes."

"Well, I have done it in restaurants, bathrooms, lavatories, different types of amusement places, such as a bar."

"Have you done it in residential areas?"

"Yes," he replied impassively, "looking into windows."

"What were you looking at?"

"Women."

"What were the women doing?"

"They were either clothed or partly clothed."

"And you would masturbate yourself then?"

"Yes."

Then Van Hazel asked his client to tell the jury where else in public he had pleasured himself.

"I have done it by the sides of schools," he replied, "grammar schools and high schools. In my car while I was watching young females."

"How old were they, would you guess?" asked Van Hazel.

"From seven to ten."

"Did you ever expose or exhibit yourself on those occasions?"

"A few times."

"What would you do?"

"Open the car door."

"How would you be dressed?"

"Pants down to my knees."

Van Hazel then asked if there was a certain type of pornography that turned him on. Garrido replied that he particularly loved looking at bondage pictures.

"Women in handcuffs, chained," he told the jury. "There [are] the positions that the women are in the magazines . . . the different positions."

"Did this sexual fantasy," asked Van Hazel, "or whatever you want to call it, become increasingly real to you, so you could visualize without pictures, just by closing your eyes?"

"Yes."

"Were you increasingly obsessed with it?"

"Yes. It started the first time I went to a drive-in and started masturbating myself. I found that from that point on, I just increased it into a realm that I didn't even realize."

Then, gently guided by his attorney, Garrido admitted getting in Katie Callaway's car at Ink's Market, and seizing her when she stopped to let him out.

"Did you handcuff her?" asked his attorney.

"Yes."

"Bind her with a strap?"

"Yes."

"Did you take her with tape on her mouth across the line into Nevada?

"No," answered Garrido. "She had no tape on her at that time. I didn't tape her until I got to the gas station, and then I pulled into it, and only taped her for the few minutes that we were there until we left."

Garrido admitted taking her across the state line against her will, saying he was powerless to resist his sexual impulses.

"I have had this fantasy," he told the jury, "and this sexual thing that has overcome me."

"Didn't you know you could be caught and criminally punished for it?" asked Van Hazel.

"Criminally," replied Garrido, "yes, I did know that."

"Didn't you think it was wrong?"

"No."

"Well, who told you it was right?" asked the defender. "Did your parents bring you up to believe that was morally right to do?"

"No," replied Garrido. "My parents never instructed me sexually at all. But just from my parents bringing me up—no."

"You didn't learn in school it was right, did you?"

"No."

"But you didn't think it was wrong?"

"Not at that point in time, no."

Garrido then admitted telling Katie Callaway he was unable to control his behavior.

"Did you tell her you were sorry you were doing this?" asked Van Hazel.

"Yes."

"Why were you?"

"Because she was so nice to me."

"But you weren't sorry enough to stop, were you?"

"No."

The attorney then asked why he had not just had sex with her in the bushes while they were still in California, as she had offered.

"Because I couldn't help myself," replied Garrido, showing the first hint of emotion since he took the stand. "I had this fantasy that was driving me to do this. Inside of me. Something that was making me do it . . . no way to stop it."

Then the attorney asked if he had wanted to be caught, giving his victim several clues to his identity, like his real name and wife's occupation.

"No," said Garrido. "She was convincing me that she was enjoying what she was doing, and I just didn't know what I was doing to be able to tell her that."

"You really thought she wanted to do that?"

"In my own mixed-up mind, yes."

Finally, Van Hazel asked why he didn't get his sexual gratification from the legal brothels in Nevada.

"I went once when I was younger," he answered, "and it never did do nothing for me. I have had the advantage of being with many women . . . with their will."

"But that isn't your sex thing?" said his attorney. "That isn't what drives you?"

"No," said Garrido, shaking his head excitedly.

"And yet," said Van Hazel, "you have stated, 'I live a clean life.'"

"Besides this fantasy, yes," he replied. "I don't go breaking into people's houses. I don't go to hurt anybody."

Before starting his cross-examination, prosecutor Leland Lutfy asked Judge Thompson to allow questions about his failed kidnap attempt, an hour before this alleged offense. Judge Thompson said he needed to hear some of the psychiatric testimony before making his decision.

Then the jury were summoned back into the courtroom and Lutfy began questioning the defendant.

"Do you know what the terms 'right and wrong' mean?" he asked.

"Yes," replied Garrido nervously.

"Do they have any meaning for you?"

"Yes."

"Is it right to beat your wife?"

"No."

"Would it be wrong to beat your wife?"

"Yes."

Garrido testified that he and his wife Chris had "an understanding" about his sexual activity.

"Did she know where you were the night you kidnapped Miss Callaway?" asked the prosecutor.

"No," answered Garrido. "The only thing my wife knew was that I went to South Lake Tahoe to get LSD."

The prosecutor then asked at what point had he taken the four hits of LSD on the night of the abduction.

"Right after the abduction," claimed Garrido.

"You didn't take it before the abduction?"

"No."

"Do you have sexual relations with your wife?"

"Yes."

"Does she restrict your sexual activities with her?" asked Lutfy.

"No."

"Does she let you do what you want to do?"

"Well," replied Garrido, "I don't hurt her, so she does restrict me, yes."

"Why don't you harm your wife?"

"Because I love her."

"Is it only people that you don't love that you harm?"

"I didn't feel I was harming Katherine Callaway," he said. "So I don't feel I was harming anybody."

"You didn't think you were harming her when you put handcuffs on her?"

"No."

"You didn't think you were harming her when you grabbed her by the back of the neck and pushed her neck down to her knees?"

"No."

"You didn't think you were harming her when you put that strap around her?"

"No."

"You didn't think you were harming her when you threw that coat over her in the front seat?"

"No."

"You didn't think you were harming her when you threw her in the back seat—or put her in the back seat—with that coat over her again?"

"No," replied Garrido angrily, "I didn't put the coat over her, in the first place."

"You never put any coat over her?" asked Lutfy.

"I did after the gas station," clarified Garrido.

Then he maintained that he hadn't believed he was harming his victim when he gagged her with tape and threw her on the back seat in handcuffs.

"What about the fact that you didn't put tape over her eyes?" asked the prosecutor. "Why didn't you?"

"Because she asked me not to," replied the defendant.

"She asked you not to rape her, didn't she?"

"No," he replied resolutely.

"Not at the beginning?"

"No."

The prosecutor then asked why he masturbated in his car at drive-ins and put towels in the windows, and not publicly in the middle of the street.

"To hide myself," replied Garrido. "I felt an embarrassment."

"You thought it was wrong? Did you?"

"At that time, yes."

Lutfy asked if he had ever sought psychiatric help for his sexual problems. Garrido said he had not, as he had not thought there was anything wrong with masturbating in cars or restaurant bathrooms.

"Did your parents ever teach you right and wrong?" he asked him.

"Yes."

"Did your get slapped when you were a boy when you did something your parents said was wrong?"

"Very unfortunately, no," he replied.

"Did they ever verbally tell you you were wrong, you shouldn't do this?"

"Up to the point when I was ten years old. After that I was spoiled. My father never did take any restrictions of beating me or disciplining me, and my mother spoiled me."

"Do you feel he should have done that?"

"Yes."

"Why do you think he should have done that?"

"Because of what I have learned."

Lutfy then asked if he had lied to the two psychiatrists who had examined him in jail. And when Garrido claimed to have answered every question honestly, the prosecutor asked why.

"Because I have been working very steadily," he replied, "the last two months with a minister getting close to God."

Garrido said that although he had believed in God for the last three years, it was only after his arrest and incarceration that he had found the Lord.

"In fact," asked the prosecutor, "you told Miss Callaway that you had discovered God or Jesus, didn't you?"

"I told her that I believed in him and someday I would like to turn to him," he replied.

"Someday?" asked the prosecutor. "It wasn't going to be that day, was it?"

"No."

"You think God would like the things you have done?"

"Absolutely not," he said contritely. "I am ashamed of them."

In redirect, defender Willard Van Hazel attempted to show his client had not known the difference between right and wrong during the period of the abduction.

"Mr. Garrido," he began, trying to repair the damage from the prosecution, "were you ashamed when you did what you did to Miss Callaway?"

"No," answered the defendant.

"You were not ashamed?"

"No," he continued, "I couldn't feel shame. I didn't even realize the reality of shame for what I was doing."

Garrido then denied only being ashamed now because he was scared of going to prison, saying his newfound religion was the sole reason.

"Well, what is the difference between then and now?" asked his attorney.

"Because I have come close to God," he replied. "Because I feel God. Because God has shown me he is real."

He said although he had spoken of God to his victim, he knew nothing about it at that time.

"Since November twenty-second," asked Van Hazel, "you have had contact with God?"

"Yes," said Garrido. "I have studied very hard and I have learned what it takes to find God."

The final defense witness was its own psychiatrist, Dr. Charles Kuhn. He told the jury he had spent an hour examining Phillip Garrido two weeks after his arrest, and would occasionally see him later while visiting other inmates.

"Have you observed any changes in his behavior?" asked defender Van Hazel.

"His appearance changed," replied the psychiatrist. "He looks somewhat more healthy, and he certainly seems quite lucid and pretty well together."

Then Van Hazel asked the doctor for his diagnosis of Garrido.

"Drug dependence," said Dr. Kuhn. "Both on LSD and cannabis."

The defense attorney then asked what the doctor believed Garrido's mental capacity to have been at the time of the offense. Dr. Kuhn said Garrido's sexual fantasies, voyeurism and exhibitionism had been exacerbated by his drug use.

"Without the influence of any of this drug involvement," he told the jury, "I think Mr. Garrido would pause before carrying out sexual fantasies."

Then the attorney asked the cause of the defendant's perverse sexual fantasies.

"I think that would be too difficult to explain in any short period of time," replied Dr. Kuhn. "But in any case I do not feel that the drug caused the fantasy."

Van Hazel then asked if he thought Garrido lacked the substantial capacity to conform his conduct to the standards of the law.

"Yes, I do," replied the psychiatrist. "I think the defendant did not have adequate control to conform his behavior."

Finally, Van Hazel asked if the doctor thought Garrido would be a menace to the health, safety and morals of himself and others, without psychiatric treatment.

"I certainly do," replied Dr. Kuhn.

At this point, Judge Thompson dismissed the jury for afternoon recess, so he could consider the prosecution's argument to permit damning evidence that Garrido had tried to kidnap another woman just an hour before seizing Katie Callaway.

The prosecution psychiatrist, Dr. Lynn Gerow, was then summoned into the courtroom to hear this new evidence.

"He entered her car," Assistant United States Attorney Leland Lutfy told the judge, "by again asking for a ride."

The prosecutor said that he directed the unnamed woman to a certain street, and attacked her when she'd stopped the car, exactly as he had done with Callaway.

"Mr. Garrido grabbed this woman," said Lutfy, "put one handcuff on [but] was unable to put the other one on. She jumped out of the vehicle struggling with him. After she promised she would not tell the police, or tell anybody about what he had done, he agreed to unloosen that handcuff."

He then unlocked the handcuff while the car was still moving, before jumping out and running away.

After hearing this potentially explosive new evidence, Judge Thompson asked both psychiatrists if it would have affected their diagnoses, if they had known of it before.

"Not at all, sir," answered Dr. Kuhn.

"It tells me, Your Honor," said Dr. Gerow, "part of the state of mind prior to the alleged offense, in that he formed the intent."

"Would it change the opinion you have reached?" asked the judge.

"No, sir," said Gerow.

Then Judge Thompson ruled against allowing the jury to hear about Phillip Garrido's previous kidnap attempt before taking a fifteen-minute recess.

When the court reconvened, Prosecutor Lutfy attempted to change the judge's mind, saying Dr. Gerow now believed this new evidence would "reinforce" his opinion of Phillip Garrido.

"And on that basis," said Lutfy, "we would ask that the testimony be allowed."

But Willard Van Hazel disagreed, saying he believed Dr. Gerow's opinion was quite clear and didn't need reinforcing.

The judge then asked Dr. Gerow what he felt was important about the evidence. The doctor replied that Garrido had already told him about it during his psychiatric examination.

"And you based your opinion partially on that?" asked the judge.

"All I was saying," said the psychiatrist, "was he was clear-minded and he formed the intent prior to leaving this area and going to Lake Tahoe. And he followed through with his intent, this first abduction being just one part of the sequence of events."

Willard Van Hazel countered, telling the judge that the jury had already heard that his client had come well prepared for the abduction, with handcuffs and a strap.

"There was some planning," he said. "There was a place he was going to. I think we have all of those things. The jury will now be hearing of a crime that the defendant is not charged with."

Then in a victory for defense, Judge Thompson ruled that the jury should not be told about Phillip Garrido's first abduction attempt.

The prosecution then called Dr. Lynn Gerow as a rebuttal witness. The psychiatrist told the court he had spent almost two hours examining the defendant on December 19.

"I formed some opinions about Mr. Garrido," he testified.

"I felt that he was competent to stand trial and I felt he was responsible for the act in question."

Then the prosecutor asked if he felt Garrido had "sexual aberrations."

"I don't use that word," answered the psychiatrist. "I concluded that he had a sexual disorder. He gave a history of being a Peeping Tom or a voyeur . . . of being an exhibitionist and taking his clothes off in front of little girls.

"He gave a history of impulsive masturbation. These things led me to believe that he was sexually deviant and had that mental disorder."

"One last question," said Lutfy. "Is it your opinion, as a result of any mental disease or defect, that Mr. Garrido could conform his conduct to the requirements of the law?"

"He can conform his conduct to the requirements of the law," said the doctor.

"Can he appreciate right from wrong?"

"He can appreciate right from wrong," Dr. Gerow told the jury.

In cross-examination, Willard Van Hazel asked about Garrido's relationship with LSD and sex.

"He used LSD as a sexual stimulant," said the psychiatrist. "He, without LSD, was not sexually stimulated to any great degree."

"Did you arrive at the conclusion in [your] report then that . . . chronic drug abuse," asked the defense attorney, "may be responsible for . . . mixed sexual deviation?"

"Not responsible for the mixed sexual deviation," said the doctor, "so much as I was applying just the tremendous sex drive the man had under LSD."

Finally, Judge Thompson asked if the psychiatrist had ever studied the effects of long-term LSD use.

"I was in San Francisco during what they call the 'Summer of Love,'" said Dr. Gerow. "The heyday of the Haight-Ashbury problem horticulture, and I saw a lot of people who had taken a lot of LSD."

"In your opinion," asked the judge, "can it have a lasting effect on the brain function?"

"Yes," replied Dr. Gerow. "Taken in sufficient quantity, in some individuals it will produce dementia."

The judge then asked if the psychiatric tests he had run on Garrido would have revealed any signs of this. The doctor said they would have, but there was no indication of any brain damage in the defendant.

At 4:20 P.M. the judge recessed until 10:00 A.M. the following day, when he would give the jury its final instructions before they went off to determine Phillip Garrido's fate.

On Friday morning, the federal government called Dr. Albert Peterman as its final rebuttal witness. The neurologist said he had examined Phillip Garrido and given him an EEG brainwave test.

"I was asked specifically if there was any evidence of brain damage," Dr. Peterman told the jury. "I did not feel that there was."

In his cross-examination, Willard Van Hazel asked if his neurological tests would have detected any organic brain damage from LSD or cocaine.

"In the instance of addiction to LSD," he said, "I would likely find nothing on examination."

"How about cocaine?" asked Van Hazel.

"Nothing."

Later that day, Judge Thompson sent the jury out to deliberate. And late Friday night it returned a unanimous guilty verdict on all counts. Then Judge Thompson remanded Phillip Garrido into custody for sentencing.

14

"EVERYBODY IS TRYING TO GET A POUND OF HIS FLESH"

A month later—on Wednesday, March 9, 1977—Phillip Garrido appeared in Washoe County district court for a change of plea hearing. A few days earlier, Ronald Bath, Garrido's defense attorney for the Nevada State case, had cut a plea deal with Washoe County deputy district attorney Michael Malloy. In exchange for the state dismissing the two other counts of possession of marijuana and an infamous crime against nature, his client would plead guilty to one count of forcible rape. The charge carried a minimum of five years to a maximum life sentence in the state prison.

"It doesn't matter to me," prosecutor Malloy told Washoe County judge Roy Lee Torvinen, "as long as that's what the negotiations are. He's going to plead guilty to forcible rape and the other will be dismissed."

Then Judge Torvinen asked Garrido if he had discussed his change of plea with his defense lawyer.

"Yes, I have," he told the Judge.

"Is it your desire to withdraw your not guilty plea to Count One, forcible rape?"

"Yes, Your Honor, I do."

The judge then formally read out the indictment alleging the forcible rape of Katie Callaway, asking how he pleaded.

"Guilty," declared Garrido.

Then prosecutor Malloy said the state had made no commitments to the defendant as to the sentencing it would be asking for.

"He has been found guilty by a jury in Federal Court . . . on a charge that arises out of what happened the same night," Malloy told the judge. "Whatever sentence the federal court gives Mr. Garrido, and maybe already has as far as I know, that hasn't entered in our discussions as to what to do here with this guilty plea. And no representation has been made to him by anybody that I know of as to whether the sentence would run concurrently or consecutively or anything else about the two cases."

"Do you understand the negotiations?" the judge asked the defendant.

"Yes, Your Honor. I do," replied the defendant.

"Are you satisfied with the legal representation you received from the public defender's office?"

"Definitely, I am," said Garrido.

Judge Torvinen then asked Malloy to outline the offenses committed, and the possible penalties now faced by the defendant.

"Mr. Garrido is charged in Count One with forcible rape, to which he has already entered a plea of guilty. The possible penalties, since there is no allegation of substantial bodily injury, are a term of years ranging from a minimum of five to a maximum of life in the state prison.

"The court can fix the sentence in that area. Probation is not available and the matter of how long the sentence should be is entirely up to the court and nobody else."

Judge Torvinen then remanded Garrido until April 11 for sentencing.

Two days later, on March 11, United States district court judge Bruce Thompson sentenced Phillip Garrido to fifty years in federal prison for kidnapping Katie Callaway.

The official United States District Court for the District of Nevada Judgment and Commitment Order read: "The defendant has been convicted as charged of the offense of Kidnapping. The court asked whether the defendant had anything to say why judgment should not be pronounced. Because no sufficient cause to the contrary was shown, or appeared to the court, the court adjudged the defendant guilty as charged and convicted and ordered that: The defendant is hereby committed to the custody of the Attorney General or his authorized representative for imprisonment for a period of FIFTY (50) YEARS."

Four days later, Phillip Garrido sat down in his cell at the Washoe County jail and wrote a three-page letter to federal public defender Kenneth C. Corey, firing his attorney Willard Van Hazel and announcing his intention to appeal his sentence. In his slanting longhand, he wrote:

My appointed councel [sic] from the beginning to end has not been in my behalf, Von Haizel [sic] has tried to his best to keep me from Trial. By telling me there was no defense. I stayed with him because I have no insight on the law. We went to change my plea to guilty. The Judge talked with me, and did not want to accept my plea. So we returned to not guilty. In this case Van Haizel [sic] did not even come to see me until the last four days before trial. He did not even work on my defense until then. At that time he still tried to change my mind in any way he could.

He was unhappy with my case from the start. Van Haizel [sic], felt I should go to prison, just by the way he talked. And put no effort to really help me.

At the time of sentencing I asked him to see if federal time could be run with state time. The man told the judge that request, and then on his own, not in [sic] my behalf, aginst [sic] my will told the Judge that he felt I should not be granted this request, for his own reasons. Not once did he try to help me. But instead did only what he had to so he him self [sic] would not look bad in his line of dutey [sic].

I asked him about modifacation [sic] of sentence [sic], and he also tried to tell me it would do no good.

All in all the man is not wanting to help me.

On these ground's [sic] I ask for dismissal of my appointed councel [sic]. And please respectfully request new appointed councel [sic].

I need some one [sic] right a way [sic] so I can file an appeal. I respectfully ask for legal forms to file:
  A. Rule 15 for modifacation [sic] of sentence [sic].
  B. Availability to Federal Law book & legal transcripts while being without funds to secure same.
  C. Availability to file legal papers & legal representation while being without funds to secure same
  I only have till the 21, to file an appeal. I ask only with respect, to please help me.
  Yours Truly Phillip Garrido

The following day, Willard Van Hazel formally resigned from the case, and Phillip Garrido's appeal was officially filed in the United States Court of Appeals for the Ninth Circuit.

At 9:15 A.M. Monday, April 11, 1977, Phillip Garrido was back in Washoe County Court for sentencing on one count of forcible rape. After reviewing the presentencing reports prepared by the Nevada Department of Parole and Probation, Judge Roy Lee Torvinen asked Garrido's defense attorney, Ronald Bath, if he had anything to say before his client was sentenced.

"Yes," replied the public defender. "First of all, we're not making light of the offense that Mr. Garrido has pled guilty to. However, I would like to point out to the court that this is one of the things that took place across the state line and everybody is trying to get a pound of his flesh, but he's presently under a fifty-year sentence in the federal jurisdiction."

The defense attorney asked Judge Torvinen to accept the report's recommendation, that the state sentence imposed today should run concurrent with the fifty-year federal one. Bath said he had discussed the matter with Washoe County deputy district attorney Michael Malloy, and they both hoped that if the court agreed to let it run concurrently, Nevada would release Garrido into the custody of the federal marshal to begin his fifty-year sentence.

"Unfortunately," said Bath, "California is waiting to go on the same kidnapping, and at this point everybody should realize that there is only so many years of someone's life to sentence him." (Ultimately, California state prosecutors did not file any charges.)

The defender told the judge that his client was now "extremely remorseful" about the offense, which was caused by "extreme use of drugs."

"He's hoping to benefit from the time spent in prison," said Bath, "and to better his life. And I think he's a candidate for the court's consideration in this matter."

Then prosecutor Michael Malloy stood up to address the judge.

"I don't know which one of us is getting the impound of flesh," he said, "the federal government or the state of Nevada or both. But anyway, I don't know that I'm getting a pound of flesh. I don't mean to make light of it either, but this is an extremely serious offense."

Then Malloy told the judge that during the plea negotiations, he had never committed himself to the Nevada sentence being served concurrently.

"I do believe that it would be concurrent," said Malloy. "In light of the fact of the sentence in the federal court, and I assume there will be a hold placed on Mr. Garrido if he is released to the federal authorities, and should he be paroled, which he will undoubtedly be from the federal prison. If he would not have been paroled from the Nevada prison by that time, he will have to come back to the Nevada state prison to serve whatever time before he is or isn't paroled."

Then Judge Torvinen asked the prosecutor for his input as to whether Garrido should begin serving his sentence in the state prison system or the federal one.

"As crowded as the state prison is," said the prosecutor, "it doesn't matter where he does his time and the federal prisons aren't as crowded. And I don't object to sending him to the federal prisons first and have the state of Nevada place the hold, but I think the sentence should be for the crime committed, and maybe by the time he's released he won't be so dangerous, because right now he's a dangerous man."

Defender Ronald Bath pointed out that when his client was sentenced in the federal court, Judge Thompson had been unable to decide if the fifty-year sentence should be concurrent with the state one.

"If in fact the district court judge wanted to do that," said Bath, "he had nothing to run it concurrent with."

Then Malloy told Judge Torvinen what his and the defense attorney's understanding was of when Phillip Garrido would be eligible for federal parole.

"Your Honor," Malloy said, "Mr. Bath informs me that he has to do a minimum of two-thirds of the federal sentence before paroled."

Malloy told the judge that as Garrido would be eligible for parole in just five years on the Nevada offense, it would be far better if he started serving his time in the federal system, as it would be for far longer.

Then, before passing sentence, Judge Torvinen asked Phillip Garrido if he wanted to address the court.

"Well," began the defendant, slowly rising to his feet, "the only thing I do say is that I'm very fortunate that this happened to me because my life was in a crash course. Before I ever came into using marijuana my life was clean. I had no arrest record, but association with marijuana led me to harder drugs, and I've used LSD for the last seven years and if it wasn't for the drug LSD I wouldn't be here right now.

"But this has given me a chance to find something more important than anything and that is God—and the most important thing, I can straighten my life out."

The judge then turned to Garrido for sentencing.

"Upon the entry of the plea of guilty," Judge Torvinen began, "to the indictment, Count One, forcible rape, a felony, it is the judgment of the court that the defendant is guilty, and it is the sentence of the court that he be sentenced to the Nevada State Prison for a term of life.

"As I understand that statute, it is with the possibility of parole, that the sentence run concurrent with the sentence of the interstate kidnapping by the federal government that I understand is fifty years."

Bath then asked the judge to release the Nevada State hold

on his client, so the federal marshal could transport him to a federal prison, to start serving his sentence.

"He was sentenced first from the federal court," said the judge, "and it will be the order of the court that he fulfill the federal sentence before required to maintain the balance of his term under the Nevada state sentence."

The judge then formally dismissed counts 2 and 3 against Phillip Garrido, who then stood up to have the final word.

"Your Honor," he said. "I would like to say one more thing that I didn't want to say before. But I feel I will be helped more in the federal prison because of the facilities and psychiatric treatment."

"All right," said the judge, as the court bailiffs led him away to start serving his fifty-year federal sentence.

At 5:00 P.M that afternoon, Judge Roy Lee Torvinen signed the official judgment, sentencing Phillip Garrido to life, with the possibility of parole, for the forcible rape of Katie Callaway. The life sentence would run concurrently with the federal one.

Both the judge and prosecutor Malloy mistakenly believed it would be at least thirty-three years until Garrido would be eligible for federal parole before being returned to Nevada to complete his sentence. But under the law at that time, Garrido would be eligible for parole after serving just a third of his federal time or ten years of a life sentence, or of a sentence of over thirty years.

And the misunderstanding that day would prove a tragic mistake with huge consequences.

15

LEAVENWORTH

On June 30, 1977, Phillip Garrido started serving his time at Leavenworth Federal Prison in Kansas. Located twenty-five miles north of Kansas City, Kansas, Leavenworth is the biggest maximum security federal prison in the United States.

Built at the beginning of the twentieth century, the tough prison's most notable inmates have included Robert Stroud, the notorious Bird Man of Alcatraz, and gangsters George "Bugs" Moran, who fought Al Capone for control of the city's underworld, and George "Machine Gun" Kelly.

Thirty-foot-high walls surround the 22.9-acre prison facility, housing almost two thousand of America's most dangerous prisoners. Its domed main building is the original "Big House" and also nicknamed the "Hot House," during the steamy hot summers, because of its poor ventilation.

By all accounts, Phillip Garrido was an exemplary prisoner. He soon settled into the Leavenworth routine, where inmates are released from their cells every morning at 6:00 A.M. and free to roam around the prison compound until lights out at 10:00 P.M.

A month after he arrived, Inmate Garrido was officially designated for "close custody and regular duty status." The prison classification team assigned him to work in the carpenter shop, recommending he seek further education to prepare himself for college.

On August 1, he embarked on a half-day educational program, and a month later he began seeing psychologist Dr. John B. Kiehlbauch, of the Mental Health Division, to work on his substance abuse problems.

"He is verbal from the outset of contact," Dr. Kiehlbauch later wrote. "He is cooperative, candid and volunteers information readily, even if self-critical."

Imprisoned 1,750 miles east of Reno, Phillip Garrido's only contact with the outside world were monthly telephone calls to his beloved mother, Pat, and weekly letters to other family members. He received no visitors.

During his free time, he played guitar and wrote new songs. He regularly attended church services, becoming an active member of a devout group of Jehovah's Witnesses. He exercised in the prison yard, as well as attending weekly movie shows.

A few months after Phillip Garrido's incarceration, his wife Chris filed for divorce.

"I went to visit her," recalled former Rock Creek guitarist Eddie Loebs. "And she seemed generally pleased and happy that he was finally out of her life. She was just happy to be rid of him."

Loebs asked what she was going to do with his valuable collection of vintage guitars and Marshall stack amplifiers and speakers.

"She said she was going to sell his equipment," he said, "and move on."

That summer, Garrido's fifty-seven-year-old mother Pat married a businessman named Herschel Franzen, moving into his home in Antioch, California. She found a job with the local school district as a maintenance worker, regularly writing letters to her youngest son in Leavenworth. And she assured him that he could move in with her and her new husband when he was released.

On August 8, United States Attorney Lawrence J. Semenza and his assistant Leland Lutfy, who had prosecuted Garrido at his federal trial, filed a sixteen-page answering brief to counter Garrido's appeal, filed by his newly appointed defense attorney James Hollabaugh.

"Appellant asserts that the government's reference to the rape was 'inflammatory,'" read the brief. "Indeed, what could be more inflammatory than his own testimony."

In late November, the United States Court of Appeals Ninth Circuit rubber-stamped Garrido's federal conviction. The three-judge panel found no merit in his argument that because he had raped and assaulted Katie Callaway after crossing the state line, the federal case became "irrelevant."

"Our analysis of the record convinces us," wrote the judges in their opinion, "that appellant's assignments of error are groundless. The judgment of conviction must be affirmed."

Four months later, Phillip Garrido filed a motion to the United States District Court for Nevada, asking to reduce his fifty-year-sentence by half, making him eligible for parole in eight years. His motion was pursuant to Rule 35 of the Federal Rules of Criminal Procedure, allowing the court to reduce a sentence within 120 days of it being imposed, although a year had already passed.

As part of the motion package, he included a handwritten letter to Judge Bruce Thompson, claiming to be a changed man.

Honorable: Bruce R. Thompson.

When living at home and going to school, my life was free from the influences of drugs. I had been raised in the country and lived in a very clean home. I was the baby of the family and spoiled in the long run.

In 1969 marijuana was reaching out to the rural area in Calif. From that point on my life was slowly changing. The drugs would bring more asocation [sic] and in turn more contact with drugs. It wasn't long before a few months pasted [sic] and L.S.D. had become a part of my life.

Slowly it began to take me to another style of living and thinking, in the long run I lost much of my reasoning powers. Seven years of using made me fall from reality.

On my own I have been seeing Dr. Kiehlbauch of Men. Health. We have private one hour sessions, in which we have progressed very well.

At this time I have started and finished high school in order to prepare for college.

I have been working at the carpenter shop as I desire to learn the trade. So I have inrolled [sic] in an apprentice carpentry program lasting four years. Along with that I inrolled [sic] in drafting school as I felt it was a very important part of carpentry.

This summer I start college. After my four years of drafting and carpentry I plan on a two year computer course.

I have set my goals and find myself well on my way. It shall take seven years of schooling to complete these courses.

In all respects my life has changed. Of course that is because I wanted to, knowing this is my chance to get my life in line. Drugs have been my down fall [sic]. I am so ashamed of my past. But my future is now in controle [sic].

If I may please, all I ask is to be given the chance. By writing and asking for a report on me from Dr. Kiehlbauch and all departments would be giving me the fairest examination I could hope for.

Sincerely,
Phillip C. Garrido.

In the March 24 motion to reduce his sentence to twenty-five years, Phillip Garrido carefully listed reasons why Judge Thompson should do so. He noted that when he committed the crime, he was "suffering from the effect of marijuana and a drug known as LSD," claiming they cause him to withdraw from reality, so he lacked the capacity to conform his conduct to the law.

Garrido also "prayed" for the reduction in his sentence, claiming that a lengthy stay behind bars would interfere with his further education and future plans.

"The Petitioner's long sentence denies [him] certain training and rehabilitation," stated the motion. "It is the Petitioner who has set his own goal to reform his old way and live a new life on his own. [He] could become a very useful citizen and be rehabilitated if he could have his sentence reduced to twenty-five (25) years, which would make him a parole date in eight (8) years, where he could be released to the State of Nevada as an Educated Person and being a rehabilitated person."

On April 5, 1978, Phillip Garrido turned twenty-seven. The same day, he received a glowing progress report of his first year in Leavenworth. His senior case manager, R. S. Rose, wrote that he was making good progress and had a clean conduct record.

"Mr. Garrido has demonstrated an above average adjustment in all areas of his confinement," read the official report. "Mr. Garrido has maintained a clear conduct record while at Leavenworth."

Garrido now worked as an apprentice carpenter, responsible for woodworking equipment, cabinet-making and installation.

"His work supervisor has rated him average," stated the report. "He shows regular attendance on the job, gets along well with others, reacts well to authority, and accepts responsibility. Mr. Garrido is presently receiving Meritorious Good Time for his responsibilities within the Carpenter Shop."

The report also applauded Garrido's recent academic accomplishments, as he now pursued college-level courses.

"Mr. Garrido has been successful in significantly elevating his academic level of performance," noted his education supervisor.

It noted that on March 16, Inmate Garrido had been reassigned from the basic educational program to the Drafting Vocational Training Program. And he had also enrolled in eight hours of college course work for the upcoming summer session.

"He is an exemplary student," stated the report, "and cooperative in all respects."

Two weeks later, Leavenworth clinical psychologist Dr. J. B. Kiehlbauch prepared a detailed four-page psychological evaluation of Garrido, to help U.S. district judge Bruce Thompson decide whether to reduce his sentence.

"Mr. Garrido is the product of a prosocial middle class family, now broken," wrote Dr. Kiehlbauch in his report, "from which he inculcated generally appropriate values, though he described himself as over-condoned and pampered by his parents. A high school graduate, he has no military service or work record of consequence, describing himself as a 'semi-professional musician.'

"There seems little question that Mr. Garrido was 'a spoiled child.' It is characteristic of him to go to extremes in whatever commitments are made or programs are undertaken; depending on the character of the pursuit, this can be contributory to excellence or extreme derogation.

"At this point in time, only occasional feelings of depersonalization, cognitively construed hallucinations, and nightmares plague him from the earlier toxicity. He has good management of impulses in the psychosexual realm, and appropriately oriented toward their prosocial expression throughout his future years.

"In effect, it does appear the instant offense evolved from the potentiation by drug use of what were comparatively normal drives to abnormal forms of expression and intensity."

Dr. Kiehlbauch appeared much impressed with his patient's positive progress in his first year at Leavenworth.

"He has gained measurably with respect to these over his period of service to date," wrote Dr. Kiehlbauch. "Highly significant is Mr. Garrido's record of accomplishment in training, education, and treatment since his arrival here. He has achieved conspicuously in educational self-development, on-the-job training in carpentry, and in a drafting vocational training course."

And the psychologist also noted how the convicted kidnapper and rapist was now a devout Jehovah's Witness, participating in religious ceremonies with other inmates.

"The depth of his religious commitment and his impact on his life philosophy are clear," noted the doctor, "and his style of dealing with these phenomena, is on balance, quite healthy. He sees himself as one whose life is and will be based on his strongly held religious beliefs."

As to his progress in treatment, the doctor noted that Garrido had been "regular, active, and highly productive." And taking into account his long fifty-year sentence, their work had involved developing his personality, resolving areas of conflict and reevaluating his lifestyle patterns.

Dr. Kiehlbauch reported that his patient was "acutely conscientious," his "prime concern" being that their lengthy sessions together were "inconveniencing his supervisor," as it kept him away from his work detail.

"Mr. Garrido follows a very active work and leisure activities schedule," he explained, "and seems quite healthy in his interests."

The doctor also reported positive results for a barrage of psychological testing Garrido had recently undergone. The Minnesota Multiphasic Personality Inventory Test—used to identify deviant personality traits—showed Garrido's personality was "healthy," falling within normal limits.

Garrido was also given the Bender Motor Gestalt Test, developed in 1938 to screen children for developmental disorders or brain damage.

"Activity and approval-seeking behaviors were a strongly recurring phenomena," wrote Dr. Kiehlbauch. "The protocol reflected careful attention to detail and manner of presentation without significant derogatory indicators."

Dr. Kiehlbauch also put his patient through the Rotter Incomplete Sentence Test, where he was given forty unfinished sentences to complete. Developed in 1950, this test is commonly used to test sex offenders and evaluate their state of mind.

"The Incomplete Sentence Test," wrote the psychologist, "reflects Mr. Garrido as a sensitive young man, who is deeply committed religiously and goal oriented in management of life's problems and aims."

Dr. Kiehlbauch reported that the test also revealed Garrido becomes "driven" and "compulsive" when he commits to a cause or purpose, approaching it with "extreme zeal and diligence."

"Appropriate degrees of secondary narcissism," wrote the

doctor, "and considerable conflict with regard to his current marital situation are also clear."

Summarizing his report, Dr. Kiehlbauch expressed great surprise when Phillip Garrido rejected his offer to help him transfer to a far easier mental health facility. Instead his patient had insisted on spending a minimum of three more years at Leavenworth, allowing him to complete his religious education and development program.

"All things considered," Dr. Kiehlbauch wrote, "this examiner recommends 1) a modification of the current sentence to indeterminate parole eligibility, and 2) a recommendation that he be paroled when treatment and training goals are accomplished, unless there is some dramatic change in his condition in the interim."

Dr. Kiehlbauch also recommended that on his eventual release from prison, Garrido should receive psychological treatment and parole supervision to ease his transition back into the community.

"Prognosis for successful transition to the community is considered very good," reported the doctor. "The likelihood of further extralegal behaviors on Mr. Garrido's part is seen as minimal."

Three weeks later, on May 10, Assistant United States Attorney Leland Lutfy filed a motion in district court urging Judge Thompson to deny Phillip Garrido's plea to reduce his sentence. He pointed out that the defendant had filed his motion well past the 120-day limit after sentencing, and was therefore void.

"While defendant Garrido's motion might at first blush appear to be made by a repentant criminal," wrote Lutfy, "the Court should keep in mind the nature of the crime for which Garrido was convicted and the circumstances surrounding it."

The prosecutor then reminded the judge how cruelly and viciously Garrido had treated his victim during her kidnapping.

"Garrido treated this girl no better than he would a side of beef," read his motion, "and the Court's imposition of sentence was equal to Garrido's actions."

Judge Bruce Thompson agreed, ruling that Phillip Garrido's fifty-year federal sentence would remain.

16

NANCY

On July 20, 1979, Phillip Garrido's mother Pat, now fifty-eight and nearing retirement, and his new stepfather Herschel Franzen, purchased a three-bedroom gray cinderblock house in Antioch, California, for $68,000. Built in 1951, 1554 Walnut Avenue was a 1,457-square-foot home in an unincorporated rural part of town. It fronted almost one acre of land in its backyard.

All the houses in Walnut Street have large extended backyards, where chickens and other domestic animals wander around freely.

Dale and Polly White moved into their house on Viera Avenue around the same time. And their back garden backed directly onto the Franzens', sharing a back fence.

"I used to work at the post office," said Polly White. "Pat had a post office box there and I'd see her occasionally and ask how she was doing. We were not friends but I just knew who she was."

After losing his fight to have his sentence reduced, Garrido, now twenty-eight, settled down at Leavenworth to serve his time. He regularly exchanged letters with his mother, who wrote him all about her new home in Antioch, which would one day be his.

In early 1980, a few weeks after Garrido's divorce was finalized, a cellmate introduced him to his attractive twenty-five-year-old niece Nancy Bocanegra, who was visiting him in Leavenworth.

Garrido struck up an immediate rapport with the shy, soft-spoken petite beauty, who lived in Denver, Colorado. The willowy, dark-haired, olive-skinned girl was also a devout Jehovah's Witness, and over the next few months Phillip Garrido assiduously courted her with romantic love letters.

He told the withdrawn and impressionable woman how he had now found God, putting his former life of sex and drugs behind him. And when he proposed marriage, saying it was God's plan for them to be together, she had no hesitation in saying yes. Soon afterwards he wrote to his ex-wife to tell her the news.

"He found God," said Christine. "He was marrying a Jehovah's Witness lady, somebody he met who visited Leavenworth."

Now that he had exhausted all his appeals, the ever-calculating Phillip Garrido had embarked on another tack. For if he had a loving wife and a stable home life awaiting him on the outside, his chances of parole would be far higher than they were at the moment.

Nancy Bocanegra was born on July 18, 1955, in Bexar County, Texas, one of six children of Mexican-American parents. There was little that stood out about the pretty, dark-haired girl, as she grew up as what her brother David would later describe as "an all-American girl" in a "loving" home.

"[She was] a normal kid," remembered David Bocanegra. "A teenager going out with her friends, working, having a good time."

When she was seventeen years old, the Bocanegra family moved to Denver, Colorado. Nancy found a job as a nursing aide and according to her brothers never got in any trouble with the police.

"I don't think she even had a speeding ticket," said David.

"Not even a parking ticket," added another brother, Rey.

But after Nancy met Phillip Garrido at Leavenworth, everything changed. In the fall of 1981, twenty-five-year-old Nancy Bocanegra began making frequent trips to Leavenworth, Kansas, to visit her fiancé.

"I knew Nancy," said Garrido's father Manuel. "She came

down to visit him in prison. I took her to lunch. I got to know her."

Manuel Garrido says he got on well with Nancy and approved of the match. But her family was horrified at the prospect of her marrying a convicted kidnapper and sex offender.

"Once she met Phillip," said her brother David, "that was it. It was like she was no longer around."

On Wednesday, October 14, 1981, Phillip Garrido married Nancy in a religious ceremony performed by Senior Pastor Nanfore Craig, of the Leavenworth Prison Interfaith Church. A couple inmates acted as witnesses, and after the ceremony a prison official took a wedding photograph of the newly married couple.

A few days later, Phillip Garrido proudly sent it to his father, who had refused to attend the wedding. He wrote on the back, "All our love, Phillip and Nancy Garrido."

Four years of prison had aged Garrido, and he had lost his youth. He now sported a Western-style mustache, his shirt unbuttoned revealing a rugged hairy chest. The newly wedded couple have their arms around each other, as Phillip stares coolly at the camera and Nancy, her hair scruffily parted in the middle, looks at her new husband adoringly.

"It's the only picture that I have," said Manuel Garrido in 2009. "When he got married that's what he sent me."

Straight after the wedding, Nancy returned to Denver, remaining in daily contact with Garrido. She was now working as a state licensed nurse's aide, regularly making the nine-hundred-mile trip east to Leavenworth to visit her husband.

And Phillip's unwavering confidence that it was all part of God's plan and he would soon be free, so they could start a family, helped her get through the tough times.

In May 1984—just seven years and two months into his federal sentence—Phillip Garrido had his first parole hearing at Leavenworth. His parole application was considered by the five-member Nevada State Parole Board, who denied his request on the grounds that he was still a danger to the public.

The board also took into account the severity of his crimes, that he had injured his victim, his previous criminal history and that he had not shown signs that he had reformed.

"The board finds that further evaluation of your progress is necessary," read its report. "Release at this time would depreciate the seriousness of the crime."

A year later, Nancy Garrido moved to Leavenworth to be nearer her husband. She easily found work as a nurse, renting a cheap one-bedroom apartment in a converted townhouse. Over the several years she lived there she kept to herself, leaving little impression.

Her Leavenworth landlord, John Saunders, barely remembers Nancy Garrido, assuming she must have been a good tenant to get her deposit back.

Nancy could now visit her husband in the federal penitentiary as often as regulations would allow, and became even more under his control. And Phillip always gave her tasks to do, ordering her around like a servant.

In March 1986, Inmate Garrido was turned down at his second parole hearing, with the board again ruling him a danger to the public.

"In the opinion of the parole board," read the State of Nevada Parole Board report, "continued confinement is necessary to protect the public from further criminal activity."

A few days later—on March 19, 1986—he was transferred to Lompoc Medium Security Federal Prison in Santa Barbara County, Southern California. Nancy followed him to California, moving into her mother-in-law Patricia Franzen's home at 1554 Walnut Avenue, Antioch. She found work as a nursing and physical therapy aid for disabled patients, and was well-regarded by her employer.

The Lompoc facility lay three hundred miles due south of Antioch, and Nancy would drive her mother-in-law there for visits. On the face of it, Inmate Garrido now appeared to have a loving family waiting on the outside, ready to give him the stability he would need if he was ever released on parole.

17

"I'LL SEE YOU AGAIN, KATIE"

On November 5, 1987, two examiners from the U.S. Parole
Commission met Phillip Garrido at Lompoc Penitentiary to
determine if he was ready for parole. During the thirty-five-
minute prison interview, Garrido freely discussed his crime,
as well as his experience as an inmate and his hopes for
the future.

The thirty-seven-year-old inmate told the commissioners
that he was now happily married, and, if granted parole,
planned to go and live with his mother and stepfather.

Neither federal prosecutor Leland Lutfy or Garrido's public defender attended the hearing, and it is doubtful if the commissioners were even shown Garrido's psychiatric reports or
reviewed a transcript of the trial. For apparently they knew
nothing of the horrific details of Katie Callaway's kidnapping
and rape. And they seemed unaware of Garrido's own admis-
sion at trial of being a Peeping Tom, exposing himself in public and masturbating to girls as young as seven.

The highly articulate inmate charmed the commissioners,
telling them that all his troubles were the result of drugs, which
were now in his past. And he persuasively spoke of his hard
work in prison to earn a further education diploma before learning the drafting and carpentry trades.

He told them how he had been spiritually reborn after finding the Lord behind bars, saying his arrest had been a true
blessing in disguise.

* * *

Two weeks later, the U.S. Parole Commission examiners unanimously voted to grant Phillip Garrido federal parole, transferring him to a Nevada state prison to finish his potential life sentence. Their report painted a highly positive portrait of Inmate Garrido as living proof of how the prison system at its best can rehabilitate and reform.

Ironically, federal parole was abolished that same month, with sentences becoming far longer and mandatory. But Garrido slid under the wire, as he was already serving his sentence when the far tougher regulations came into effect.

Under the old system, parole suitability was determined by a numerical formula, factoring the inmate's age, high school diploma and history of heroin/opiate dependence. Phillip Garrido was rated category seven, actually making him eligible for parole as early as 1985, although he had been required to serve at least ten years.

On January 20, 1988, the commission officially granted Phillip Garrido parole, after serving just ten years, eleven months of his fifty-year sentence.

"Phillip Craig Garrido is eligible to be paroled," read the U.S. Parole Commission's Certificate of Parole. "[The] said prisoner has substantially observed the rules of the institution, and in the opinion of the Commission said prisoner's release would not depreciate the seriousness of this offense or promote disrespect for the law, and would not jeopardize the public welfare."

Two days later, he was discharged from federal custody.

"Before you lies the opportunity," the U.S. Parole Commission wrote Garrido, "to plan and re-establish the course of your life toward goals approved by society and in accordance with the principles of good citizenship."

He was then transported to a medium security state prison in Carson City, Nevada, for the life sentence he owed Nevada for forcible rape. But astonishingly he was already eligible for parole in Nevada, for his time served in federal prisons.

Two days later, on January 22, Garrido was photographed for a Nevada Department of Prisons mug shot. In the photograph he has short hair and a small mustache. He is wearing regulation prison garb, staring at the camera impassively, his eyes giving nothing away.

On August 4, seven months after his transfer to the Carson City prison, Phillip Garrido attended his third Nevada State parole hearing. And the state board commissioners now reassessed Garrido, designating him "moderate" risk. Under the Nevada State assessment criteria, he scored a six out of a possible perfect ten low risk score.

Had the commissioners known that in 1969 he had served time in California's Clayton Farm Facility for drug offenses, it would have added two points to his score, making him a "high risk" parolee with a score of four.

After considering his case, the Nevada State Parole Board voted three to two to free Phillip Garrido from prison and into federal parole.

In the official State of Nevada Board of Parole Certificate, Phillip Garrido was granted parole with surprisingly few restrictions. He had to reside in California with his mother and maintain steady employment. He was also required to submit to searches and regular drug testing, as well as attending outpatient substance abuse sessions and mental health counseling. But there were absolutely no restrictions on his contact with children.

On August 29, 1988, Phillip Garrido walked out of the Carson City Prison, after serving just seven months and four days of his Nevada life sentence. He then traveled 210 miles west to the ECI Halfway House in Oakland, California, entering a community treatment program for sex offenders.

Garrido was now virtually free to come and go as he pleased, as long as he attended his treatment sessions. During that time he reportedly had one violation of his parole agreement, being sent to San Francisco City Jail for a short time, before being allowed back to the ECI Halfway House.

During the brief stay at the halfway house, he and Nancy visited his father Manuel and brother Ron several times in the Brentwood house where he had grown up.

"After he got out of prison," said his father, "I saw him a few times. But then he went to live with his mother and I didn't see him any more."

After Phillip Garrido's trial, Katie Callaway had tried to put her nightmare behind her, but she found herself haunted by him day and night. Even though he was serving a fifty-year sentence halfway across the country, she constantly cried and had recurring nightmares of Garrido chasing her.

"I was hoping if I just forgot it," she said, "it would just go away. It didn't."

The first Christmas after the trial, Callaway sent Officer Clifford Conrad a holiday card, thanking him for saving her life. She was now back at the casino, but was wary of strangers, unable to stand within ten-foot "grabbing distance" of them.

Her relationship with her boyfriend David Wade had broken up under the pressure. And all the tension at home led to her young son, who knew what had happened, getting into trouble at school.

"He didn't know why Mommy was crying all the time," Callaway said later. "He acted out by going to school and getting into fights."

In 1980, she moved to England to start a new life, but still couldn't forget her nightmarish memories of the rape.

"I walked around like a zombie," she recalled. "I had to tell everyone I met what had happened to me—because I didn't feel like myself. It was as if I had to explain why I wasn't 'normal.'"

After five years abroad, Callaway, now in her late thirties, returned to South Lake Tahoe, as she missed family and friends. She found a job as a casino dealer at Caesar's Palace, Lake Tahoe, and tried to get on with her life.

But Phillip Garrido still haunted her and in 1987 she registered with a federal victim notification program, to contact her if he was ever released. They assured her his earliest possible parole date was 2006, so she stopped worrying.

A year later on a Friday afternoon, she was working a roulette wheel at Caesar's casino when a tall, thin man came up and sat down beside her. She immediately knew it was Phillip Garrido, the hairs on the back of her neck standing up.

"He walked right up to my table," she remembered, "and he said, 'Hi, Katie.'"

The man bought a pile of chips and ordered a cocktail.

"You know, Katie," he said, staring her straight in the eye, "this is my first drink in eleven years."

Katie froze in fear, hearing his unmistakable voice again and realizing that her worst nightmare was coming true—that somehow the man who kidnapped and raped her had escaped from prison and was sitting just feet away.

"It was creepy," she said. "He tried to engage in small talk but I was guarded. After he got his drink, he cashed out, leaned towards me, and said, "I'll see you again, Katie."

In a panic, Callaway summoned her pit boss, saying she had just seen the man who had kidnapped her. The casino security then chased the man down, checking his driving license. But as he was not carrying Phillip Garrido's ID, so they let him go.

"I'm sure it was him," said Callaway. "I'm convinced he came back to see me."

Still shaking with fear, she resumed her shift at the roulette wheel. On her twenty-minute work break she dashed to the nearest pay phone, calling Lompoc Penitentiary. She was told Garrido had been released to San Francisco City Jail, pending parole. Appalled that her attacker could possibly be out on parole so soon, she then called San Francisco City Jail, which informed her that he was now living in an Oakland halfway house.

When she contacted the halfway house she was given Garrido's parole agent's phone number, so she called and made an appointment. A few days later she met with his parole agent, who told her Garrido had gotten a degree in psychology in prison, teaching classes to other inmates.

"That's how he got out so early," she said. "[I was] scared to death. I was terrified."

According to Callaway, the parole agent described Phillip

Garrido as "a sick puppy," saying he was certain to reoffend, although he didn't think she was in danger.

"He thinks he's smarter than everyone else," Callaway says the parole officer told her. "And the thing is when he doesn't get his own way his whole persona changes."

After the meeting, Katie Callaway returned to Lake Tahoe and tried to resume her life, but was too scared knowing Garrido was out there and knew where she was. So three months later, she packed up her belongings and moved to a small town in central California, making her friends and family promise not to tell anyone where she was living.

"I knew how dangerous this man was," she later explained. "I had to put my invisible cloak on and disappear."

18

THE SECRET BACKYARD

Phillip Garrido was also lying low. On December 16, 1988, he was finally released on federal parole, moving into his mother's three-bedroom house at 1554 Walnut Avenue, Antioch.

"He came to live with me," said Pat Franzen in 2009, "because he had nowhere else to go. And Nancy was looking after me, so it seemed the best thing at the time."

Phillip and Nancy Garrido soon settled down into a comfortable anonymity, and could not have picked a better place for what he had in mind.

Antioch was founded in 1850 by twin brother itinerant ministers William and Joseph Smith. They arrived during the great California gold rush, naming the town Smith's Landing. But a year later it was overrun by malaria, killing Joseph and most of the population.

Making a fresh start, William Smith threw a town-naming picnic on July 4, 1851, on the bluff overlooking the San Joaquin River. The town's entire population of thirty-five men, women and children came to decide on a new name for their community. And at Smith's suggestion they renamed it Antioch, after the fourth-century Syrian city, known as the cradle of Christianity.

In 1859, rich deposits of coal were found in the hills to the south of Antioch, and a prosperous mining industry sprang up. That led to the creation of several new towns around Antioch, including Black Diamond, now renamed Pittsburg.

In 1876, a railroad was built from Antioch to the coal mines, to improve efficiency. And toward the end of the nineteenth century copper ore was discovered, making the town even richer.

The town's fortunes waned in the twentieth century, as copper supplies ran out and coal mines closed down. This led to an exodus of people leaving Antioch, looking for better opportunities in San Francisco.

By the time Phillip Garrido arrived, Contra Costa County was a modest bedroom community for Oakland and San Francisco, easily accessible through the State Route 4 corridor.

Although on the surface Antioch was a respectable blue-collar city with a population of around 90,000, a large slice of semi-rural unincorporated areas surrounded it and was a throwback to the Wild West. And with its scruffy wooden cabins, trailer homes and crude cinderblock houses, Walnut Avenue was *the* perfect place for Phillip Garrido to slip under the radar of law enforcement.

The unincorporated part of town is the boondocks, stretching for about four miles along the San Joaquin River. There is little if any police presence, as the nearest police station is miles away. There are also no schools, libraries or post offices.

Walnut Avenue and neighboring Viera Avenue, Santa Fe Avenue and Bown Lane are virtual dirt roads without sidewalks. Many driveways are littered with rusting trucks, with chickens roaming around overgrown lawns, reined in by wire mesh fences.

Cheap housing attracts people on the edge of the law, including many coming out of prison. With few opportunities in the rundown area, the main industry is crystal meth, and drug abuse is rampant. There is a proliferation of home-based labs, turning out large quantities of methamphetamine and crack cocaine. It was not quite what the federal parole authorities had in mind when they made it a condition of Phillip Garrido's bail that he move there to live with his sixty-seven-year-old mother.

In unincorporated Antioch, everybody keeps to themselves, minding their own—often shady—business. And over the next several years, Phillip Garrido would have no trouble transforming his mother's back garden into a fully functioning prison compound. This time he would do it properly, making sure that police would not stumble into his pleasure palace again, like they had in Reno.

Phillip and Nancy Garrido soon settled into their new lives at 1554 Walnut Avenue. Nancy's nursing job with the disabled was going well, and although her fellow workers thought her withdrawn and slightly strange, she worked hard and was well-respected.

"She was quiet but she would always talk to me," remembers Maria Christenson, who worked in the same building. "She worked for the handicapped people and was nice. But I would be the one doing all the talking, she'd be the one nodding or whatever. She never said much."

Helen Boyer, who lived next door, had been friends with Pat Franzen when her son and daughter-in-law suddenly moved in without any explanation.

"He was always in a hurry," she said, "and just different. But he was a good neighbor. [Nancy] was distant and I never had a conversation with her. She was just real cordial."

The federal parole authorities had designated Phillip Garrido moderate risk, placing few restrictions on him. He was required to attend outpatient mental health counseling, but there is no evidence that he ever had a counselor to supervise him. His supervision reports, covering the first three years of his federal parole, were satisfactory, as he logged month after month of "difficulty free" life in the community.

As conditions for his parole, Garrido was now subject to drug testing and was forbidden from drinking alcohol. It would take him more than a year to officially register as a sexual offender, as required by law.

Soon after he arrived at 1554 Walnut Avenue, Phillip Garrido embarked on a series of home improvements. Working under cover of night, Garrido erected an eight-foot fence, as well as planting a line of shrubbery and other foliage, dividing his backyard into two.

"It was just there one day," remembered Polly White, who shared a back fence with the Garridos. "He also installed a fence that was eight foot high, and the boards overlapped each other. And then in the places where he didn't have the board he just nailed up pieces of wood. And it was all overgrown."

Garrido had effectively created a backyard within a backyard, completely screening the large area at the back from the prying eyes of neighbors. Over the next few months, he also built a ten-foot-by-ten-foot soundproofed shed, as well as a primitive outhouse and shower, stringing yards of green electricity cables along the ground from the house for power.

He dragged an old mattress into the soundproofed shed, installed restraints and fitted security bars on all the windows of his mother's house, to stop law enforcement breaking in.

Occasionally his older brother Ron and his wife would visit the house, and were shocked at how Nancy seemed under Phillip's control like "a robot." Years later, their father Manuel Garrido told the *New York Post* that Phillip had once propositioned Ron to have three-way sex with Nancy.

"[Phillip] wanted them to go back and have a threesome at the house," Manuel would claim. "Ron said no, and Phil then started screaming and asking if Nancy wasn't good enough for him."

On November 19, 1988, a few weeks after Phillip Garrido was paroled, nine-year-old Michaela Garecht and her best friend Katrina Rodriguez rode their scooters to the Rainbow Market in Hayward, California. They left the scooters outside the convenience store, going in to buy sodas, beef jerky and taffy.

When they came out a few minutes later, Michaela's scooter had been moved across the parking lot, by an old battered sedan car about thirty feet away. So the pretty, blonde-haired blue-eyed girl walked over to retrieve it. Suddenly Katrina saw a tall man in his late twenties appear out of nowhere.

"You looking for your scooter?" the man asked. "It's over by my car."

Then Michaela screamed as the man suddenly grabbed her and threw her into his car.

"She was just kicking and screaming," Katrina recalled. "And he shoved her in the car, got in the car himself and pulled out. I just stood and watched, frozen in shock."

A massive manhunt ensued, but there were no clues except a partial palm print on the missing girl's scooter. Later Katrina helped a police artist compile a sketch of the abductor. Years later she said it bore an astonishing resemblance to Phillip Garrido, then living just sixteen miles away, in an Oakland halfway house.

Michaela Garecht's disappearance was the first in a series of mysterious abductions over the next year.

At 3:00 P.M. on January 30, 1989, thirteen-year-old Ilene Misheloff left Wells Middle School in Dublin, California, to walk home for ice skating practice. The freckled teenager with brown curly hair was last seen walking toward a ditch at Mape Park, commonly used as a shortcut. Later her backpack was found on a path, but Ilene was never seen again.

Although the Alameda Sheriff's Department interviewed hundreds of suspects after her disappearance, they never questioned convicted abductor and rapist Phillip Garrido, who was living just forty miles away, in Antioch.

Ten months later, six-year-old Jennifer Chia and her eight-year-old brother Charles disappeared into thin air in Reno, Nevada. They were last seen at 3:20 P.M. October 18, getting off their school bus, by their home at the Timber Hills apartment complex in southwest Reno. It was just three and a half miles away from where Phillip Garrido had once lived. On July 25, 1990, their skeletal remains were discovered off Highway 70 in Plumas County, California—fifty miles west of Reno.

And two months later, seven-year-old Monica DaSilva was snatched from her bed in the middle of the night, as her little brother James slept next to her. Her battered remains were later found in a canyon outside Reno.

It would be another twenty years before detectives reactivated all these cold cases, to see if Phillip Garrido was the man responsible.

Part Two

19

JAYCEE LEE DUGARD

In the summer of 1979, Kenneth Slayton, a ruggedly handsome thirty-three-year-old decorated Vietnam veteran, was going through a difficult divorce. So he went on a camping vacation to Lake Havasu, Arizona, to get away from it all. At the resort he met a twenty-year-old graphic artist named Terry Dugard, embarking on a passionate affair.

"I met Terry at a lake," remembered Slayton. "I was in the middle of a divorce and we had a fling for about two weeks. She was a very sweet gal."

After the camping trip the lovers returned to their respective homes, soon losing touch with each other. But about a year later, Slayton heard through friends that Terry had given birth to a baby girl, who looked exactly like him.

But by that time he had met his future wife, and never attempted to see the baby.

On May 3, 1980, Terry Dugard gave birth to a healthy baby girl whom she christened Jaycee Lee. As an unmarried mother, living outside Los Angeles, Terry scrimped and saved, working as an art designer. She brought up Jaycee alone, helped by her sister Tina, a teacher who lived nearby.

Growing up, Jaycee Lee was a striking girl who turned heads with her flaxen blonde hair and piercing blue eyes. She was naturally shy and nervous, with only a few close friends at school.

"[She was] an introverted child," said Terry. "Very shy, but once she did make friends she made them for life. She would pull you into her own little world."

When Jaycee was seven years old, Terry married a handsome forty-year-old carpet contractor named Carl Probyn, who was also a Vietnam vet. They moved into a house in the Los Angeles suburb of Garden Grove.

At first Jaycee resented her new stepfather, feeling he was coming between her and Terry.

"My wife and [Jaycee] were more like sisters," explained Carl, "because I didn't come in her life until she was about seven years old. I used to tease them that I couldn't get a quarter between them on the couch. They were really close."

Terry soon became pregnant again, giving birth in 1989 to a baby girl they named Shayna. Nine-year-old Jaycee adored her baby sister, often helping her busy mother take care of her.

In June 1990, the Probyn family vacationed in Lake Tahoe, falling in love with its serene rural beauty and deciding it would be the perfect place to bring up their family.

"The mountains and the clean air and a small town," said Carl, "someplace where we'd be safe. Where the kids would be safe."

The Probyns now saw their future living in the idyllic lakeside resort, on the Nevada-California border. Every summer the low-crime town drew gamblers and beach lovers, replaced by skiers and snowboarders in the winter. With a population of just 25,000, it had a friendly small-town atmosphere where everybody knew everybody. And Carl and Terry agreed it would be far safer than the concrete big city.

"We just decided to take the chance and move up there," said Carl, who soon found work, hanging wallpaper and working nights at the American Legion Hall.

That September, the Probyn family moved into a house on tree-lined Washoan Boulevard in the peaceful South Lake Tahoe suburb of Meyers. Jaycee was now ten years old and her baby sister Shayna was eighteen months.

A few weeks after they arrived, Terry enrolled Jaycee in the fifth grade of the Meyers Elementary School. At first she found it hard being the new girl in town, and her teachers were concerned.

"Jaycee was very quiet," recalled her fifth-grade teacher, Sue Louis. "I remember having to talk to her mom about trying to encourage her to raise her hand more, because even if she knew the answer, she didn't want to raise her hand."

The bashful, introverted girl also had problems making friends.

"She was a new kid," said her fifth-grade classmate Nicole Sipes, "so she didn't have a lot of friends. [She was] very soft-spoken . . . kind of kept to herself a little bit."

But Jaycee was highly intelligent, inheriting her mother's artistic gifts.

"She was a decent student," recalled Meyers Elementary School principal Karen Gillis-Tinlin. "She was well liked but didn't have a lot of friends."

But Jaycee enthusiastically joined in many school activities, becoming a Girl Scout and playing on the soccer team.

That holiday season, Carl Probyn put up a Christmas tree in the front room, and Terry and Jaycee helped trim it. Since moving to South Lake Tahoe, Jaycee's relationship with her stepfather had improved dramatically, and she had now accepted him as her father.

On Christmas morning a smiling Terry donned a Santa hat, as Carl shot home movies of an excited Jaycee and Shayna opening their presents.

"A boombox," exclaimed a delighted Jaycee as she unwrapped a gift, before helping Shayna with hers.

"Moving to Tahoe felt like freedom and safety," said Terry. "And Jaycee was blossoming."

By the spring of 1991, Phillip Garrido's plans to turn the backyard of 1554 Walnut Avenue, Antioch, into a prison were well advanced. He was already back into drugs, his new favorite being crystal methamphetamine, which gave him a manic energy for all the heavy work necessary.

Nancy was now working at an abused children's center and had started drinking heavily, after discovering she was infertile. Phillip had told her it was God's wish that they have children, and if they could not have them naturally, they must seize a young girl to bear their fruit.

On May 3, 1991, Jaycee Lee Dugard celebrated her eleventh birthday, with a party for her friends at the Round Table Pizza restaurant. There was a birthday cake and a joyous Jaycee blew out the eleven candles on it.

Now at the end of her first year at Meyers Elementary School, Jaycee was finally coming into her own and had become more outgoing.

Every morning she walked up Washoan Boulevard to the school bus stop with her friend Jamie Smith. And her teacher, Sue Louis, was pleased with Jaycee's progress.

"She's every teacher's dream," said Louis. "She was responsive in class [and] always did her work on time. She was cooperative and she worked well with other kids."

On Friday, June 7, Jaycee attended a sleepover party for her friend Kelly Brosnahan's eleventh birthday. A photograph taken that night shows a laughing Jaycee dressed in a pink top and light blue trousers, sharing a joke with her friends.

"We had fun," Brosnahan recalled. "And we were playing Nintendo and just the normal things you'd do at a sleepover."

That weekend Jaycee helped her parents run a stall at a local arts fair. And later several people would remember an intense dark-skinned woman with jet-black hair lurking around it.

On Sunday night Jaycee told her mother she wanted a pet dog. But the little girl seemed unusually distracted, refusing to say what was wrong.

"Something was on her mind," Terry would later say. "I wonder if she wanted to tell me she'd been approached by this woman at the fair."

A few weeks earlier, Jaycee had been asked to list her likes and dislikes for a school assignment.

She wrote: "Blond hair. Blue eyes. Freckled. Sibbling [sic] of Shayna. Lover of chocolate, cats, horses. Who feels happy on holidays. Pain when hurt. Who needs loving care. Friends. Family. Who fears bumble bees, spinach and spiders. Who would like to see my friends. Less homework. More trees."

20

THE ABDUCTION

Just after eight o'clock the next morning, Phillip Garrido's shabby gray Ford sedan was parked across the street from Jaycee's house. It was a bright sunny day and the street was empty, as he watched the front door of the girl's house, while Nancy sat in the passenger seat clutching a stun gun.

Then they saw the beautiful girl they had followed the day before. She was wearing a pink windbreaker, stretch pants and white sneakers, looking far younger than her eleven years.

The predators watched her go into the garage, before coming out of the driveway and heading up the steep hill.

At 8:12 A.M. Garrido turned the ignition key to start the engine, slowly driving down Washoan Boulevard. He made a U-turn by the house and then drove back up the hill towards Jaycee.

As he pulled alongside the tiny four-foot, seven-inch, eighty-pound girl, he suddenly turned the wheel around sharply, cutting her off. Then the little girl screamed in terror, as Nancy threw the door open and snatched her into the car.

Nancy pushed the defenseless child to the floor, shooting a bolt of electricity from the stun gun to subdue her. Then Phillip Garrido slammed down the accelerator, speeding off down Route 50 toward Antioch.

After witnessing Jaycee's abduction, Carl Probyn jumped on his mountain bike in a burst of adrenaline, giving chase up the twisted mountain road. But he was no match for the silver sedan which had sped off at high speed.

"I couldn't catch them," he later explained. "My energy was gone after seeing what happened."

So in a panic he rode back down the hill to a neighbor's house, screaming to call 911 as there had been a kidnapping. By the time he reached his neighbor's front door, she already had emergency services on the phone.

"My daughter was just kidnapped," Carl breathlessly told the dispatcher. "Top of the hill. It was a gray Ford. A man and a woman in the car."

Jaycee's abduction was also witnessed by some of her Meyers Elementary classmates, who were waiting at the bus stop on Pioneer Trail. Nicole Sipes was already on the bus when it arrived at the stop a couple of minutes later.

"The twins from across the street ran onto the bus," she remembered, "and started yelling, 'They took her! They took her!'"

Then an El Dorado County sheriff's officer arrived and boarded the bus, ordering the frightened pupils to stay put.

"Everybody was scared," said Sipes. "A police officer gets on and says we all have to stay on the bus. You know something bad has really happened."

Within minutes of Carl Probyn's 911 call, an all points bulletin was broadcast for a two-tone silver Ford sedan, with a male driving accompanied by an Arab-looking woman with jet-black hair and a little blonde girl dressed in pink.

The Tahoe Basin is shaped like a giant bowl and has only seven roads in and out. But instead of sealing off these roads, the El Dorado Sheriff's Department, which was soon joined by the South Lake Tahoe Police Department, focused the search within.

Ironically, El Dorado deputy sheriff Jim Watson had been on his way to Meyers Elementary School with his wife when the emergency distress call came over his police radio. He immediately made a U-turn back to his office, where he was appointed lead detective on the search for Jaycee Lee Dugard.

The experienced forty-seven-year-old investigator immediately drove to Washoan Boulevard to interview the abducted girl's stepfather, Carl Probyn, the only eyewitness to her abduction.

Still in deep shock, Probyn described the kidnappers' car as an early '80s or late '70s silver two-tone Ford Grenada. He said he had not seen the man driving, but had got a good look at the woman passenger, describing her as between thirty and thirty-five years old, with an olive complexion and dark straight hair. Later a police artist used his detailed description to make composite a drawing of the woman for the media.

Terry Probyn was at her desk at work when an El Dorado County sheriff's officer walked in.

"We have reason to believe your daughter was kidnapped," said the officer.

In that moment, Terry Probyn's world fell apart.

By 10:00 A.M., California and Nevada highway patrols and law enforcement officers from all neighboring counties had joined in the search for Jaycee Lee Dugard. Police helicopters and planes took to the air, and officers started canvassing door-to-door for any leads. Local radio stations broadcast descriptions of Jaycee, the suspected female abductor and the car used in the kidnap.

Meyers Elementary School was in total lockdown, with the children in a panic.

"I had walked into the office," recalled principal Karen Gillis-Tinlin, "and the secretary said, 'We've got a problem. One of our children has been abducted.' [I was] sickened. This just doesn't happen in Tahoe."

Then the school bus Jaycee should have been on arrived, after police finally allowed it to complete its journey.

"I remember the kids coming from Jaycee's bus," Kelly Brosnahan later told *Dateline NBC*. "They heard somebody got kidnapped, and then another group of kids said they thought it was Jaycee."

As word quickly spread around the South Lake Tahoe community, anxious parents began arriving at school, concerned it was their child who had been abducted. And television news crews descended on the school, trying to interview anyone they could.

"My students were scared," said Jaycee's teacher, Sue Louis. "Some of the kids already knew about it because they had witnessed it at the bus stop. The kids were very agitated and upset."

Later that morning, counselors arrived to help Jaycee's classmates try and cope with her abduction.

"I had kids in my office within a few hours," said Gillis-Tinlin, "asking, 'Can we pray for Jaycee?'"

Jaycee's classmate Stephanie Spees said the children were too young to fully comprehend what was happening.

"The news crews were coming up to the school," she said. "Counselors were coming and talking to us. It was intense for being so little."

At around 11:00 A.M., Phillip and Nancy Garrido pulled up in front of 1554 Walnut Avenue, Antioch. All through the 160-mile drive from South Lake Tahoe, a petrified Jaycee Lee Dugard had been restrained by Nancy in the backseat.

When they arrived at the house, Phillip carried the tiny girl through a secret blue tarpaulin entrance into the hidden prison compound he had so carefully prepared. Then he threw her into the tiny soundproofed shed, placing her in restraints and locking the door behind him.

It would be eighteen months before they would allow her out to see daylight again.

21

"IF YOU CAN HEAR MOMMY"

After Terry Probyn learned of her daughter's abduction she went into deep shock. Later she would describe it as having open-heart surgery, without being sewn back up again. That first agonizing day she chain-smoked and drank heavily, in a desperate effort to cope with the heartbreak of losing her beloved daughter.

By the afternoon, when there was still no sign of Jaycee Lee Dugard, calls from her kidnappers or ransom notes, investigators became increasingly concerned for her safety. They realized that there was a clock ticking, with each passing hour decreasing the chance of getting her back alive.

South Lake Tahoe was in virtual lockdown, as investigators set up checkpoints on all roads. They searched scores of old two-tone Ford sedans, showing motorists a picture of Jaycee that her mother had provided.

Specially trained police dogs walked the abduction site, in the hope they might pick up a trail. And detectives were also running down a report of a suspicious vehicle seen near the Probyn house on Sunday.

At 3:30 P.M., someone reported seeing a man driving a sedan with a woman and a little girl in pink by Fallen Leaf Lake, just five miles from where Jaycee had been snatched. Teams of investigators rushed there, but there were no signs of Jaycee or her abductors.

It would be the first of hundreds of false leads over the next few months, and investigators would faithfully check out each and every one of them.

Within hours of the abduction the FBI had been called in, and Special Agent Chris Campion of the Sacramento office was assigned case agent.

"From the very first call," said Agent Campion, "our agents were out there covering leads shoulder-to-shoulder with the sheriff's department."

Agents from the FBI's Reno and South Lake Tahoe offices were also drafted in to help in the search.

"Basically everybody with a badge within fifty miles," said Agent Campion, "was somehow involved in this case."

Late that evening, FBI spokesman Special Agent Joseph T. Sheehan held a press briefing. Without revealing Jaycee Lee Dugard's identity, he told reporters that her stepfather had witnessed the dramatic abduction. He said a man and woman may have been working together to kidnap the eleven-year-old girl, but so far no ransom demand had been received.

He appealed for anyone with any information to call the El Dorado County Sheriff's Department or the Sacramento FBI Office, giving out special hotline phone numbers.

At nine o'clock that night, Terry and Carl Probyn invited a local television news crew into their home and made a plea directly to their daughter and the kidnappers.

"Jaycee," sobbed a distraught Terry, dabbing her eyes. "If you can hear Mommy, I love you, and I want you to come home tonight safe and sound. It's been thirteen hours and that's too long. She's got to be scared."

Then Carl told how he had witnessed Jaycee's abduction, but had been powerless to save her.

"I saw the dust," he said choking up, "and I heard one scream and I realized I couldn't catch them. She's eleven years old. She's a pretty little blonde and some psycho came down the hill, saw her . . . and just snatched her."

Then he pleaded with the abductors to return Jaycee unharmed.

"Drop her off," he said. "Let her go back home. Don't hurt her."

On Tuesday morning, the *Sacramento Bee* metro section carried a front-page story, headlined "Girl, 11, Abducted On Way To School Near Lake Tahoe." In the story, FBI agent Joseph Sheehan was quoted as saying that the unnamed girl lived with her stepfather and mother in Meyers.

"Her natural father resides in Southern California," he said. "At present, the father is not a suspect in the case."

The *Tahoe Daily Tribune* also reported the story, with FBI special agent Albert Robinson asking for sightings of any suspicious people in town over the last several weeks.

"Even though it may seem trivial," he said, "[it] may fit into our puzzle."

That day hundreds of FBI investigators and law enforcement agents from California and Nevada, as well as volunteers, searched the whole Lake Tahoe area for any signs of Jaycee Lee Dugard. Investigators now believed that the man and woman suspected of the kidnapping might have been local and still in the area.

"We had a command post of between one hundred and two hundred officers [going] out door-to-door searching," recalled lead detective Jim Watson. "We had dog teams and horse teams out searching the woods all around the area."

Leads were coming in from the public by the minute, and every one was followed up. But twenty-four hours after the abduction, Watson knew that time was running out.

Later that morning, Terry and Carl Probyn held a press conference at the El Dorado Sheriff's Department's South Lake Tahoe station. They were accompanied by Carl's mother, Wilma, and Jaycee's little sister, Shayna.

Clasping Jaycee's favorite stuffed bunny to her chest, Terry tearfully announced the family was posting a $5,000 reward for any information leading to her daughter's safe return.

"Please don't hurt her," wept Terry. "She's a good girl. Just drop her off. No questions. No nothing."

Then she told reporters how Jaycee would check the microwave oven clock in the kitchen every morning, starting her walk to the school bus stop at precisely 8:05 A.M. And she described how Carl had watched in horror as he'd witnessed Jaycee's abduction.

"My husband heard her scream," said Terry, "and that's it."

Then Terry burst into tears, as she spoke directly to her missing daughter.

"If you are out there and you can hear me," she sobbed, gazing longingly into the camera, "you know I love you and want you to come back soon. She's out there somewhere. The baby has been asking for you, Jaycee."

El Dorado County Sheriff's Department sergeant Larry Hennick told reporters his officers had been working around the clock, setting up checkpoints all over the Lake Tahoe area.

A reporter then asked if investigators believed Jaycee's disappearance had anything to do with a domestic dispute. FBI special agent Joseph Sheehan replied that Jaycee's natural father had already been questioned but was not a suspect.

"At this point," said Agent Sheehan, "we are less inclined, if we ever were inclined, to see this as a family matter."

Suddenly, from the back of the room, a smartly dressed female TV tabloid show reporter started yelling at Carl and Terry Probyn.

"What are you hiding in that house?" she shouted accusingly.

As everyone turned around in amazement, the woman continued, lambasting the police for not allowing her camera crew to film inside the Probyns' home.

In the hours after Jaycee Lee Dugard's abduction, South Lake Tahoe plunged into shock and disbelief. Nobody could believe that something so horrible could touch the tranquil town, where serious crime was virtually unknown. And from now on parents started taking their children to the bus stop or directly to school.

"Kids were very, very worried," explained Meyers Elementary School principal Karen Gillis-Tinlin. "They walk to the bus every day. It was a common thing . . . and then it went awry."

For the rest of the week, all special events marking the end of the school year were cancelled. And Jaycee's fifth-grade class became a continuing group therapy session, as her teacher and classmates tried to make some sense of her disappearance.

"It was a very scary time," recalled Meyers fifth-grade teacher Sue Louis. "We did personalize—'My gosh, this could have been my child.'"

Then suddenly pink ribbons started appearing all over South Lake Tahoe, on trees, poles and posts. It was reminiscent of the yellow ribbons for the American Embassy hostages in Iran, twenty years earlier.

"We had pink ribbons on the kindergarten fence within twenty-four hours," said Gillis-Tinlin. "The students knew that her favorite color was pink. Pink ribbons were everywhere."

Jaycee's heartbroken classmates also tied a pink ribbon to her chair, writing letters to their lost friend as a way of expressing their feelings.

"The kids needed to talk about it," said Louis. "What an incredibly scary thing to have happen in a small town."

Jaycee's classmates even drew their own missing persons posters for their lost friend. And in a heartbreaking photo opportunity for the Associated Press, three of them posed holding them up.

"Pleas [sic] look for her. It is worth it," read one little girl's poster. "Tahoe Girl Kidnapped," read another. And another classmate's poster had drawings of a heart and a flower, alongside the words, "Jaycee Lee Kidnapped. Please Look."

Another classmate, Kristina Rhoden, who had attended Jaycee's eleventh birthday party a month earlier, said South Lake Tahoe was never the same again after she disappeared.

"It was horrible," she explained in 2009. "There was an overflow of fear. That bus stop in Pioneer Trail was a major stop. We realized it could have been anybody who was taken. We just couldn't believe someone we knew was kidnapped—that no one was really safe."

* * *

On Wednesday, June 12, two days after Jaycee Lee Dugard was taken, the El Dorado Sheriff's Office released the composite drawing of the suspected female kidnapper based on Carl Probyn's description. The drawing showed a thin-faced Arabic-looking woman in her thirties, with piercing dark eyes and long black hair. It was circulated to all law enforcement agencies in California and Nevada, as well as television stations and newspapers.

The El Dorado County Sheriff's Department—the official lead agency of the investigation—were now receiving an average of one new lead every five minutes from all over America.

"We are checking all of them out," Special Agent Tom Griffin of the FBI told *The Sacramento Bee*. "But I am afraid that we have nothing positive to report right now."

After Terry Probyn's heartfelt television plea to the kidnappers, two families from Lake Tahoe and Sacramento, who wished to remain anonymous, had pledged $10,000 each, bringing the total reward money to $25,000.

As the long agonizing hours turned into days, Terry Probyn chain-smoked, drinking herself senseless. Her friends and family tried to comfort her, but she was inconsolable. Her mood swings alternated between panic, hope, anger and despair.

"Basically my wife collapsed," recalled Carl Probyn. "She was just beside herself."

On Wednesday afternoon, Terry Probyn received a visit from Trish Williams, who ran a San Jose–based nonprofit agency called Child Quest International, dedicated to the recovery of missing children.

After spending some time with Terry, Williams decided she needed to be occupied doing something constructive, instead of drowning her sorrows in alcohol.

"We wanted to get her out of the house," she later told author Robert Scott, "and doing something . . . positive."

So she drove Terry to St. Theresa's Catholic Church, where dozens of volunteers had gathered to walk the streets, distributing Jaycee's missing poster, as well as the sketch of her suspected female kidnapper.

Jaycee Lee Dugard's missing poster, which would also be used on a t-shirt, bore two recent photographs and read:

ID INFO

Jaycee is a white female, 4'7" tall, weighs 80 pounds, has straight blonde hair and blue eyes. She has a gap in her front teeth, a chicken pox mark between her eyes and a birthmark on her right arm below her elbow. She also has a mole on her back and was last seen wearing a pink jacket, pink stretch pants, a white t-shirt and white canvas tennis shoes.

CIRCUMSTANCES

Jaycee was last seen by her step-father walking up a hill to her school bus when a gray on gray vehicle made a U-turn and the person on the passenger side grabbed her and put her in the car and sped off. The step-father gave chase but lost sight of the vehicle. Jaycee has not been seen or heard from since.

IF YOU SEE THIS CHILD, OR MISSING PERSON, OR KNOW WHERE SHE IS LOCATED, PLEASE CONTACT THE EL DORADO SHERIFF DEPARTMENT.

For the next few days, Terry Probyn helped distribute the posters, which soon started appearing on walls, trees, convenience stores and motels all over California and Nevada, and later as far away as the East Coast.

22

AMERICA'S MOST WANTED

By Thursday morning, seventy-two hours after the kidnapping, investigators had made little progress in their search for Jaycee Lee Dugard. Although there had been hundreds of reported sightings of the little girl or the kidnappers' car, nothing had checked out.

"Everyone was so concerned," said the FBI's lead investigator on the case, Chris Campion, "because it was such a tragic and shocking case for the community. We got tons of calls, and we really diligently followed every lead that we possibly could to its logical conclusion."

At his daily press briefing, El Dorado County sheriff Don McDonald said all investigators really had to go on was Carl Probyn's description of the getaway car, now believed to be a two-tone gray 1980s Mercury Zephyr. He said that although investigators still believed the kidnappers might be holding Jaycee in the area, all the roadblocks and door-to-door searches had stopped.

Now-retired FBI special agent Mary Ellen O'Toole was part of the team of profilers working the Jaycee Dugard case. She thought it "striking" that a couple, especially a woman, was involved in such a crime. O'Toole, who would later co-write an FBI manual on child abduction, said investigators had been working on the theory that Jaycee's kidnappers had also taken Michaela Garecht, three years earlier.

"We had this cluster of child abductions," O'Toole told

Dateline NBC in 2009, "and of course one of the primary questions . . . were they committed by the same individual."

The FBI investigators were also astonished at the apparent "high-risk behavior" of the kidnappers.

"It occurred in broad daylight," she observed. "Plus, it occurred in front of other people who could provide us with information about the car, about Jaycee, about the abductor."

On Thursday afternoon, Anthony Batson, a producer on Fox Television's highly rated *America's Most Wanted* (AMW), flew into Sacramento with his crew. They then drove to South Lake Tahoe to interview Carl and Terry Probyn at their Washoan Avenue home. It would be the first of three AMW segments on Jaycee over the next few years.

"It was my first time dealing with the parents of a missing child face-to-face," Batson remembered. "We talked to Jaycee's parents. . . . They were devastated and desperate."

Batson and AMW correspondent Lena Nozizwe interviewed the Probyns in their pine-tree-canopied backyard about the fateful morning their daughter had disappeared.

"Tears flowed throughout the interview," said Batson. "Some of them were mine."

Then they filmed Carl in the garage, where he had witnessed the abduction.

"Once the car opened," he said, "I really panicked. I reached for my car keys. Didn't have any. They were in the house."

The AMW crew then moved to Jaycee's bedroom, interviewing her tearful mother on her bed, surrounded by her daughter's beloved teddy bears and dolls.

"We do feel she's alive," said thirty-two-year-old Terry holding Jaycee's teddy bear. "You know, I feel her in my heart. And that's what keeps me going."

The segment, which would air the following night, included home video of Jaycee's recent birthday party, with a slow-motion shot of her blowing out birthday cake candles.

"It was edited in such a way," said Batson, "as to grab the viewer's attention, make them look closely at the cute blonde girl on the screen, and motivate them to pick up the phone and call our free 800 number, if they had the slightest detail they thought investigators could use."

In 2009, Batson, now a senior producer with CBS's *The Early Show*, would admit that at the time he secretly believed Jaycee was already dead.

"The FBI says the first seventy-two hours is crucial in a missing child case," he explained. "After that, the chances of recovery are next to zero."

On Monday, June 3—one week before Jaycee Lee Dugard's abduction—a two-year-old girl had been playing alone in the garden of the Beverly Lodge Motel in South Lake Tahoe. Inside her mother was paying a bill at reception, when she saw a dark-skinned woman pick up the child and start walking toward the hotel entrance.

She dashed out to challenge the woman, who immediately handed over the child, saying she had just been looking for the mother. Then she got into a white pickup truck and was driven away by a Caucasian man.

After reading about Jaycee's abduction and seeing the sketch of the suspected woman, the mother had called investigators to report the earlier incident.

And on Friday morning, at its daily briefing, the El Dorado County Sheriff's Office appealed to the mysterious woman to come forward, so she could be eliminated from the investigation.

Lieutenant James Roloff then told reporters that the investigation had been "scaled down," due to a lack of promising leads. And investigators were now hoping that evening's *America's Most Wanted* telecast would revitalize the search.

"If there are no developments over the weekend," reported *The Sacramento Bee*, "investigators will reevaluate the effort Monday."

That night millions of viewers all over North America watched the moving *America's Most Wanted* segment on Jaycee Lee Dugard's abduction.

"Have you seen Jaycee Lee Dugard?" asked AMW host

John Walsh. "Jaycee's eleven years old. She has blonde hair and blue eyes. She's four-and-a-half feet tall and weighs eighty pounds."

The dramatically powerful piece generated hundreds of leads, none of which came to anything. One viewer mailed in an ad from a swingers magazine, saying the photo of the dark-haired woman in the advertisement resembled the composite sketch.

There were no windows in Jaycee Dugard's prison, and it was stiflingly hot that summer. Her only sense of time was when Phillip and Nancy Garrido would unlock the shed door to feed her. They gave her old clothes to wear and a rotting mattress to sleep on, only allowing her out of the filthy shed to use the makeshift toilet and shower. And investigators believe that Garrido may have fed his captive tranquilizers and other prescription drugs to keep her compliantly under his control.

Within a month of her abduction, Phillip and Nancy Garrido entered the shed with a tape player. They then turned it on to play one of his country-and-western-style love songs. In his deranged way, Garrido tried to create a romantic setting to have sex with his eleven-year-old prisoner.

He then forced the little girl down on the mattress, telling her it was the will of God, and mercilessly raped Jaycee.

At first Jaycee tried to scream for help, but he had sound-proofed the shed so effectively, no one could hear her. Several times a day he would come to abuse his slave, subjecting her to unimaginable sexual cruelty.

What went through the little girl's mind is anybody's guess. But as the days turned into weeks, and the weeks into months, and then years, the gentle child stopped fighting back, eventually resigning herself to her fate.

23

THE SUMMER OF TERROR

Two weeks after Jaycee Lee Dugard was taken, there was still no sign of her. But although she seemed to have disappeared off the face of the Earth, her smiling toothy grin and enchanting blonde-haired, blue-eyed looks were known to everyone. Her distraught family regularly joined hundreds of volunteers, handing out "missing" fliers. Jaycee's poster blanketed almost every tree and fence in Tahoe and neighboring towns. And children all over the area were now wearing "Have You Seen Jaycee?" buttons, emblazoned with her photo.

"I never knew I had so many friends," Terry told *Sacramento Bee* reporter Mark Glover.

Each day Terry and Carl Probyn sat by the phone, waiting for news and fielding calls from reporters. But with absolutely no word of their daughter, every day was yet another torturous ordeal for them to face.

"I was walking the floors, ranting and raving," Terry recalled, "thinking the worst."

On Tuesday, June 25, Sheriff Don McDonald admitted the investigation was no nearer finding Jaycee than it had been on the day she was taken.

"We've had literally hundreds of leads," he said. "But we have none right now that we think are really promising."

The sheriff said that the fifty-officer investigation had now moved into another phase. Investigators were checking if any vehicles in the area fitting Carl Probyn's description were registered to sex offenders. And they were also looking into the files of seven children who had gone missing in the Reno area over the last several years.

He said his department had also been receiving calls from psychics, claiming to know where Jaycee was being kept.

"We'll have a psychic call," said the sheriff, "say[ing] she's being held in a large building in a metropolitan area. There's really no way to check that out."

Terry Probyn was also receiving a flood of upsetting calls from all over the country, making things even worse.

"They were driving me crazy with satanic theories," she told *People* magazine in November 1991. "One woman called and said she felt that Jaycee was in a trunk of a car at a casino. So we spent the day knocking on trunks of cars at casinos."

Years later, Reno psychic Dayle Schear—who later worked on the O. J. Simpson case—would claim that Terry Probyn had consulted her soon after Jaycee's disappearance. The celebrated psychic says she did a psychic reading for the Probyns, in which she described the man and woman holding Jaycee near a white bridge.

"I described the general area and how she was being held," Schear said. "I said it was sexual. I knew she was being held at force and she could not get to a phone to call."

Another psychic Terry and Carl consulted several times told them that they both knew the abductors. And several years later, Jaycee's stepgrandmother Wilma Probyn would also visit a psychic, who said the little girl was still alive and living with a couple in Northern California.

One Sunday, about a month after the kidnapping, Terry Probyn decided to sober up for the sake of her family. So she came down from her room, dried her eyes and took control of the situation.

"I was by myself," she remembered, "and I suddenly got this inner strength to quit crying and get on with it."

Over the next few months, Terry and Carl Probyn embarked

on a mission to keep Jaycee's story in the media, never turning down an interview. It was part of their strategy to find her, after the police investigation stalled through lack of leads.

"This was [our] whole goal from the very start," explained Carl. "I mean we did interviews from day one and we've done them all the way through. Our job right now is to get her picture out there and get these interviews to get her back."

On July 3, Terry was interviewed by the Associated Press. It went out on the national wire on Independence Day and was picked up by newspapers coast-to-coast. Accompanying the story was a photograph of Terry sadly tying a pink ribbon to a tree on Highway 50, the road Jaycee's abductors had taken three weeks earlier.

Terry, who had taken a leave of absence from her job, also joined a dedicated group of volunteers who met every Wednesday at a South Lake Tahoe church hall. There they prepared mailers containing Jaycee's photograph and information to be sent out to truck stops, convenience stores and campgrounds throughout North America. The group averaged five thousand mailings a week.

A local Tahoe rock band called The Movers gave a benefit concert to raise money for the Jaycee reward fund. And a silent auction was held, with all attending children fingerprinted as a precaution against future abductions.

That summer, South Lake Tahoe lived in terror that Jaycee Lee Dugard's abductors would strike again. Parents never let their children out of their sight, and everyone started locking their doors.

"It was a summer of a lot of fear in Tahoe," recalled Meyers Elementary principal Karen Gillis-Tinlin. "Parents didn't just let their children walk down the street. Didn't let them out on their bike to just ride freely in the neighborhood. We really did keep our children close to us that summer."

Jaycee's former classmate Meghan Dorris said she and all her friends lived in fear.

"We were petrified to be alone," she recalled. "We were petrified to walk anywhere by ourselves, to do anything by ourselves, because we thought we were next . . . [that] we'd be picked off the street one by one."

Investigators then turned their attention to Carl Probyn. As the last person to see Jaycee, he soon became a suspect, and some of his in-laws even hired a private investigator to check him out.

Over the next few months, Carl would be subjected to four FBI-administered lie detector tests, as well as tough questioning from law enforcement under hypnosis.

"I think in any investigation you have to look at everyone as a suspect," explained lead detective Jim Watson. "And you have to look at stepfathers. The person I was working for was Jaycee, and if it meant questioning the stepfather, Carl, it was simply to find out where Jaycee was at."

Probyn says that although being under suspicion made him nervous, he totally understood why.

"The FBI put me through the wringer," he later recalled. "I was the last person to see her alive. I went through hell. They asked me if I'd take a lie detector test. And I remember they asked me questions like, 'Do you ever wish she wasn't around?' 'Did you ever forge a document?' And I'm thinking, 'Why don't you guys ask me a straight question?'"

After the first examination, investigators told Carl he was holding something back, asking him to return for another test the following day.

"I said sure," said Probyn. "So I took another one and then [another] the next day. And basically the same kinds of questions."

One theory investigators considered at the time was that Jaycee had been snatched by a drug gang to whom Carl owed money.

"They were fishing," he said. "I can't knock them for what they were doing."

And Terry became obsessed with the nagging question of whether Carl could possibly have done more to save Jaycee. She would lash out at him, even though she realized that he had done his best to chase the abductors uphill on his bicycle before calling 911. Carl himself was racked by guilt, thinking if only he had had his car keys in his pocket, he could have jumped in his vehicle and gone after them.

August 10 marked the two-month anniversary of Jaycee Lee Dugard's abduction. Carl and Terry Probyn attended a moving silent candlelight vigil along Highway 50, to keep hope alive for the safe return of their daughter.

By fall, when there were still no clues to her whereabouts, many investigators secretly believed she was dead, and the search had almost ground to a halt. But the Probyns soldiered on undaunted, working around the clock to keep Jaycee's name and picture in the public consciousness. A public service announcement was running on California and Nevada TV stations, appealing for any information about Jaycee. And her photograph was now on milk cartons and grocery bags all over America.

In one interview, Carl Probyn desperately attempted to communicate with Jaycee through *Sacramento Bee* columnist Anita Creamer. If she ever got to read the story and happened to be in a department store, he told her "to raise hell" and "start screaming."

Several months later, Carl and Terry Probyn helped restage Jaycee's disappearance for the popular TV series *Missing Reward*. Each week the thirty-minute show highlighted a missing person or fugitive, using actors to portray the real characters. But Carl and Terry Probyn insisted that they play themselves in a reenactment at their home, which took twelve hours to shoot.

"We didn't want somebody else portraying our part," explained Carl, "because I saw what happened. An actor couldn't take my place and do the same things."

Terry also felt it was important for them to play themselves in the segment.

"We felt this is what we can do to get Jaycee back," she said. "This has got to be it . . . our one break."

A few weeks later, Terry and Carl held a fundraiser at a local crafts fair. Wearing a "Missing" T-shirt with a large picture of her daughter, Terry held up a poster with her daughter's favorite Boo Boo Bunny poem.

It's difficult to calm a child
Even when the pain is mild,
When a lump, a bruise, or little knot,
Appears in almost every spot.

On November 25, 1991, *People* magazine published a major story on Jaycee Lee Dugard's abduction. It would be the first of several the magazine would run over the years. The double-page feature, bearing the headline "Too Cruel a Theft," was a candid account of the day of the kidnapping, and the terrible toll it had taken on the Probyns.

"At first nothing could stop the pain," read the article by Karen S. Schneider. "The day Terry learned of her daughter's abduction, she smoked cigarette after cigarette and drank herself into a stupor."

It vividly described Terry's ordeal over the first few days of her beloved daughter's disappearance, and how she had been inconsolable.

"Day after day the despondent mother sank in a dark hole of drunkenness," it read, "tears and heavy, troubled sleep."

It also reported the unbearable pressures Carl and Terry Probyn had been under, not made any easier by his being a suspect in his stepdaughter's kidnapping.

"It made me nervous," Carl told *People*. "I had to say, 'Sure, there were times I'd wished Jaycee wasn't in our lives.'"

The lead detective, Sergeant Jim Watson, was quoted as saying investigators were now "99.9 percent sure" there was no family involvement in Jaycee's abduction.

The Probyns said they were haunted by not knowing where Jaycee was or if she was still alive. Even Jaycee's twenty-two-month-old half-sister Shayna knew something was wrong, said Terry, telling how the toddler would occasionally take a "Have You Seen Jaycee" button and kiss it.

"It breaks my heart," she sobbed, "when she asks for her 'siss.' We just say she'll be home soon."

Terry said that her only source of comfort was the possibility there was a woman involved. She speculated that the female abductress might have lost her own child, and was caring for Jaycee.

"Maybe she took Jaycee because of her grief," said Terry. "If that is true, all I can say is, 'Please let my child go. You may like her, but I love her.'"

The week the *People* article ran, Carl Probyn was rushed to the hospital with a burst appendix. He had two emergency operations, but within days he was out of the hospital and had rejoined the search for his stepdaughter.

Tuesday, December 10, marked the six-month anniversary of Jaycee Lee Dugard's abduction, and the investigation had stalled. Lead detective Sergeant Jim Watson said the El Dorado County Sheriff's Department and the FBI had received around six thousand tips since the kidnapping, generating six hundred good leads. But even with the help of the latest FBI computers, nothing had come of any of them. There was, he told the *Sacramento Bee,* one tip from the very beginning that was still under investigation. But he refused to elaborate further.

To mark the somber occasion, Carl and Terry Probyn held another emotional candlelight vigil on Route 50, attended by scores of sympathetic friends and well-wishers.

A crew from *America's Most Wanted* was also in South Lake Tahoe for the sad anniversary, filming an update to the story, which would air the following Friday. Once again there were hundreds of calls to investigators with new tips, but nothing ultimately panned out.

Sacramento bounty hunter Leonard Padilla was so moved by Jaycee's story, he posted a further $100,000 reward for any information leading to her being found.

A few days before Christmas, Jaycee Lee Dugard joined sports legends like Joe DiMaggio, Joe Montana and Nolan Ryan as a trading card collectable. For *America's Most Wanted* had started its own set of trading cards, with Jaycee's color photo joining thirty-four other missing children in the two-hundred-card set.

"The whole idea is to get her picture out there," explained Carl Probyn. "If just one person sees her, or sees the kidnappers . . . anything that helps do that is a good idea."

The trading card set was being distributed through sports card stores nationwide. And the missing children's set was endorsed by superstar sportsmen Larry Bird and Lawrence Taylor.

That Christmas, Terry Probyn retreated to Jaycee's room and cried. Unlike last year there was no tree, festive decorations or holiday joy.

"I can't bring myself to have Christmas not knowing where she is," Terry told *The Sacramento Bee*, adding that she believed Jaycee was still alive. "It's the people showing up to help . . . someone they don't even know that helps me focus."

Facing his first Christmas without Jaycee, Carl said the uncertainty of not knowing what had happened made it so much worse.

"If she got hit by a car," he said, "it would tear your heart out, but there would be an ending. But there is no ending here."

Between 4:30 and 5:00 P.M. on December 27, four-year-old Amanda Campbell left her brother to ride her bicycle around the corner to a friend's house. The chubby little blue-eyed, blonde-haired girl never made it there. Her bicycle was found later that evening in a nearby field.

The little girl, who was never seen again, was abducted from Fairfield, California, just a forty-five-minute drive from Walnut Avenue, Antioch.

24

STOCKHOLM SYNDROME

One hundred and seventy miles away in her filthy Antioch dungeon, Jaycee Lee Dugard never knew it was Christmas. Imprisoned in her windowless jail each day was just like the last, with little sense of time.

Soon after Phillip Garrido had started to rape her, the eleven-year-old had learned to cope by distancing herself from her nightmare. At first she prayed her parents would soon come and rescue her from this nightmare. But eventually she began to wonder if anyone was even searching for her. And perhaps nobody even cared.

Phillip and Nancy cruelly played with her conflicted emotions, using them as an effective method of control. First Phillip would brutally rape her, and then he and Nancy showed her kindness, bringing her little presents and fussing over her.

Naturally shy and submissive, Jaycee was not a fighter and never tried to confront her jailer—probably the key to her survival. Later there was speculation that Garrido had fed her various drugs, like Valium and other addictive tranquilizers, making her even more docile.

As the days turned into weeks, and the weeks into months, Jaycee somehow bonded with Phillip and Nancy Garrido. Her jailers literally held the power of life and death over her, easily brainwashing their young sex slave.

"The moment he snatches her right from her parents," explained renowned forensic psychiatrist and best-selling author

Dr. Keith Ablow, "her whole world crumbled. In a sense she had to dispel belief here in order to live there and not go crazy, utterly insane, you'd have to believe yourself to be safe. You have to convince yourself you're in a good situation."

There are limits to the human mind's ability to cope, and few children have ever suffered like Jaycee Dugard.

"An eleven-year-old who is abducted," explained Dr. Ablow, "and held against her will has little alternative but to bond with her captors. To maintain one's desperation and grief and rage for many years would be too damaging to the human mind—so the human mind tells itself a story about safety and contentment to safeguard itself."

Dr. Ablow believes that over the first few months of her captivity, Jaycee Dugard may well have suffered a classic case of Stockholm Syndrome—a psychological condition where in order to survive a hostage bonds closely to his or her captors. The condition was first identified in 1973, when a team of bank robbers took employees at the Kreditbanken in Stockholm, Sweden, hostage for six days. Over that period they became emotionally attached to their captors, ultimately resisting rescue attempts by the police, later refusing to even testify against the robbers.

The term was first coined by Swedish psychiatrist Nils Bejerot, a police adviser during the incident.

Perhaps the most famous case of Stockholm Syndrome came the following year, when American newspaper heiress Patty Hearst actually joined the radical Symbionese Liberation Army, who had kidnapped her. She took part in several bank robberies, eventually serving a two-year jail sentence, later commuted by president Jimmy Carter.

"He's God to Jaycee," said Dr. Ablow of Garrido. "Her first sexual experience is with this man. He was not only her kidnapper and rapist, but the man who kept her fed and clothed and kept her makeshift hovel dry when it rained. When she wept, it may have been he who comforted her and reassured her that everything would be all right—because he loved her."

* * *

In January 1992, a Reno songwriter named Larry Williams wrote a moving tribute song to the missing girl, entitled "Jaycee Lee." The catchy song had a rousing chorus of "Jaycee—Jaycee Lee. Soon the tears of joy will rain and we'll fulfill our dreams."

Williams then recruited a local band called Perfect Circle to record it, inviting Terry and Carl Probyn to attend the recording session. And in the middle of the song, Terry spoke this moving message directly to her daughter.

> Listen to your heart baby and hear me say.
> That every minute of every day.
> Every moment and in every way—we are with you
>   Jaycee.
> You're in our thoughts, you're in our prayers and we
>   won't rest until you're home.
> Until you're safe. And in the arms of the ones that love
>   you.

In early 1992, Herschel Franzen died, leaving 1554 Walnut Avenue to his widow, Patricia. And soon after that Garrido brought Jaycee out of the shed, formally introducing her to his mother as his and Nancy's daughter.

At 6:00 P.M. on Wednesday, April 22—ten months after the abduction—an anonymous caller telephoned the Contra Costa County Sheriff's Office with a new tip. The tipster reported seeing a little blonde girl staring intensely for a long time at Jaycee's "missing" poster in the forecourt of a gas station, on Highway 4. The girl then walked to a yellow Dodge van and was driven off by a man.

The caller was convinced it was Jaycee, but did not have a license plate number or know which direction the van had taken.

By the time a deputy arrived, there was no sign of the yellow van and the caller had left.

* * *

Two months later, on the first anniversary of Jaycee Lee Dugard's abduction, more than four hundred people gathered in South Lake Tahoe for a special service and candlelight vigil. Carl and Terry Probyn attended the grim ceremony with their little daughter Shayna, later giving an interview to a Sacramento television station.

"I'm scared," said Jaycee's thirty-three-year-old mother, having visibly aged over the last year. "I'm scared that it is going to go on forever and ever and we're never going to have an ending. We are living our worst nightmare. Unfortunately it's gone on for too long."

She also announced she and her Wednesday volunteer group had begun mailing out missing fliers to seventy thousand liquor stores from coast to coast.

Carl said their daughter's disappearance had affected every part of their life, including their marriage, jobs and finances. And not a day went by without him thinking about her.

"It's like being tortured every day," he said. "You know she's gone. I don't know what they're doing to her, but we're being tortured every day not knowing what's happening to her."

That fall, Terry Probyn went back to work as a graphic designer. She still ran the search for Jaycee, but with each month passing without news, it became harder and harder to motivate herself. And her marriage to Carl was starting to fracture under all the pressure and uncertainty.

That second Christmas without Jaycee, Terry took a week off work and stayed at home, crying.

"She was a basket case," Carl said later. "The first ten years . . . she didn't celebrate Christmas. She would take a week vacation, and stay home. On Jaycee's birthday she would stay home a week and just cry."

It would be eighteen months before Phillip Garrido was satisfied that he had successfully brainwashed Jaycee. Soon after she arrived, he had renamed her Alyssa, further distancing her from her old identity. She was now under his total control.

He finally let her out of the shed and into the sunshine, although she remained captive in his secret backyard prison, living in a motley collection of sheds and shabby tents.

One hot summer's afternoon, nine-year-old Patrick McQuaid was outside playing when he saw a little blonde-haired girl on the other side of a chicken wire fence, separating his yard from the Garridos.

"I thought she was pretty," recalled McQuaid, who had never seen any other kids playing there before. Hoping to make a new friend, he asked if she lived there or was just visiting. The girl said she lived there and that her name was Jaycee.

Then suddenly Phillip Garrido appeared and took her into the house. The next day a new privacy fence suddenly appeared, preventing the little boy from seeing the Garrido backyard again.

"I was young and didn't think anything of it," said McQuaid. "Kids came and went all the time. But she sure was pretty."

25

"MY BABY BLUE"

On March 18, 1993, a federal arrest warrant was issued for Phillip Garrido, for breaking his parole conditions. Not only had he failed to report to a federal probation officer, but he had tested positive for marijuana and was not going to aftercare counseling sessions as required.

Garrido was then taken into custody at the federal detention center in Dublin, California. And on April 1, he appeared at a probable cause hearing, which ordered him incarcerated in the Pleasanton Federal Correctional Institution.

For the next month, Phillip Garrido remained behind bars, leaving Nancy alone with Alyssa. She now assumed her husband's duties as jailer, closely guarding the little girl and making no attempt to free her.

Every morning, before leaving for her nursing job, Nancy would feed Alyssa and bring her a change of clothes. She had become genuinely fond of her husband's sex slave, believing it was God's will they should all be a family.

Nancy was also grooming her "daughter"—now just a couple of months shy of her thirteenth birthday and going through puberty—to be ready to bear their children once Phillip was released.

During his four weeks behind bars, Phillip Garrido composed a dozen new songs, many about his beautiful young sex slave.

As he strummed his bass guitar in his cell, he wrote country-and-western-type songs about Alyssa and his twisted sexual obsession for her.

"I will tell you about the only one," begins "Baby Blue," his love song to Alyssa. "She's a dream, dream come true. With a note saying you're my Baby Blue."

The lyrics to another song appear to describe the abduction.

"Leavenworth is a long way from Nashville/ here I go tra la la/ But I get my jollies in a motorcar/ feeling good tra la la/ Stopped and sucker for a candy bar."

Another of his bizarre love songs bears the lyrics, "For every girl in the world/ They want to be in love, yeah/ You're just the same, go play a game/ Just tell me that you want me."

But perhaps the most chilling is the one entitled "Mother," in which he describes the little girl's imprisonment and repeated rapes.

"Mother in your eyes, deepness in your pride/ played well when I first met ya/ Saved from the days, I kept you, but in the darkness you remain/ Everybody pays in the human race/ Being abused and used as devices."

On April 29, Phillip Garrido was released to home confinement supervision and ordered to report to a halfway house in Oakland a day later. The U.S. Parole Commission case analyst then withdrew the arrest warrant, reinstating his parole subject to 120 days supervision and electronic monitoring.

Although Garrido was technically still under Nevada state parole, the federal parole authority had never informed them of their parolee's drug violation. If they had done so, Nevada could have revoked his parole, returning him to a state prison to finish his life sentence.

A few days later, Phillip Garrido was allowed to return to 1554 Walnut Avenue and resume his life in the community.

On May 3, 1993, Alyssa turned thirteen years old, and the Garridos brought her a little kitten as a birthday present. She was delighted. Her manipulating captors used her love for pet animals as a powerful weapon to win her trust. They also told her what they had paid for the kitten, making her even more beholden to them.

Over the last two years, they had so successfully robbed Alyssa of her past that she now believed they were treating her better than her own parents ever had.

"I got [a cat] for my birthday from Phil and Nancy," Alyssa wrote in a secret journal she had started keeping. "They did something for me that no one else would do for me, they paid $200 just so I could have my own kitten."

Soon afterward Alyssa became pregnant with Phillip Garrido's baby, making her even more emotionally dependant on him and Nancy. As an experienced nursing aide, Nancy was well qualified to care for her during the pregnancy, as Phillip never allowed any doctors into the secret compound.

As Phillip's seed took root in Alyssa's body, the Garridos finally owned her body and mind.

Although Phillip Garrido had finally freed Alyssa from the shed, where she'd been held since her abduction, he still confined her to the backyard. There she camped in all weathers in a ramshackle assortment of small tents, wooden shacks and other ad hoc structures.

Phillip kept his expensive musical instruments and recording equipment in the soundproofed shed, and he loved to plug in his bass guitar and play his songs, with Nancy and Alyssa as his appreciative audience.

The now pregnant thirteen-year-old girl was rarely allowed inside the adjacent three-bedroom house, where her jailers lived comfortably with Phillip's aging mother.

"I always wished I could have a daughter," Pat Franzen later said of Alyssa's emergence. "So when Alyssa appeared one day it was amazing. I was pleased she was around."

In late 1993, Carl and Terry Probyn appeared on the *Geraldo Rivera Show*. It would be the first of several appearances over the next few years, with Carl forming a friendship with the famous talk-show host.

During their interview, it became apparent that Jaycee's disappearance was now threatening the Probyns' marriage.

"Terry," asked Geraldo, "I wonder what kind of stress must that put on a marriage. What can it do to you?"

"It could destroy us if we let it," she replied. "The whole focus is to stay together and . . . work together to keep the hope alive."

She said they also had to be strong for Jaycee's younger sister, Shayna.

"When Jaycee comes home she's going to need that family life," said Terry. "She can't afford for us to be split up."

As if the Probyns didn't have enough to contend with, now there were vicious rumors that they had something to do with Jaycee's disappearance. One theory was that they had sold her into prostitution in Central America, to pay off drug debts. Another accused the El Dorado County Sheriff's Department of being in cahoots with them, ensuring the case never went anywhere.

But the vast majority of the South Lake Tahoe community had stood by Carl and Terry Probyn, sharing in their terrible heartbreak. Her abduction still haunted the town, and pink ribbons and Jaycee Dugard "missing" posters were everywhere.

On October 1, 1993, twelve-year-old Polly Klaas was abducted from her bed in Petaluma, California—190 miles from where Jaycee was taken. A strange man wielding a knife burst into her bedroom, while she was having a slumber party with two friends. He then tied up the girls, placing pillowcases over their heads, and escaped with Polly.

The terrified girls finally managed to untie themselves, waking up Polly's mother who called the police. Over the next two months, there was a massive nationwide search for Polly, reminiscent of the one for Jaycee. Her kidnapping was covered on *America's Most Wanted* and *20/20,* and she became the first missing child to have a picture posted on the Internet.

On November 20, police arrested a drifter named Richard Allen Davis for a parole violation, matching his palm print to one discovered in Polly's bedroom. He was then charged with her murder, and four days later he led police to where he had strangled the little girl and buried her in a shallow grave.

Terry and Carl Probyn followed the Polly Klaas abduction closely, as it resembled Jaycee's. And when they read of Davis's arrest for Polly's murder, they were devastated, waiting by the phone to find out if he had been at large in June 1991.

Finally, investigators told the Probyns that Allen could not possibly have had anything to do with Jaycee's abduction. Once again hope had been sucked away, leaving them no nearer to knowing what had happened to Jaycee than before.

"I'm glad Polly's parents have a resolution," said Terry at the time. "I wouldn't want anyone to go through not knowing. It's hell."

Polly Klaas's kidnapping and subsequent murder reopened all the old wounds for Terry, and as Christmas approached she hit rock bottom. She took her annual vacation, sending Carl and their daughter Shayna to stay with relatives in Southern California, leaving her alone at home to cry.

On December 11, 1993, *Sacramento Bee* columnist Anita Creamer interviewed Terry once again, to see how she was coping this holiday season.

"She still calls the sheriff's department every week," reported Creamer, "checking to see if they've got new leads. But the trail is cold, the case is old, and Terry Probyn tells me she's about sixty percent sure Jaycee is never coming home."

On January 4, 1994, Carl Probyn took his daughter Shayna to the California state capitol of Sacramento, for a rally demanding that lawmakers pass new legislation to protect innocent children from criminals. There he met Polly Klaas's father Marc and David Collins, whose ten-year-old son Kevin had been snatched off a San Francisco street in February 1984.

And from now on they would all keep in touch, working together in the fight to protect other children from being attacked by heartless predators.

In August 1994, fourteen-year-old Alyssa gave birth to Phillip Garrido's baby daughter. Nancy delivered the baby in the filthy soundproofed shed prison, without any painkillers or medical equipment.

Phillip was overjoyed to be a father at forty-three, naming the child Angel. And for a brief time, as Alyssa recovered from the painful birth, he stopped raping her.

A few days after Angel's birth, Phillip Garrido decided to take Alyssa as his second wife. In a bizarre wedding ceremony in the garden, Garrido put on his best clothes to perform the ceremony, insisting Nancy attend as witness.

He then picked up his guitar and sang a new song he'd specially composed for the occasion, before making Alyssa promise to always love him, fulfilling God's desire for them to always be together.

Finding herself a mother at just fourteen, Alyssa rose to the task at hand. She now had a young baby to take care of, and the responsibilities of motherhood in captivity empowered her. Nancy, who had been unable to bear children of her own, would now compete with Alyssa for Angel's love and attention.

Although her education had been cut short in the fifth grade, Alyssa was a highly intelligent girl and eager to learn. She persuaded Phillip Garrido to bring her books about cats and other animals into the compound, as he refused to let her read anything else.

That December, Nancy, now thirty-nine, found a new full-time job at Contra Costa ARC, as a nursing and physical therapy aide for the disabled. And she came with excellent job references, dating back to 1981, the year she married Phillip Garrido.

"She was a good employee," said Barbara Maizie who hired her, "and she was well-liked by the people she worked with."

The soft-spoken nurse came with a valid California nurse aide license and an impressive history of working in nursing homes. Before hiring her, the nonprofit agency ran a routine state background check, including a criminal records check, all of which came back clean.

For the next three and a half years, the slightly disheveled, eccentric nursing aide would impress everyone with her dedication and caring attitude toward her adult patients.

* * *

Jaycee Lee Dugard's classmates and teachers at Meyers Elementary School would never forget her. One year, the school planted a little memorial garden in Jaycee's honor by the multipurpose room. And at the center was a plaque reading: "Some people come into our lives, and quickly go. Some stay for awhile and leave footprints on our hearts, and we are never, ever the same."

On each anniversary of her abduction, the whole school would gather in the memorial garden for a sad vigil of pink ribbons and candlelights. But as the years went by, few thought they would ever see their classmate again.

26

"THE POWER OF ADVERTISING"

In the summer of 1995—four long years after dragging her into his dark abyss—Phillip Garrido finally brought Alyssa out into the real world. After Angel's birth and their marriage, he now allowed Alyssa to occasionally leave her backyard prison during the day to clean his house. But she always had to go back afterward, to sleep in a tent with her baby daughter.

Although he had granted her limited freedom, the fifteen-year-old remained in a secure mental prison, created by her jailer. After sharing her first sexual experiences with him and bearing his child, Alyssa now loved Phillip in some twisted way.

But even though Phillip had managed to wash her brain clean, he could never reach the furthest corners of her mind, where she still vividly remembered her old life and her family.

Her captor also had an ulterior motive for allowing her slightly greater freedom. For Garrido had decided to start a printing business from one of the sheds in his garden, and he wished to exploit Alyssa's natural talent for graphic design, which she had inherited from her mother.

So he bought a cheap printing press, setting it up in one of the squalid tents in his back garden. Then he bought an old computer and a book of instructions, which he gave to Alyssa to learn. Eventually his printing business would occupy three small tents in the backyard, for printing, paper and stenciling.

Naming his new enterprise "Printing For Less," he appointed Alyssa design director. Her first project was to design an ambitious four-color sales brochure, with a comprehensive price list, well undercutting all competitors.

"The Power Of Advertising Is Now Affordable" was his newly adopted slogan.

He also had Alyssa run up a batch of Printing For Less business cards, with a seductive photograph of a young blonde model from one of his favorite girlie magazines.

"Printing For Less—Affordable Advertising," boasted the erratically capitalized brochure, "Will take the hassle out of all your printing needs. No One Beats our Quality, Services Or Prices! Just Schedule An Appointment And Start Your Layout."

Phillip Garrido started driving his red 1988 VW van around Antioch and the neighboring towns of Pittsburg, Concord, Walnut Creek and Oakley, pitching for business. And with his with zero overheads and literal slave labor, he could offer the lowest prices in town for personalized stationery, even throwing in free incentive gifts like notepads.

Local businessman Marc Lister, who ran a full-service glass company, had first met Phillip Garrido a few years earlier after selling him some new windows for his van.

"He had just got out of prison," said Lister. "And this guy would never give his phone number."

Over the next few years, Garrido telephoned Lister periodically for glass, coming into his store to have it fitted into his various vehicles.

Then one day in 1995, he arrived proudly announcing his new printing business.

"He solicited myself and my business," Lister recalled, "as well as several businesses in the area to do their printing work and business cards. He did a good job for me and I was more than happy to introduce him to my friends in the automotive industry."

Phillip Garrido's new business soon prospered, helped by referrals by word of mouth. And he told his new clients that all the design and printing was being done by his talented daughter Alyssa.

"[Everyone] started using him for their fliers, pamphlets

and business cards," recalled Lister. "He was cheap, reliable and there was never any graphical errors or misspelled words."

One afternoon in late 1995, a shabbily-dressed Phillip Garrido turned up at the East County Glass and Window company in Pittsburg, asking to see the owner.

"He just walked in with some fliers," said company president Tim Allen. "He described his business and what type of services he offered . . . any kind of printing we would need, he could take care of us. He was very polite. Very courteous."

Allen did not buy anything that day, but three months later he decided to give Printing For Less a try, placing a small order for some business cards.

"It was acceptable," he recalled. "The price was good and the service was excellent."

Tim Allen viewed Garrido as a "self-employed entrepreneur," admiring his professionalism and efficiency. The printer would always arrive on time to pick up the materials, returning a few days later with the finished order to collect his check.

And East County Glass and Window company was soon using him for all its printing supplies, including envelopes, letterhead, coupons and business cards.

"Everybody here thought he was a little bit strange," said Allen, "but it's not illegal to be strange. He acted a little bit different, but he didn't act dangerous or anything."

A few days later, Garrido walked into a nail salon in Antioch with his brochures and a book of his sample business cards.

"He was talking to the owners of businesses in the area," recalled local businesswoman Janice Gomes, who was having a manicure and knew Garrido from high school. "He said his wife had just had a baby and they were starting a new business."

Gomes asked for one of his cards, and was impressed by his polite, low-key approach.

"He seemed very friendly," she said, "very open and wasn't pushy. 'Oh, don't make a decision now. If you find that you are interested, give me a call.' "

A few months later, Gomes called the number on his business card, leaving a message on his answering machine for him to call back.

"You always got a recording," she said. "At least for the first few years. Later on you were able to get someone on the phone."

Then Gomes ordered some plain business cards, which were half the price of the company she had been using. And when they came back she was highly impressed by the results.

"So I told everyone about him," she said, "and they told their friends. He's very competitive, so over the years quite a few people were using Phillip's services."

In the winter of 1995, Terry and Carl Probyn took part in a six-minute video on missing children. Produced by Doug Broomfield of the Veeple Video Company, the short film used actors to re-create the abduction, as part of a special project to track down missing children.

In a highly emotional interview, Jaycee's tormented mother was filmed in her daughter's bedroom, clutching her favorite stuffed bunny.

"A piece of me is missing," Terry said tearfully. "A piece of my heart feels like it's been ripped. And I don't feel like a complete person."

Lead detective Jim Wilson was also interviewed about the current state of the investigation, saying he had become personally involved in the case.

"It's just hard to deal with," he said. "We're still actively investigating leads and reevaluating. I mean we're in a phase now where we're going back and we're reevaluating everything we did."

Trish Williams of Child Quest International, who had been involved from the beginning, said her organization had received more than ten thousand Jaycee Dugard sightings.

"Unfortunately, in your stranger abduction," said Williams, "rarely do you have a good ending."

A few months after the short film was made, Carl and Terry Probyn split up. They had been in counseling for months

Rock Creek bassist Phil Garrido dreamed of being a rich and famous rock star.
Tommy Wilson-O'Brien

Phillip Garrido's January 1998 Nevada Prison mug shot, just weeks before he was freed on federal parole.
Nevada State Prison System

Phillip and Nancy Garrido moved to Antioch, California, soon after he was released. They lived on Walnut Avenue, a quiet California backwater where everyone minds their own business. *Contra Costa County Department of Conservation and Development*

The cage found in the Garridos' backyard, where investigators believe Jaycee was first imprisoned after she was abducted in June 1991. *Contra Costa County Department of Conservation and Development*

Garrido erected an eight-foot-high fence to create a secret backyard within a backyard. *Contra Costa County Department of Conservation and Development*

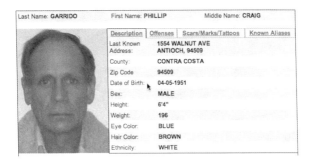

Last Name: GARRIDO	First Name: PHILLIP		Middle Name: CRAIG
	Description	Offenses	Scars/Marks/Tattoos	Known Aliases
	Last Known Address:	1554 WALNUT AVE ANTIOCH, 94509	
	County:	CONTRA COSTA	
	Zip Code:	94509	
	Date of Birth:	04-05-1951	
	Sex:	MALE	
	Height:	6'4"	
	Weight:	196	
	Eye Color:	BLUE	
	Hair Color:	BROWN	
	Ethnicity:	WHITE	

Many of his neighbors knew Phillip was a registered sex offender, from his listing on a law enforcement website.

California Department of Justice

Jaycee's office, where she successfully ran Garrido's "Printing For Less" business.
Contra Costa County Department of Conservation and Development

Phillip Garrido handed out this business card, falsely claiming it had his daughter's picture on it.

John Glatt

Deepal and Mala Karunaratne often met Jaycee, even entertaining her at their home.

John Glatt

Jaycee designed this wedding shower invitation for the Karunaratnes' daughter.

John Glatt

Janice Gomes was a long-time customer of Phillip Garrido, who once gave her advice on how children should protect themselves against kidnapping.

John Glatt

Maria Christenson did her best to avoid Phillip after he suddenly made inappropriate confessions to her.

John Glatt

The remains of the children's swimming pool and toys after investigators had torn the backyard apart, looking for clues to many unsolved murders.

Contra Costa County Department of Conservation and Development

Tim Allen often humored Phillip Garrido when Garrido preached his bizarre religious beliefs.

John Glatt

Phillip Garrido visited his client Tim Allen's showroom a few months before his arrest.

Tim Allen

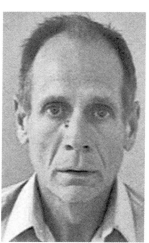

Phillip's mug shot after his arrest in August, 2009.
El Dorado County Sheriff's Office

Nancy Garrido was stunned and amazed when she was arrested.
El Dorado County Sheriff's Office

KIDNAPPING

June 10, 1991
South Lake Tahoe, California

JAYCEE LEE DUGARD

Recovered

DESCRIPTION

Date of Birth: May 3, 1980
Sex: Female
Height: 4'6" (at the time of her disappearance)
Weight: 80 pounds (at the time of her disappearance)

Place of Birth: Anaheim, California
Hair: Blonde
Eyes: Blue

Race: White

THE DETAILS

Jaycee Lee Dugard was last seen as she walked to her bus stop in South Lake Tahoe, California, on June 10, 1991. It has been claimed that she was abducted by two individuals, a male and a female) who were driving a car. However, extensive law enforcement investigations since the time of her disappearance have neither identified any abductors nor revealed the location of the victim.

REMARKS

Jaycee Lee Dugard was last seen wearing a pink windbreaker, a white t-shirt, pink stretch pants, and white sneakers.

Individuals with information concerning this case should take no action themselves, but instead immediately contact the nearest FBI Office or local law enforcement agency. For any possible sighting outside the United States, contact the nearest United States Embassy or Consulate.

[Sacramento Field Office] [Kidnapping and Missing Persons Investigations]
[FBI Home Page] [FBI Field Offices]

The FBI's kidnapping poster for Jaycee Lee Dugard was updated after she was found in August, 2009.

Federal Bureau of Investigation

with their daughter Shayna, but all the stress and pain of Jaycee's disappearance had finally proved too much.

So Carl moved out and got his own place, although they remained friends and never officially filed for divorce.

"This broke our marriage up," Carl explained later. "We had a great marriage. My wife and I have never sat down and talked about it. It's too painful. My wife's personality is the same as Jaycee's—she's mellow, she's easy-going. I mean we never argued."

Phillip Garrido doted on his aging mother, who was now being looked after by Nancy. And Pat Franzen, who had always spoiled her favorite son, apparently had no idea that Alyssa had been kidnapped and been forced to bear her granddaughter Angel.

"That was her world," said Pat's longtime friend and neighbor Helen Boyer. "He really catered to her—he and Nancy both."

The gray-haired seventy-four-year-old pensioner was frequently seen driving her son's old gray two-door sedan around Antioch. Now long retired from her maintenance job for the local school authority, Pat loved puttering in her back garden. And her pride and joy were the grapes she was growing by the far wall of the back garden, near the white-roofed shed where Alyssa and her daughter Angel lived.

One day she asked Dale and Polly White, whose garden backed directly onto hers, to cut down a paradise tree growing through a shared fence, as it was interfering with her vines.

"Well, actually the tree started on her side of the fence and came through our side," observed Polly White. "So my husband said he'd cut it down. He told me he didn't know why she asked him to cut it down, as it was growing on her side. I said, 'Well, perhaps she doesn't have anybody else to cut it down.'"

Mike and Glenda Shelton rented the house next door to the Garridos from 1996 to 1998, sharing a driveway with them. They both thought Phillip "weird" and "defensive," as he refused to allow anyone near the gate to his backyard.

"You could always tell there was something funny about

him," recalled Mike Shelton. "One time the lock on the gate was broken, and Garrido appeared to be in a panic until it was fixed."

In March 1997, sixteen-year-old Alyssa became pregnant again. And with his second child on the way, Phillip Garrido started enlarging the hidden backyard compound to cope with his growing family. He built another shed and over the next few years would add several more tents, as well as installing a plastic swimming pool, a yellow slide and a set of swings.

His printing business was flourishing and Alyssa now spent most of her time on the computer, designing clients' stationery and setting up the printing machinery. The artistic teenager loved designing logos for customers, often adding her own unique, charming touches.

A childish-looking graphic for a local recycling center had a large picture of the earth lying inside a blue recycling bin, alongside other rubbish. Another graphic for Wayne's Barbershop in Pittsburg had a smiling face on the end of a barber pole—resembling the Democratic political pundit James Carville—brandishing a cut-throat razor and electric clippers.

Barbershop owner Wayne Thompson first met Phillip Garrido when he came into his shop for a haircut, and began pitching his print company. Then, after shaking Thompson's hand, Garrido immediately washed his hands in the sink.

"He was a germ freak," explained Thompson. "He looked like he bought his clothes at Goodwill."

Garrido handed him a Printing For Less business card, boasting that the beautiful blonde on it was his daughter Alyssa.

"He told me," said Thompson, " 'I put my daughter's photo on it to show customers how I can display their photos on their business cards. I got Alyssa all fixed up to look glamorous.' "

Thompson pinned the card on his notice board, and was soon ordering all his stationery from Printing For Less.

Since being released from his 1993 parole violation, Phillip Garrido had steered cleared of trouble. His federal parole officer visited 1554 Walnut Avenue on occasion, but never saw anything out of the ordinary.

Once a parole agent had actually been inside Garrido's secret prison compound behind the house, drawing an accurate diagram of it and its proper dimensions. Even the shed—used to imprison Alyssa—was included. But apparently the agent had not been suspicious, placing the diagram in Garrido's federal parole file where it gathered dust.

In fact Phillip Garrido's only run-in with law enforcement was a traffic citation, issued on February 10, 1997.

If the convicted kidnapper and rapist was no longer under suspicion, Carl Probyn certainly was. On March 18, 1997, a team of investigators from the El Dorado Sheriff's Department arrived at his old Washoan Boulevard residence to dig up the front porch of the house. They refused to reveal what they were searching for.

"We're going back and trying to put some closure to some leads," said Lieutenant Fred Kollar obliquely. "Sometimes you want to have someone else come back and look at the case."

When the *Tahoe Daily Tribune* asked Carl Probyn if he was still a suspect in Jaycee's disappearance, he replied that he probably always would be.

"There is about one percent of Tahoe who think we had something to do with the kidnapping," he told a reporter. "And this just gives them fuel for the fire."

Terry Probyn brushed off the renewed search, which turned up nothing, saying it did not bother her.

"We never had any doubt that the family had nothing to do with it," she said. "But some people in town expressed concern that somehow the family was."

Although her estranged husband Carl had now returned to Southern California, Terry said she felt "bound" to South Lake Tahoe until the mystery of Jaycee's disappearance was solved.

"It's hard to move with life," she explained, "when you are still stuck on the past."

But Terry Probyn was determined that something positive

should come out of her daughter's abduction. And in 1997, she donated $3,400 from her Jaycee Dugard search fund to the Soroptimist International chapter of South Lake Tahoe, to launch the Fighting Chance program.

Terry Probyn was the keynote speaker at that year's Soroptimist International meeting, where she officially announced the program in Jaycee's memory.

"It is really time to tell our children," she told the meeting, "that at the very moment they are in the grasp of an abductor, it is important to free themselves."

Now taught to all fourth through sixth graders in Tahoe schools, the hands-on abduction prevention course instructs kids how to fight back if they are ever abducted. And since the program was launched, thirty-five hundred students have gone through it, and it is credited with preventing the abduction of at least three local children.

"The whole community was really touched by Jaycee's abduction," explained local teacher Charma Silver, who helped formulate the program. "We wanted to do something proactive to make sure this wouldn't happen again."

In the final lesson, under the supervision of the El Dorado County Sheriff's Department, students are placed in a trunk of a specially designed training car, and told to fight their way out. Other lessons include kicking out the taillights or ripping out the car's electrical wires.

"If a person tried to pull a child into a car," Terry told the meeting, "that child should try and run in the opposite direction from where the front of the vehicle is pointed. If a person tries to pull a child off a bicycle, the child should hold onto the bicycle as long as possible."

In 1998, Terry finally left South Lake Tahoe, moving to Southern California to live with her sister Tina. A few years later she made a self-help video for children with martial arts expert Ken Bowers.

"If I would have given [Jaycee] the knowledge to help herself," she told viewers in the video called *A Child's Life*, "she would be with me today. Jaycee was caught off guard. She wasn't expecting someone to come up behind her and cut off

her path. She froze. I'd have given her the knowledge to run
the other way or possibly help herself find an avenue out after
she had been taken."

On Thursday, November 13, 1997, Alyssa gave birth to a baby
girl, under Nancy Garrido's helping hand. Phillip Garrido
named his second daughter Starlit and it would be their last.
Later there would be speculation as to whether Garrido might
have disposed of any male children he had sired, thinking of
them as possible threats when they grew up.

Investigators would also explore whether he had been responsible for a series of four gruesome murders around the
Antioch/Pittsburg area, officially naming him a "person of interest." The unsolved murders were all along stretches of Highway 4—the main corridor through Contra Costa County—that
Garrido drove up and down every day, making calls for his
printing business. One of the bodies was found in a dismantling yard where he sometimes worked.

On November 6, 1998, fifteen-year-old Pittsburg High
School sophomore Lisa Norrell disappeared after attending a
coming-of-age party at an Antioch social club. After she was
insulted by a boy, the teenager stormed out of the party and
was last seen walking along Highway 4, towards her home in
Pittsburg. After she failed to arrive home that night the FBI
was called in, and later her shoes were found dumped on the
dark, lonely stretch of road.

A week later, Lisa's body was discovered facedown in an
industrial park, just four miles away from Garrido's house. She
had been asphyxiated, and at the time police refused to release
any information about the injuries, as they were too horrific.
Years later it would emerge that Lisa often visited her aunt
Kathy Russo, who lived directly opposite the Garridos in Walnut Avenue, Antioch.

The murder shocked Contra Costa County, and former
California governor Gray Davis put up a $50,000 reward for
any information leading to her killer's arrest. And though several man were charged with her killing, they were never brought
to trial, as there was insufficient evidence.

Four weeks later came the first in a series of savage prostitute killings in the Pittsburg area, over a two-month period. On December 5, the body of twenty-four-year-old Jessica Frederick was found stabbed and beaten in an another industrial park in Pittsburg. Once again, investigators even withheld the autopsy report from her family, as it was too gruesome.

Ten days later, thirty-two-year-old Rachael Cruise was discovered strangled to death in a ditch, close by where Lisa's body had been found. And in January 1999, twenty-seven-year-old Valerie Dawn Schultz, who used the professional name "China," was found murdered. She had been stabbed and asphyxiated. A few days later, a fifth woman was found barely alive, after being brutally beaten and left for dead.

The FBI were convinced that a frenzied serial killer was on the loose. Although hundreds of local men were interviewed by investigators, there is no known record that convicted kidnapper and rapist Phillip Garrido was ever questioned.

Jaycee Lee Dugard should have graduated high school in 1998, and her former classmates were determined to remember her anyway. Now students at South Lake Tahoe High School, they were still haunted by their beautiful friend, who had vanished so mysteriously seven years earlier.

"Thoughts of Jaycee followed me everywhere through school," said her old friend Kristina Rhoden. "Her name would come up or I'd read about another kidnapped child, and I'd wonder, 'Where is she now?'"

So it was arranged that a photo of Jaycee be printed in the 1998 class yearbook, alongside the caption, "Even though you may not be walking with us down the graduation aisle, you will always be walking with us in our hearts—From the Class of 1998."

27

"A PRODUCTIVE CITIZEN"

In March 1998, Nancy Garrido quit her job at the Contra Costa ARC to look after Phillip Garrido's mother full-time. Pat Franzen, now seventy-seven, was suffering from the early stages of dementia, requiring round-the-clock nursing. So Phillip had decided Nancy should became primary caregiver, also allowing her to help out with the printing business.

Phillip Garrido's old beat-up van was now a common sight doing its daily rounds up and down Highway 4. He and Alyssa worked hard and his printing business was easily turning a profit, with little overhead and no wages to pay.

To the outside world, the convicted felon now appeared to be successfully rehabilitated back to society, and a fine example of the parole system at its best.

On March 9, 1999, Phillip Garrido was officially discharged from federal parole, receiving a certificate of early termination from the U.S. Department of Justice.

"You are hereby discharged from parole," read the certificate signed by U.S. Parole Administrator Raymond E. Essex. "By this action, you are no longer under the jurisdiction of the U.S. Parole Commission."

The letter lauded him for his good behavior and what he had achieved over the eleven years he'd been under federal parole supervision.

"After a thorough review of your case," it continued, "the Commission has decided that you are deserving of an early

discharge. You are commended for having responded posi-
tively to supervision and for the personal accomplishment(s)
you have made. The Commission trusts that you will continue
to be a productive citizen and obey the laws of society."

After his early discharge from federal parole, Phillip Garrido was officially returned to the jurisdiction of the Nevada
parole board. The Nevada Department of Public Safety, Division of Parole and Probation now requested that California assume parole responsibilities for Garrido, under the terms of the
interstate parole compact—which had only been written into
law a month earlier. Under the compact, which runs in all fifty
states, the receiving state can take over the parole duties of visitation and supervision if the parolee resides and works there.

When the interstate compact authority refused to assume
responsibility for Garrido, Nevada's Division of Parole and
Probation appealed, urging them to reconsider.

"Since granted parole," wrote Julie Johnson of the Division
of Parole and Probation, "the subject has complied with parole
requirements and displayed a stable lifestyle."

She wrote that Parolee Garrido was a "legitimate and successful" self-employed design artist and printer, who had been
granted an early release from federal parole because of his
"positive" performance.

"Ordering the subject to return to Nevada to await acceptance from your state," wrote Johnson, "would be disruptive
and unproductive for the subject who has managed to change
his behavior. Please reconsider your decision."

That same day, Assistant Supervisor David M. Albright
sent a memo to Johnson, telling her to have Phillip Garrido
report to the Concord, California, parole office the following
afternoon at 1:00 P.M. for his first meeting with his new California parole agent, Al Fulbright.

On June 9, 1999, on the way to meet his new parole agent for the
first time, Phillip Garrido finally registered as a sex offender
with law enforcement, under penal code section 290. From then
on he would register each year without fail, as the law required.

When he met Parole Agent Fulbright, Garrido angrily complained that a serious mistake had been made. He explained that after the federal government had released him from parole, the Nevada authorities should also have discharged him from all parole supervision. He said he had only signed the official transfer forms to California under duress.

In his official report, covering that first meeting, Agent Fulbright noted that Garrido was now "seeking counsel of an attorney."

Straight after the meeting with Agent Fulbright, Phillip Garrido wrote to the Nevada Parole Commission, demanding to be released from all parole supervision. And he even claimed that continuing parole supervision would prove psychologically detrimental to him.

This letter is to inform the Parole Commission that I Phillip Garrido was released from the Federal Sentence and all supervision completely.

The reason for my release 26 years early, was due to the complete recovery and successful reorientation back into the community. Years of hard work went into this recovery. At this point every professional involved in my case recognized any further supervision would no longer be of any benefit to me, and so I was released back into the community under no supervision.

At this point it is obvious to me and the professionals handling this case that I will receive no benefit from continued supervision, but in fact is nothing more than a poor reminder of what I have been told to put behind me, thus psychologically and realistically is of no benefit to my success.

I sign under duress, because the threat that Nevada would for no other reason violate my parole.

Bottom line is if Nevada would have been the one to supervise my parole it is now becoming obvious that they do not have the resources nor the desire to truly help people orientate back into society for under your present system I would have fallen through the cracks. On the other hand the Federal Government has the resources and stayed off my back until they were able to isolate a bi-chemical problem.

*So now after all this you're informing me the reason for
this continued supervision is to help me back into society.
Frankly your laws are outdated and need to be reviewed by
professional psychologist [sic] and the Federal Government.*

Five days later, Agent Fulbright filed a progress and conduct
report for his new parolee, noting he was "stable" and his "prognosis of success is good."

Over the next five months, Parolee Garrido kept the parole
agent busy with all his objections, so he had no supervision
whatsoever.

That November, the California parole department recommended that Nevada discharge Phillip Garrido from parole. In
the five months since taking over the case, parole agent Fulbright noted Garrido had made "good parole adjustment," ad-
vising that he be reduced to minimum risk—the lowest level for
a sex offender—until his discharge date.

But under the California parole department policy, Garrido
should have been classified as high control for a minimum of a
year, because of his earlier convictions for kidnapping and rape.

In his November 9 report, Agent Fulbright noted that Garrido lived with his wife, Nancy, and mother, Pat, and was the
self-employed owner of a full-service printing shop.

"Garrido has completed over 10 years of Federal Parole
Supervision," wrote Fulbright, "and was successfully discharged on 3/09/1999. He is available for supervision and in
compliance with his conditions of parole. Recommendation:
Discharge from parole supervision."

This would be the first of four official recommendations
from California over the next nine years that Garrido be discharged from parole. But Nevada turned a deaf ear to all of
them, continuing to enforce his parole.

In late 1999, Phillip Garrido hooked his Printing For Less business computer up to the Internet, allowing Alyssa to deal with
their clients online. She was a busy working mother, with Angel
now five years old and Starlit two.

Alyssa had been with the Garridos for more than eight

years and felt part of their family. And she had long become used to living in tents outside in the hidden backyard, where she was raising her daughters as best she could.

Most nights Phillip Garrido would arrive in the back garden and take Alyssa into his soundproof shed, where he would force her to have sex. Often Nancy would babysit the little girls, before Phillip and Alyssa joined them for dinner.

Printing For Less was doing so well that Phillip Garrido decided to expand, buying new camera and printing equipment. He also took on a number of new clients.

"All of a sudden he appeared with his business cards," remembered Cheyvonne Molino, owner of J & M Enterprises—an auto-wrecking yard—in Willow Pass Road, Pittsburg. "And he started doing our printing."

Around the same time, Maria Christenson, who owns a recycling center in Pittsburg, happened to mention to a friend that she was looking for a printer.

"And the next morning," recalled Christenson, "Phillip was here waiting for me."

So she started placing orders with Printing For Less, and liked the quality of work and rock-bottom prices.

"At first he seemed like he was always in a hurry and looked kind of jumpy," she said. "But he was very, very businesslike at the beginning."

For the first few years, Christenson hardly ever saw Garrido in person. She would call his office and place her print orders. Then a few days later she would arrive at work, to find it waiting outside the front door.

"The only thing that was odd," she said, "was that he would deliver at strange hours. I'd come in and there was a pile outside the door. He probably brought them in the middle of the night or early, early in the morning. The only time I saw him was when he came to pick up the check."

Antioch realtor Deepal Karunaratne, who also ran a marketing business, hired Phillip Garrido after a recommendation from a business contact.

"Phillip came to my house," recalled Karunaratne. "He told me that he has a home-based printing press and showed me some work he has done. Very good quality work. So I started trying him out and it worked very well. I gave him a lot of work and I referred him to a lot of other clients."

Over the five years they had done business, Marc Lister had developed a good relationship with Phillip Garrido. In fact, one day he was invited to visit 1554 Walnut Avenue for a business meeting with the company design director, Alyssa.

"I went inside the house," he remembered, "and [Alyssa] was sitting across the table from me."

Nancy was busy dusting and cleaning the old furniture, while Angel and Starlit played in the corner. Then with a dramatic wave of his hand, Phillip Garrido introduced his wife and two fair-haired daughters, leaving Lister under the impression that the pretty blonde Alyssa was his wife, and Nancy his cleaning lady.

"I sat across the living room table," recalled Lister, "and talked to [Alyssa] about what I wanted on my cards—color changes. She made a couple of suggestions."

Over the next few years, Lister would often visit the house, forming the impression they were a happy family.

On December 9, 1999, seven-year-old Xiana Fairchild was kidnapped from a bus stop in Vallejo, California, thirty miles west of Antioch. Her disappearance triggered a massive police hunt around Northern California, with hundreds of volunteers scouring the countryside for the little girl.

Child safety advocate Janice Gomes, founder and president of the National Community Empowerment Programs, Inc., was appointed a search team leader. So she decided to update the group's child safety fact sheet, going to her printer Phillip Garrido's house to brief him on the project.

"We had just been talking about Xiana Fairchild, who was abducted from a bus stop," said Gomes. "And he said, 'Next time you might want to add a couple of things. You know children should never walk to a bus stop alone, because they're no match for an adult.'"

He then declared it was a myth that children were safer traveling around in groups.

"If an adult approaches a group," Garrido told her, "they all scatter and you just grab one. That's all you want anyhow."

Gomes said she would consider his advice, but his strange comment raised no red flags.

"Phillip was strange," she explained, "but you wouldn't put him under the category of rapist, murderer or kidnapper. He told me he had A.D.D. but I felt he had A.D.H.D., because he was definitely very hyper."

After their meeting, Garrido went into his backyard, handing a rough copy of the new child safety fact sheet to Alyssa to typeset and print. As she typed it into the computer, she would have had to read the copy.

"The predators victimizing people today," stated the fact sheet, "are using methods never heard of before. There is a need to apply safety awareness and survival knowledge to children of all ages."

And under the "Reported Facts" section, it stated there are approximately 850,000 children reported missing each year. Out of those, 4,600 abductions are by non–family members, and three hundred of those unfortunate children either disappeared for long periods or were murdered.

"Remember," ended the fact sheet, "everyone is someone's child and crime can victimize you at any stage in life. Let's get together to make a safer future for our children today!"

In 2001, Xiana's remains were found in a reservoir in Santa Clara County. Four years later, drifter and self-confessed serial killer Curtis Dean Anderson pleaded guilty to kidnapping, molesting and murdering Xiana. He was sentenced to fifty years to life in prison—the same sentence Phillip Garrido had received twenty-five years earlier.

On May 3, 2000, Jaycee Lee Dugard turned twenty years old. Investigators used a newly developed computer technique of age progression to show what she might look like today.

The picture—showing a beautiful, smiling blonde woman—was added to her missing poster, alongside a photo of how she had looked when she disappeared.

* * *

Five days later, on May 8, California parole agent Al Fulbright visited 1554 Walnut Avenue, Antioch, for the first time since taking over the Garrido case, almost a year earlier.

When the agent informed Garrido that he would now have to undergo regular drug testing, the parolee replied that he would probably test positive as he was taking tranquilizers to calm him down. Then Nancy came in and talked to the agent briefly.

Later, in his official report, Agent Fulbright voiced his frustration at having to deal with Garrido, his most difficult client, writing, "Why did I take this case?"

28

CREEPY PHIL

Phillip Garrido's increasingly eccentric behavior was beginning to attract attention. Months earlier, he had confided to his friend Marc Lister that he was taking medication for schizophrenia and had it under control. But Lister suspected he often didn't take his prescribed drugs, self-medicating with illegal ones instead.

"I watched Phil go off on his tangents," recalled Lister. "I would say, 'Phil, get back on your meds.'"

Garrido would now burst into song at the slightest opportunity. He loved singing Madonna songs in particular. He was also writing songs for Britney Spears and mailing them off to her management.

"'Like a Virgin' was his favorite," said Janice Gomes. "He would sing very high and very off-pitch. He sang to everybody and it made me very uneasy."

He also ordered Alyssa to prepare a new business card with Madonna's headshot, having her touch up the eyes and mouth to avoid possible copyright problems.

It became commonplace for Garrido to serenade his clients while delivering orders. One day he was chatting to Tim Allen across his East County Glass and Window company showroom counter, when Allen happened to mention that his son played guitar and sang in his punk band.

"He went nuts," recalled Allen. "Phillip got all excited. He said, 'Hey, I used to be in a band and I write songs. I play guitar and I record my own songs."

Then Garrido started snapping his fingers and tapping his toes and burst into song to the amazement of the other customers.

"They were snappy songs," said Allen. "And he had a pretty decent voice and he'd sing pretty loud. He came in and sang to us a couple of times."

Betty Upingco and her family moved onto Walnut Avenue in 1999, and before long she met Phillip Garrido, who lived opposite.

"I saw him downtown singing in the grocery store," she remembered. "Just singing very loud. I thought he was weird. I just didn't like the aura that I felt about him."

At the time Upingco owned a concrete business and ordered some business cards from her neighbor, as they were such good value.

"He brought them to my house and left," she said. "It was very scary. I never even knew he was in my yard and I was at home."

The local children were also scared of Garrido, who had started practicing tai chi moves in his front garden every morning. They started calling him "Creepy Phil," after he told some boys to be careful what they said about him, because he could hear everything.

In summer 2000, Janice Gomes ordered business cards for her National Community Empowerment Programs action group. But when Phillip Garrido delivered them, she noticed her color portrait was far too dark and "Child Safety" had been spelled "Child Saftey." So she sent them back. A few days later, when he returned it redone, the color was better but it was still "Child Saftey."

"So I asked Phillip," she said, " 'Why are all my business cards spelled wrong?' And he says, 'Well, my daughter's doing them.' "

As he'd already told her his daughter helped out in the business, Gomes asked why he had someone so young doing her business cards. Garrido thought for a second, and replied that she was very smart.

"Well," she told him, "she's not a good speller."

"She's a good speller for six," he replied.

The child advocate kept the misspelled cards, as she thought it was sweet.

In January 2001, a new parole agent in charge of the Garrido case officially reevaluated him as a low-risk offender. He completed a "Sex Offender Risk Assessment" form, determining if the current level of supervision was appropriate. And although Garrido had been convicted of violent rape and kidnapping, the agent decided the following low-risk description most applied to him:

"One or possible registerable [*sic*] sex offenses in the record along with other non-sex-related offenses. Controlling offense is non-sexual. Offending sexually is more opportunistic or situational than a primary deviant sexual orientation. These cases can be reasonably handled on a control service caseload."

From then on Phillip Garrido's supervision became even less intensive.

June 10, 2001, marked the tenth anniversary of Jaycee Lee Dugard's abduction. And more than a hundred supporters walked in a solemn pink ribbon procession along U.S. 50. The somber parade began in front of Meyers Library, where a permanent plaque to remember Jaycee had been set up by a rock.

Terry Probyn, now forty-two, returned to South Lake Tahoe for the sad occasion, walking the parade route with the former Meyers Elementary School principal, Karen Gillis-Tinlin.

"I walked with Jaycee's mom," she remembered, "and part of our conversation was just needing closure."

Later, Terry addressed the marchers. In the ten long years since her daughter had been abducted, Terry had visibly aged with worry lines lining her forehead.

"Someone out there knows what happened," she told the crowd. "We need peace. Give us that gift."

* * *

That year, Alyssa's oldest daughter Angel turned seven. Later investigators would question whether Phillip Garrido now transferred his sexual attentions toward her. For at his 1976 trial, Garrido had readily admitted to being obsessed with seven-year-old girls and masturbating outside schools.

"As [Alyssa] gets older," explained Michael Cardoza, a former San Francisco major crimes prosecutor, who was later briefed on the case by the FBI, "he becomes less interested in her. Because of his sickness he wants the younger girls."

29

1554 WALNUT AVENUE

Occasionally, Phillip Garrido would breakfast at the Bridgehead Café, a small diner a few blocks away on East 18th Street, Antioch. Over the years, café owner Murray Sexton got to know the eccentric local printing entrepreneur, who was always in a hurry.

"He'd come in and sit down and have breakfast," Sexton recalled. "Or sometimes he'd get a couple of burgers to go."

Sexton says that Garrido always came alone and he never saw Nancy, Alyssa or the two little girls.

As his daughters grew up, Phillip Garrido set up a small tent as a classroom with geography maps and assorted books, mostly about cats. There were now a number of pet animals being kept in the backyard compound, including two dogs, four cats, two cockatiels, a mouse and a pigeon.

As time went on, Alyssa persuaded her jailer to allow her and their daughters more and more freedom. Later she would tell police that she had never feared for her daughters' safety, although she eventually learned of his sexually violent criminal past, and that he'd served time for kidnapping and rape.

She even initiated serious conversations about their daughters' future, persuading him to buy the 1998 book *Self-Esteem: A Family Affair* by family relationship expert Jean Illsley Clarke. Ironically, one of the chapters in the best-selling book was "What's a Nice Family Like Us Doing in a Place Like This?"

The book's message was that children's needs are best served by parents whose own needs have not been neglected. And it offered "a range of creative and workable options," encouraging parents to build up their children's self-esteem while fulfilling their emotional needs.

Alyssa also attempted to educate her daughters in one of the tents, with the limited resources available. She taught them the alphabet and basic reading and writing skills. But Garrido censored their reading, refusing to allow them any children's novels or the typical books popular with young girls. The only books he allowed were about cats.

A makeshift bookshelf in the tent classroom was entirely devoted to feline books, including Peter Gethers's *The Cat Who Went to Paris* and English anthropologist Desmond Morris's *Catlore*. He also bought Angel and Starlit Barbie dolls, bicycles and a thousand-piece cat jigsaw puzzle.

Garrido was an avid reader himself. His bookshelf inside the house was devoted to true crime, horror and science fiction. His favorite author was the American horror-thriller author Dean Koontz. Among his almost complete collection of Koontz books was *Intensity,* featuring a demented serial killer and rapist who keeps a young girl imprisoned in his basement.

Late at night, while Garrido was out on his regular prowls around the neighborhood, Alyssa used the Internet to teach her children about the world. Her lessons included astrology, the names of the night sky constellations and basic botany.

But as Phillip Garrido refused to allow his captives to watch television, they had little concept of history, math or geography. And as Alyssa's education had been cut short in the fifth grade, she could only teach them the basics that she had learned.

On cold winter nights, Alyssa and her girls would wrap up in sleeping bags and huddle together in their tent, as she told them stories she remembered her mother telling her as a little girl.

The two blonde girls grew up believing that Phillip was their father, Nancy their mother and Alyssa their older sister. They never knew she had been kidnapped against her will and they were all prisoners, as Alyssa wanted to protect them from the truth.

Around that time, Phillip Garrido instituted a list of rules that Alyssa and the girls must always follow. If anyone ever came to the front door, they had to immediately run out of the house into the backyard. And in the event Alyssa was ever asked about Angel and Starlit, she was to say that they were hers and she was fine with them being around Garrido. He later created a second cover story, that they were his nieces.

And in the event that he was ever arrested, Alyssa was ordered to get an attorney, so he could continue to communicate to her through lawyers, with attorney-client privilege protecting them from prying law enforcement.

That summer, Phillip and Nancy Garrido began taking Angel and Starlit out in the evenings to promenade up and down Walnut Avenue.

"My daughter remembers seeing him and his wife," said Betty Upingco, "walking down the street in the evening with a toddler in a stroller. But his girls never came out and played on the street like the other kids."

As the years went by, Phillip lessened his hold on Alyssa and their daughters, confident they were under his complete control. They were still living rough in his secret backyard, but in measured acts of kindness he built them an above-ground swimming pool, installed a trampoline and gave them various bicycles and other toys.

Often, on lazy hot summer afternoons, Pat Franzen would sit outside in the backyard, watching Alyssa playing with Starlit and Angel. Later she would claim that her son had told her they were his children by an old girlfriend.

"I saw all three girls as my granddaughters," she explained. "Out back the two youngest went out to play in the garden. They didn't have lots of toys, but they spent their time reading books or sitting with Alyssa."

Dale and Polly White, who shared a back fence with the Garridos, often heard the little girls laughing and splashing around in the pool.

"We used to hear children back there playing in the pool," said Polly White. "We thought they were just there visiting Pat."

That June, the Contra Costa Fire Department was called to 1554 Walnut Avenue, after a little girl injured her shoulder in a swimming pool accident. The fire department later wrote up a report of the visit, but apparently it was never read by Phillip Garrido's parole agent.

On June 11, 2002, one day after the eleventh anniversary of the abduction, Phillip Garrido met his new parole agent, Agent R. Rodriguez, at the Concord parole office. While there he completed a drug test, again explaining his prescribed medication would always give a positive result.

"To evaluate his testing," wrote Agent Rodriguez in his report, "we need to see the other drug use. Testing once per month at home."

On June 19, Garrido's test came back from the laboratory positive. Rodriguez duly noted that he informed his supervisor, who asked him to note the incident, but that no activity report was needed.

One month later—on June 22—Agent Rodriguez paid an early morning visit to Parolee Garrido's house. It was the first time any parole agent had gone to 1554 Walnut Avenue in more than a year. When no one answered the front door, Rodriguez left his business card, instructing Garrido to call him.

When Agent Rodriguez next visited the Garrido home at 8:51 A.M. on August 22, Pat Franzen answered the door, saying her son was not home.

"Mom showed me their room," the agent later reported. "First room off the living room. Big house."

Five weeks later, when Agent Rodriguez paid his next visit, Parolee Garrido was at home. This time he met Nancy, noting that they were "Doing ok." Once again Garrido was unable to provide a urine sample, promising to come into the parole office and give one, which he did three hours later.

During one of his visits, Agent Rodriguez drew a simple sketch map of the Garrido house in pencil. Through the front door he drew a large living room, backing on to the kitchen/

dining room area. Phillip's bedroom backed onto the porch with another, presumably Nancy's, to the right of it. A bathroom separated that bedroom from the one at the front, occupied by his mother.

Behind the porch, the agent noted the "backyard door"—the door that lead out to the secret prison where Alyssa and her two daughters were being held.

Lorenzo Love and Christine Meacham, who own a transport and tow company in Oakley, California, became friends with Phillip Garrido after hiring him to print their business cards and invoices. And before long he opened up about his past life.

"He told us he had a drugs, gambling and sex problem," recalled Meacham. "There's a few people that come into this office, and if I don't feel comfortable I'll ask them to walk outside and do the transaction. Not once did I ever feel threatened sexually."

Every couple of weeks, the printer arrived at their office to deliver their orders. And although they thought him an old hippie who had probably taken too many drugs in his youth, they found him surprisingly businesslike and efficient.

"His business he conducted very well," said Meacham. "He was always on time. He was very presentable. His charges were cheap."

On one visit, Garrido discussed his business, saying his daughter Alyssa helped him with the printing and that he also had two grandchildren. Then he gave them a Printing For Less business card, with a smiling blonde-haired, blue-eyed woman on it.

"I was like, 'Who is that? She's gorgeous,'" said Meacham. "And he said, 'That's my daughter.'"

When Meacham remarked that his daughter should be a model, Garrido smiled, agreeing she was "very gorgeous."

Over time, Meacham and Love developed a good rapport with Phillip Garrido, who often stayed with them for an hour or more.

"We weren't like, 'Get out!'" she explained. "We'd listen to him. He'd sing his songs that he wrote to us. Gorgeous voice.

He loved our metal acoustic building and he'd just come out
and sing."

Garrido told them that he suffered from schizophrenia and
A.D.D., and was under heavy medication.

"He told us he used to take drugs," Meacham recalled, "that
he is now on a certain drug for a schizophrenic that is compa-
rable to crank. He was also balancing the Ritalin they give
you for A.D.D."

Although her partner Lorenzo Love thought Garrido was
"fucking nuts," he still liked him.

"One time he says something that kind of caught my attention," Love remembered. "He said, 'I'm high on medicine. I
started doing the crank.' "

Later, there were reports of Phillip Garrido being a
"tweaker," and using an old van in the hidden backyard as a
methamphetamine laboratory. Crystal meth is big business in
the poor unincorporated Antioch badlands, and it was rumored
that Garrido was manufacturing and selling the drug.

There would also be media speculation that he had turned
Nancy into a hard-core methamphetamine addict, so he could
control her even more.

In late 2002, realtor Deepal Karunaratne's print orders started
coming back riddled with spelling mistakes and inaccuracies.
So he complained to Phillip Garrido, asking why the quality
of his work had fallen.

"He told me that he had dyslexia," recalled Karunaratne.
"He said his daughter was the one who is handling all the
work."

Karunaratne asked to meet with Alyssa, so he could deal
with her directly. At first Garrido was reluctant, but eventually
he invited his longtime client over to his house for a meeting.

When Karunaratne arrived at 1554 Walnut Avenue, Garrido made him wait at the gate at the end of the driveway,
while he fetched Alyssa.

"He brought her out to the front of the house," recalled
Karunaratne. "He introduced us. She was very normal. A very
pretty young lady, but she was kind of dirty blonde."

Wearing gloves and dressed in ink-stained work overalls, Alyssa was polite and professional.

"We talked specifically business at the beginning," remembered Karunaratne. "She appeared very normal. I regarded her as his daughter."

Initially, Alyssa found it difficult to understand the Sri Lankan–born businessman, but they soon developed a good rapport.

"We got used to each other," he explained. "She is a very good graphic designer and understands computer graphics. She was very good at her job."

From then on Karunaratne was in touch with Alyssa at least twice a week by phone or e-mail, with the occasional meeting in Walnut Avenue. But their conversations were limited to business.

Once Karunaratne asked Garrido if he could come into the backyard to see the printing operation, but he refused.

"He said it was a trade secret," said Karunaratne.

In 2002, El Dorado County, California, implemented the Amber Alert network, to quickly track down missing children who may have been abducted. Named after nine-year-old Amber Hagerman, who was abducted in Arlington, Texas, and then savagely murdered in January 1996, the nationwide plan has saved many children's lives since it was first introduced.

If Amber Alerts had been in place in 1991, investigators believe Jaycee Lee Dugard would have been found quickly, and her abductors caught.

"Would there have been a greater likelihood we could have caught [Phillip Garrido] in the early 1990s had these systems been in place? Absolutely," the National Center for Missing and Exploited Children president Ernie Allen later told the *Contra Costa Times*.

30

"I DON'T WANT TO HURT HIM"

Phillip Garrido always talked a good game. Constantly in motion and using his hands to make points, the eccentric printing entrepreneur loved to embellish the truth. As Tim Allen got to know him better over the years, he became curious about his printing operation and just how it worked.

"Phillip would just say it was a family business," said Allen, "and they did all the work in a metal building behind the house. He kind of described the property. So in my mind I thought they actually had a printing company in a big metal building you could drive cars into."

Garrido also loved talking about his cutting-edge printing equipment.

"He was always bragging," recalled Allen, "about how he was buying new machinery—a new copy machine, new computers, new printing equipment. But I always encouraged him, as he was kind of a self-employed entrepreneur. Instead of relying on government support, he was out there beating the pavement."

Perhaps the only one of his clients to ever see his archaic printing equipment firsthand was Christine Meacham, who claims to have been in his backyard at least eight or nine times.

"I needed to check the first proofing on a print order," she said. "He took me into the backyard. I was in three tents. One tent had printing, the other had different colored paper, the other had stenciling."

Garrido also allowed Marc Lister into the backyard several times, showing off his recording equipment.

"Phil just told me," said Lister, "that shed back there was his recording studio and his print shop. You'd just have to assume he was telling the truth. There was no reason to question what he was telling me."

Another client, Ben Daughdrill, who owned a hauling and demolition company in Oakley, collaborated with Alyssa on several new advertising campaigns.

"She was the brains in the business," said Daughdrill.

Whenever Daughdrill called Printing For Less with an order, Phillip Garrido would answer the phone. Then he would hear him relaying instructions to Alyssa, who would then take over the project. From then on they would correspond through e-mail, working up the proofs and designs.

"I always got the impression," said Daughdrill, "that she was the one doing the design and the artwork."

Several times over the years, Daughdrill met Alyssa when he came to collect orders, and was impressed by her professionalism.

"She came across as just a nice, genuine person," he said. "[I] didn't see anything that was weird or like she was looking over her shoulder. Just a normal person."

On September 5, 2003, Alyssa, now twenty-three, wrote this entry in her secret journal, providing a clear insight into the mental turmoil that engulfed her. Her desperate cry for her and the children's freedom reveals her torturously conflicted feelings for her captor.

"I don't want to hurt him," she wrote. "Sometimes I think my very presence hurts him . . . so how can I ever tell him how I want to be free. Free to come and go as I please . . . Free to say I have a family. I will never cause him pain if it's in my power to prevent it. FREE."

In 2004, Phillip Garrido stopped paying property taxes on 1554 Walnut Avenue. Technically the deeds were still in his mother's name, but since she was suffering from dementia, he and Nancy were now paying all the bills.

Nancy Garrido was working at the Diamond Ridge Healthcare Center in Pittsburg as a laundress and cleaner. It was a big step down from her old career as a nurse, having not renewed her state nursing license since 1995 and letting it lapse.

"Nancy was a nice woman," her former co-worker Janie Bates later told the *National Enquirer*, "but she often looked unkempt."

Bates said Nancy often came to work looking like she had slept in her clothes and was in need of a wash.

"Nancy's hair was always oily," Bates recalled. "Her clothes were not filthy, but not fresh either. They were never ironed."

During breaks, the disheveled cleaner often spoke about her husband.

"Nancy talked about Phillip like she worshipped him," said Bates. "We all thought it was so strange the way she looked off into space when she talked about him."

Nancy also told them that Phillip was her only family, as she could not have children. She explained that Phillip promised God would bless them with children, and that God always kept his promises to her husband.

After finishing work, Nancy went home to take care of her ailing mother-in-law before going into the backyard to garden.

"Nancy worked hard in that yard when she wasn't inside," said longtime neighbor Helen Boyer, "weeding, watering, mowing."

As a young man in Reno, Nevada, Phillip Garrido had often organized drug-fuelled late-night sex orgies. And toward the end of 2004, he reportedly started throwing wild parties in his backyard, keeping his neighbors up in the early hours with loud rock 'n' roll music.

One night Mike Rogers, whose backyard backed directly onto the Garridos', was unable to sleep because of the deafening music and drunken laughter. So he peered over the fence into Garrido's backyard and was shocked.

"What I saw was not normal," Rogers later told the *News of the World*. "Eight to ten men, mostly Mexican, would gather in a line drinking beer, yelling and screaming and swearing."

Rogers says Garrido regularly threw late-night parties where groups of men would drink beer around a campfire before mysteriously disappearing into one of the tents.

"I saw them entering the tent one by one," he said. "On a number of occasions I saw them bobbing up and down through the window and I thought, 'My God, there is something sexual going on in there.'

"I thought they had a prostitute or something in there. I thought it might have been some kind of sex party or something."

Rogers said the backyard parties lasted until two in the morning. But he never reported them to the police, for fear of reprisals.

"These guys were unsavory-looking men," he explained, "and they were drinking beer and smashing the bottles on the ground. I didn't know what they were capable of."

Polly White was also kept awake by the parties, hearing stories of men lining up outside the tent for sex.

"I did hear men laughing and loud music playing," she said. "It's frightening to know something like this was happening at the end of your backyard."

On July 5, 2004, Alyssa wrote an entry in her journal, revealing the total control Phillip Garrido now exerted over her. Thirteen years after being snatched from her family into his dark realm, she still desperately struggled to keep her identity. But it was a battle she could not possibly win.

"It feels like I'm sinking," she wrote. "I'm afraid I want control of my life . . . this is supposed to be my life to do with what I like . . . but once again he has taken it away. How many times is he allowed to take it away from me? I'm afraid he doesn't see how the things he says makes me a prisoner . . . Why don't I have control of *my life*! I feel I can't even be sure my thoughts are my own."

* * *

In 2005, Angel turned eleven, the same age her mother had been at the time of her abduction. And the resemblance between the beautiful blonde child and the "missing" photographs of Jaycee Lee Dugard was uncanny.

Angel and her eight-year-old sister Starlit worshipped their father. He now regularly took them out of the backyard for trips into town, to see movies after eating lunch at their favorite restaurant.

And it was a sight to behold the gray-haired, balding six-foot, four-inch Phillip Garrido, with his two little girls trailing behind him in long, unfashionable thrift-store dresses.

"They're beautiful little girls," said Cheyvonne Molino, a local business owner and one of Garrido's clients. "Well-mannered, soft-spoken, knowledgeable. I watched them grow up."

Her husband Jim agreed.

"They call him Dad," he said. "They're just like two peas in a pod."

That year, the Garridos' aged next-door neighbor Delbert "Jack" Medeiros went into a nursing home. Phillip Garrido moved into his house as caretaker, so it wouldn't be empty. He also adopted Medeiros's dog, bringing it next door as a new pet for Alyssa and her children.

Phillip and Nancy had recently befriended the sick seventy-nine-year-old pensioner, who had grown fond of them and was only too happy for them look after his property.

While the old man was in the nursing home, the Garridos visited him regularly, updating him on his house and taking him out for short trips in their car.

There were also a number of sheds and outbuildings in his backyard next door. Phillip moved into one of the sheds for a time, bringing in a couch, a mattress, a music system and a VCR player. He also, reportedly, turned all the locks backward, so people could be locked in.

One day he invited Marc Lister over to see the house he was caretaking, showing him some firearms he was keeping there.

"I saw long rifles," said Lister. "He had them stored at the house next door he was caretaking."

Jack Medeiros's ex-wife Magdalena Miller, who was negotiating to buy the house, talked to the new caretaker several times by phone.

"He said his kids were helping him clean the house," she later recalled.

Phillip and Nancy Garrido's only friend in Walnut Avenue was Janice Dietrick, who lived across the street. The sixty-two-year-old widow was dying of cancer, and the Garridos visited her regularly at night, bringing her waffles and cream.

"I know the couple real well," said Dietrick. "We were friends and they came over all the time. Phil would do anything for me. I knew him better than anyone."

Dietrick, who was prescribed medical marijuana, shared joints with the Garridos, chatting for hours into the night in her front room.

"He would sit with me," she said. "He told me he had two girls. I loved the way he took care of the old people."

Bridgehead Café owner Murray Sexton said everyone knew Dietrick was close to the Garridos, socializing with them all the time.

"Unfortunately she's on borrowed time," he said. "[Phillip] was giving her food. Something to eat. They'd burn one together once in a while. He was good to her."

One hot summer night in 2005, Phillip Garrido arrived at an Antioch hotel with a twelve-year-old girl, checking into a single room under his own name. The hotel manager, Beth Torres, would later remember she was suspicious he was with such a young girl.

"I knew there was some sick sex thing going on," she recalled. "But I couldn't prove it at the time."

Torres said that during the night she walked past Room 140, where Garrido was with the girl, listening for any sounds of distress.

At 8:00 A.M. the following morning, Garrido checked out of the room, paying in cash, as the girl waited outside in his car.

"After he paid and started to walk out," said Torres, "he turned to look at me and it gave me the chills."

After two years at the Diamond Ridge Healthcare Center, Nancy Garrido was fired for missing four days of work without any explanation. Her co-worker Janie Bates says Nancy's behavior was becoming increasingly erratic, and it was rumored that she took pills, smoked weed and did heroin.

On the rare occasions Nancy was invited to a work function, she had refused, explaining Phillip never allowed her out socially. She also said she could never invite anybody over to the house, as her husband hated company.

"Phillip expected her home directly after work," said Bates. "We knew she had a certain amount of time to get home or Phillip would get angry."

Soon after losing her job, Nancy found a job with another local health facility, but, according to Bates, was let go after failing a random drug test.

31

"GOD'S DESIRE"

In late 2005, Phillip Garrido was reborn. Much of his life had been a struggle between sex and God. But just before his fifty-fifth birthday he announced he was giving up masturbation in order to devote himself fully to religion. He also claimed to have cured himself of schizophrenia, having invented a miraculous black box, allowing him to hear the voices of angels.

After his epiphany he spent hours drafting a rambling, often incomprehensible manifesto he called "Origins of Schizophrenia Revealed," triumphantly proclaiming he had healed himself and was no longer a sexual deviant. And he claimed his "powerful new insight" would help law enforcement, educators and therapists worldwide understand why sex offenders, like himself, were unable to control their "abnormal desires and thoughts" and committed "such dysfunctional acts."

"Twenty-nine years ago I was imprisoned for a violent crime," he wrote, "that behavioral scientists believe is not possible to end. Not only have I accomplished an end to that problem but I have established a powerful means of developing a pathway for others to accomplish the same quality control."

In his manifesto, which he later posted on the Internet, inviting the media to disseminate, Garrido attributed now being able to "process complex issues concerning love" as a key ingredient in his success.

"It is the age-old struggle between right and wrong," he wrote, "that is holding the human race back from discovering a freedom so capable that the renewing of one's mind becomes a simpler reality."

Discovering this freedom, he wrote, had "reorganized and replaced an internal thought process with such unequivocal success that it literally redefines the possibilities." There is now "solid hope" for "sexual predators," suffering from "the many forms of aggressive sexual behavior."

He then went on to address the subject of celibacy at length.

"Not all people who suffer from these types of problems," he wrote, "are happy with their behavior and do experience major depression after ejaculation."

Garrido spoke of his own remorse and self-loathing after sex, saying he was helpless to control himself the next time he was aroused. Then he described how his spiritual rebirth had led to a loving new relationship with his wife, leaving it unclear if he meant Nancy or Alyssa.

THIS IS MY STORY

It started when I began to examine issues differently due to the many moral issues and experiences I have had, the type that leads to believing in a creator who deals with reality and help a person reason correctly. Having insight of how we form thoughts and the desire to live a healthy productive life I began to discover that the human mind has an undeveloped potential, one that is subject to our own thoughts.

Because of my background I began to examine the issues of how certain behaviors cause a great deal of pain in myself and those who are victimized by those behaviors especially our family and my wife. Building from those personal experiences I prepared a way to deal with these issues in my own mind.

How? For example every time I would see a woman who was attractive I began to examine my thoughts directly, not allowing my eyes to turn aside in order to avoid those issues I needed to confront the problem. Looking allowed my self-talk to provide pictures and words that dealt with reality, saying to myself that people are beautiful and attractive. Slowly I began re-addressing the matter with reality statements such as "see how beautiful she is to look at." These messages began confirming my desire to be rid of the physical feelings the mind provided the body. I used the feedback of other realities like the harm it caused my wife and me to help supply a healthier out look [sic].

In time it began to form a new picture, slowly beginning to drop and reinforce the issues that kept opening the doors to inappropriate thoughts and desires. At first the mind (or self talk) would send out the same stimulating messages leaving me subject to the physical attractions. As time went on I gained control over my body by taking the next step, (controlling masturbation) as it is a key in opening the mind up to more problematic developing. This allowed me (after a few months) to find a new experience awaiting me the type that escapes our notice without having the experience to know what it would provide. This helped supply a completely new freedom that at first became an observation and not much more, that is until the weeks passed by and the reality started to set in.

When this was well formed within my belief system I started to notice a new freedom was being established through the subconscious mind. As this went on one day I discovered one of the most powerful freedoms imaginable, it was like the feelings one has when he is with someone new for the first time, except this time it was with my wife. When I had intercourse with her the feelings were so powerful and exciting that every time we have intercourse now it is as though I had just met her, you know the kind of excitement we all find when we first meet someone we keep thinking of them often during the day and can hardly wait to be with them.

Get ready because here is the reward: Finally one day when we were having intercourse and I ejaculated I got up and in great anger I realized I never needed to act or do the things I used to believe was so great and stimulating. At that same moment I began explaining to her how my relationship with her was all I ever needed and at that moment I knew and felt what must be the greatest freedom of all because I was able to see myself as wanting those things only! I began to weep telling her, "I am sorry for the things I did in the past" at that time a feeling of remorse came over me, one that I never new [sic] or felt before or even dreamed was possible.

Since then it has happened again and again and has become a powerful reward providing a loving interaction the kind that was meant to be between a man and a wife. The fact is I now find myself no longer wanting to separate from her after sexual intercourse, instead I keep telling her how much I truly love her, because now I find it desirable to hold her calling into play the same feelings I had just before the sexual interaction, the feelings that attracted me to desire that interaction was still there without the need to have sex, imagine that!

Research shows the desire for a man to have intimacy with his partner after sex is not usually there instead I feel the opposite and very content afterwards. You have no idea how rewarding that is especially for me as I always wanted to get away from a woman after it was concluded, no longer needing or desiring to touch.

This is just part of the progress I have made through knowledge I have gained concerning the creator and his purpose intended for mankind. I would never have changed nor would I have ever known the quality found in such freedom. Thanks to God and his Son Christ Jesus I am alive and free of these burdens.

This is the process God and his son provided me with as I cleaned the inside of the mind not just to make it look that way on the outside. God will testify for me concerning these facts. God willing I will be teaching this and other skills Christ is providing for me in the prisons throughout the U.S. as well as over seas [sic].

Soon afterward, Phillip and Nancy Garrido arrived at Maria Christenson's recycling center, asking to talk to her privately in her office. He told her he was starting a church in his backyard, asking for a $2,000 loan to build a bathroom for it.

When she agreed to lend Phillip the money, he suddenly became very emotional.

"He started talking about how he was a changed man," Maria recalled. "And he didn't masturbate any more."

Then Phillip and Nancy both burst into tears, as he told her he had once been to prison, without elaborating further.

"They were both crying and she was hanging onto him," Maria recalled. "I couldn't understand why is he in front of his wife telling me he doesn't masturbate. I tried to get rid of him really fast."

From then on Christenson tried to avoid Phillip Garrido as much as possible, telling her employees never to leave her alone with him again.

On January 31, 2006, Phillip Garrido filed the first of two applications, officially registering to create what he would call the Phillip C. Knight Institute. He submitted the forms and a $15 filing fee to the Contra Costa County Clerk's Office. It was then duly stamped by recorder Stephen L. Weir, giving him until January 31, 2011, to use the "fictitious business name statement."

Several years later, he refiled the forms, as he had forgotten to write the word "Institute" on the earlier one.

Later there would be speculation that Garrido had intended to start his own school to educate his daughters, Angel, now aged eleven, and Starlit, eight, as well as giving him access to other young girls.

To help him prepare the application, Garrido arrived at notary public David Robinson's office with some legal questions.

"We helped him fill out the paperwork," said Robinson. "We notarized it."

Then Garrido triumphantly announced that he had cured himself of his sexual addiction.

"It's kind of a conversation stopper," said Robinson's wife, Rainy, who was also there. "I thought it was something very odd to say."

One morning, an excited Phillip Garrido arrived at Jim and Cheyvonne Molino's car-wrecking yard with important news.

"He said he had a project he was working on," recalled Cheyvonne, "and it was the development of a cure for schizophrenia."

Garrido then showed them a large black box with an amplifier inside, and input jacks on either side for earphones. There was a third input for a microphone. He then explained how schizophrenics always hear voices in their head.

"So if a normal person puts this on," said Cheyvonne, "they can hear what a schizophrenic walks around hearing in everyday life. That's how he explained it to me."

Then, Garrido demonstrated his device for the Molinos. He put on one set of earphones leading from the black box, giving the other to Cheyvonne. Then he turned around to face the wall, and started whispering into the microphone.

"He'd ask you to tell him if you could hear him whispering," she said. "And he'd change his sounds."

Over the next few months, as he perfected his black box, he started making increasingly bizarre claims about it. Eventually he maintained that it allowed him to hear the heavenly voices of angels.

Nancy, Alyssa, Angel and Starlit were to serve as his devoted disciples, venturing out with him into the world to save mankind.

For his first public demonstrations of the black box, Phillip Garrido would take Alyssa and their two young daughters to parks around Antioch, giving exhibitions to the homeless. His client and friend Marc Lister witnessed about a dozen of these.

"There were a couple of parks in Antioch where the homeless hang out," said Lister. "He'd go down there and test the waters."

According to Lister, Alyssa, Angel and Starlit all participated in the public demonstrations, which soon became more ambitious. Then Garrido started driving to People's Park near the University of California, Berkeley Campus, where hundreds of homeless people gather everyday for free meals. Alyssa took charge of logistics and planning, while Angel and Starlit handed out free water and snacks.

"He'd get a group of up to fifty people together," said Lister, "by handing out sandwiches and cold drinks. Then he'd start plugging in his black box and do all his stuff."

According to Lister, Alyssa often complained about the problems she faced, organizing these public displays. And she would blame demons for trying to stop them, disseminating their message to save the world.

"She was telling me they were out at People's Park," he recalled, "and all the things they had to do to get on campus. Dealing with the police and dealing with this person and that person. It was her belief that it was demons that were putting these people—these roadblocks—in their way."

Lister attended many demonstrations, genuinely curious about how the black box worked.

"I just stood around and watched," he said. "One time Phil was in a panic because he was late. There were a lot of people there and he was busy talking, handing out sandwiches, handing out drinks. He had [Alyssa] and the girls handing out some pamphlets and literature."

Then Garrido hooked up the power cord to a generator, and switched on his black box, turned away from the crowd and started talking.

"I stood back and watched," said Lister, "and I saw people raising their hands. 'I hear you, Phil! I hear you, Phil.'"

In late June 2006, Betty Upingco threw a high school graduation party for her son, inviting the entire neighborhood. In the middle of the party, Phillip Garrido showed up by himself, and as the loudspeakers were broken and there was no music, he ran home for his.

After setting them up in the yard, he was invited to join the party. He began drinking and his behavior started getting "weird," as one attendee put it. He gave strange looks to all the young girls, and made suggestive remarks.

"He made us feel very uncomfortable," recalled Betty. "And

he kept trying to talk to the teenage girls. Finally my husband told the boys to take the speakers and give them back to him."

Garrido walked back to his house and stood by his front gate, inviting the girls inside as they walked home.

"They came back and told us," Betty said, " 'He keeps trying to lure us over to talk.' So at that point, we started escorting the girls out."

A few days later, Betty Upingco's daughter went on the Megan's Law website for sexual offenders, discovering to her horror that their neighbor was on there. He was listed as a convicted rapist, along with his photograph and a description of the surgical scar on his abdomen.

"So from that point on," said Upingco, "anytime we had female guests over, we would escort them out of the area and made sure we kept an eye on them. It was very uncomfortable."

32

"DO YOU HEAR ANYTHING?"

That June, Phillip Garrido started demonstrating his black box to his print clients, as he did his rounds. He drafted a "Declaration of Affirmation," which he asked each to sign after witnessing his invention.

"This document is to affirm," it began, "that I Phillip Garrido have clearly demonstrated the ability to control sound with my mind and have developed a device for others to witness this phenomena. By using a sound generator to provide the sound, and a headphone amplification system, *(a device to focus your hearing so as to increase the sensitivity of what one is listening to)* I have produced a set of voices by effectively controlling the sound to pronounce words through my own mental powers."

Then he left a space to be signed and dated, confirming that they had witnessed him at their place of business, "controlling a voice or set of voices that are unearthly in nature."

It also addressed Phillip Garrido's state of mind.

"Concerning the state of Phillips' [*sic*] mindfulness and his freedom to conduct himself appropriately: I will confirm that out of the many years I have interacted with him, business or otherwise, he has always acted mature and intelligent. He has a steady personality throughout the many years I have known him. He has never displayed an unsuitable, incoherent or improper cognitive behavior all the years I have known him."

One morning he arrived at the East County Glass & Window company, asking to see the owner, Tim Allen.

"He said, 'I'm doing demonstrations with the box," Allen recalled. "It was twice the size of a shoe box maybe, and it had some sort of electronics inside."

Garrido then proceeded to plug in the earphones, handing a set to his amused client to put on.

"The way he described it," said Allen, "is that he could hear people think. He could hear voices. God would talk to him and he could hear the voices through this box, and that I could understand what he was thinking telepathically."

Then, as Allen's employees looked on in astonishment, Garrido began the demonstration.

"I shut my eyes," said Allen. "I really wanted to hear something, but all I could hear were kind of hollow sounds like a shell."

But the one voice he did hear came from outside the earphones, asking, "Do you hear anything?"

"And so I opened my eyes," he recalled, "and I looked at him and he was mouthing words, but he wasn't saying anything."

Garrido asked him again if he had heard anything, and Allen said he could not.

"Then he started whispering louder," he said. "And when he got to a certain volume out of his mouth, I could hear him. So I told him, 'Phil, I can hear you.' And he said, 'Great! My box works! It's fantastic.'"

Not wanting to hurt Garrido's feelings, by telling him that it was his voice and not the black box he had heard, Allen thanked him for the demonstration, wishing him good luck with his new invention.

"I just said, 'That's great, Phil.' I didn't want to erode his self-esteem."

Later Allen would say that his purported signature on Phillip Garrido's Declaration of Affirmation that day was a forgery.

When Garrido arrived at Deepal Karunaratne's house with the black box, the realtor told him he didn't have time for a demonstration.

"He told me he could control voices with that," recalled Karunaratne. "He kept bugging me to test it."

Finally the realtor gave in, just to humor him.

"It was just like an amplifier," he recalled. "I could see that he's moving his lips. I could hear the voices like birds singing. The voices of the air. Stuff like that. I don't know what he was trying to do."

When Garrido asked him to sign his declaration, Karunaratne agreed, just to get rid of him.

A few days later, Phillip Garrido arrived at Janice Gomes's new office, which she shared with a friend named Kevin, another of his print clients.

"Phillip brought up a big black box," Gomes recalled, "and he set it down on the table. And he says, 'This is just fantastic. I want you to hear the angels speak to me through here.'

"And Kevin looked at him and said, 'Phillip, you and the angels get out of here. I'm busy.'"

When he tried to demonstrate it to Maria Christenson, who was still wary after his previous outburst about masturbation, she told him to keep their relationship just business.

"He said that I was going to be blown away," Maria recalled. "I was going to fall over backwards when he'd shown me the black box he had in the car. But I never let him, when he wanted to bring it in. So he just kind of backed off then. He was getting too weird."

He then produced his black box affidavit for her to sign anyway, becoming angry when she refused.

"I didn't want to sign one," said Christenson. "He was mad at me because he wanted to bring that box, so I could hear the voice. And I just said no."

Several months later, Christenson took her children Erika, twenty-six, and Cary, fourteen, with her to collect a print order at Phillip Garrido's house. When there was no answer at the front door, they walked over to the side, peeking over the fence into the backyard.

"We were on the fence when he came out," Maria recalled. "And he got very upset and told us to get back in the car, because he had a vicious dog."

While they waited in the car for Garrido to bring them the order, Erika begged her mother to leave immediately, saying it was just too creepy and weird.

"I just told them," recalled Christenson, " 'That guy's a Jesus freak. He's harmless.' "

Around that time, David Bocanegra called to see how his sister Nancy was doing. She now hardly ever spoke to her family, and on the rare occasions she did, Phillip was always there hovering in the background.

During their conversation, Nancy seemed very excited as she told her brother that Phillip had invented a black box that allowed him to talk to God.

"It was just really off the wall," said David. "I couldn't believe my sister was with this guy that was just nuts."

On August 22, Phillip Garrido brought eight signed Declarations of Affirmation to a notary public to be officially witnessed. Later most of his clients would deny ever signing them.

In an attached affidavit, Garrido swore under oath that each client had signed and dated it under their own free will.

"I state that each individual," read his affidavit, "clearly witnessed myself demonstrate the freedom to control and produce a set of voices unearthly in nature.

"I willingly assume full legal responsibility under the laws of perjury in the state of California that protect all humans from deliberately providing false or misleading testimony."

In late November, Damon Robinson and his girlfriend, Erika Pratt, rented Jack Medeiros's house, which Garrido had been taking care of. When Robinson moved in he was surprised to find all the locks had been turned around, preventing the doors being opened from the inside. Although the property was supposed to have been vacant for the last three years, it was obvious somebody had been living there, as there was a mattress and other old furniture in the living room.

On November 30, Erika Pratt was showing a girlfriend around their new home, when they looked over the fence into

the Garridos' backyard. And to their surprise they saw two
little blonde-haired girls, who were obviously living in a tatty
collection of sheds and tents. They also saw several pit bulls
roaming around.

"He had little girls and women living in that backyard,"
Pratt, twenty-five, later told the *San Francisco Chronicle*,
"and they all looked kind of the same. They never talked and
they kept to themselves."

"Freaked out" by what she had seen, Pratt called her boyfriend, who told her to call the police.

She then called 911, reporting her neighbor Phillip Garrido
was a "religious psychotic with a sex addiction," with young
children living in tents in his backyard.

A deputy from the Contra Costa County Sheriff's Department was duly dispatched to 1554 Walnut Avenue to investigate. He questioned Garrido in his front yard, never asking to
enter the backyard, as he did not consider there was any reason to do so.

But before leaving, he did warn Garrido about possible
code violations if he had people living outside in a residential
neighborhood.

Then the deputy, who had no idea that Phillip Garrido was
a registered sex offender on parole for rape and kidnapping,
got in his squad car and drove off.

Later, Pratt contacted the Contra Costa County Sheriff's
Department to find out what had happened.

"[They] told me they couldn't go inside because they didn't
have a warrant," she said. "So they just told him they'd keep
an eye on him."

After such a close call with law enforcement, Phillip Garrido
was badly shaken up. He now became convinced that it was
only a matter of time before the truth came out about his kidnapping Jaycee Lee Dugard, fifteen years earlier.

In hindsight, Tim Allen believes that the November 30 visit
from law enforcement changed everything.

"My opinion is that Phil felt they was onto them," said Allen. "And I think that also coincides with some other things."

Now approaching sixty, Garrido's libido was waning, accounting for his more civilized attitudes toward women.

"He had two young daughters that he loved dearly," said Allen. "I could see that in his eyes. So I think his whole attitude and outlook on life changed, as he realized he had done some terrible, terrible things that he could not hide or get away with."

And as Starlit turned ten and Angel thirteen, he knew it was only a matter of time before they wanted to break away and live their own lives away from his backyard.

"He really loved those girls," said Allen. "That was something that was starting to happen that he couldn't stop."

As Angel and Starlit did not even officially exist, with no birth certificates or Social Security numbers, they could never go to school, get medical attention or get a driver's license.

With his ailing mother now confined to bed with dementia and declining, Garrido knew that when she died, his and Nancy's world would come crashing down. The deeds of 1554 Walnut Avenue were in Pat Franzen's name, and as a convicted felon, if he ever tried to transfer the property over to himself, there would be too many probing questions, exposing his secret family.

An appraiser would examine every inch of the house and the backyard, and many years of tax returns would have to be shown. It would soon become obvious that he had never claimed for these three females living with him, who did not exist bureaucratically.

"So his back is up against the wall," said Allen. "So I think he's planning his retirement. So he does schizophrenia and acts really weird around a bunch of people. He starts talking to God in a box. Starts a church. He's got the whole mental defense going that he's crazy."

A few weeks after the deputy's visit, Phillip Garrido asked Marc Lister to manage his music career, giving him three CDs with about twenty of his songs.

"When he gave them to me," said Lister, "he said, 'What makes these so valuable, Marc, is that I recorded these while I was in prison.' I looked at him and I said, 'Come on, Phil.' And he said, 'Other than Johnny Cash, I'm the only other person who recorded music in prison.'"

Lister declined the offer, saying he was too busy with his own business.

"He told me to hang onto them," Lister recalled, "as some day they are going to be worth a lot of money. I just threw them in my storage room and forgot about them."

Phillip Garrido also shared his music with Deepal Karunaratne, this time claiming he had recorded it in his backyard studio.

"He comes here to bring my stuff," said Karunaratne, "he has earphones and his little Walkman. So I asked what he was listening to."

Garrido replied that it was his own music, and put his headphones on Karunaratne so he could listen.

"He's a very good singer," said Karunaratne. "I asked, 'Where do you record this?' He said, 'I have a soundproof recording studio in my backyard.'"

33

THE MAN WHO SPOKE WITH HIS MIND

On February 7, 2007, Phillip Garrido took his black box public, registering four sites with Blogger.com. Over the next eighteen months "The Man Who Spoke With His Mind"—as he now called himself—would regularly write about his religious beliefs on his main blog, "Voices Revealed." But he also registered other blog domains, with names like "Charging The Angels With Error," "The Truth Will Set You Free" and "Exposed."

"The Creator has given me the ability to speak in the tongues of Angels," he proudly announced on Voicesrevealed. blogspot.com, "in order to provide a wake-up call that will in time include the salvation of the entire world."

And at the same time, he mailed out a comprehensive media package to newspapers and television stations around the Bay Area. His kit included press releases, his photo and his eight client affidavits, complete with a notarized jurat certificate.

Under the headline, "Origin of Schizophrenia Revealed: Voices Are Real," Garrido declared that he had made "one of the most powerful discoveries of this century."

But he stipulated that media outlets could only reprint his six-page media pack in its entirety, without any rewrites.

In a cover letter to editors, Garrido wrote: "This is the beginning of a powerful discloser that concerns the entire inhabited Earth. It will address the stigma's [sic] surrounding the phenomenon and controversy afflicted with hearing voices."

He offered to arrange black box demonstrations for the "news media," urging reporters to "approach this with an open mind," and witness his great discovery themselves.

And to make it easier, he even wrote a news story, complete with a twenty-year-old photograph of himself, inviting reporters to contact him via e-mail at voicesrevealed@hotmail.com.

A Bay Area man has made a major discovery concerning the phenomenon of voices. He has documented the discovery with signed and notarized affidavits. The declarations are from established business owners in the greater bay area [sic]. They should not be taken lightly as this is a very serious matter that concerns the lives of human beings all over the globe who may be at this very moment under pressure and moving towards harming themselves and/or others. Any attempt to express concern is welcome but be advised the statements concerning the facts of the affidavits are true and require serious responses that would pertain solely to proving quality interactions by qualified educators that are prepared to provide answers for the millions who suffer from these disorders usually characterized by withdrawal from reality.

In the interests of public disclosure, Phillip also informed the media that he had been under the care of a psychiatrist for the past fifteen years for Attention Deficit Disorder.

But when his press package failed to generate a single story, he went back to the drawing board.

Over the next few months, Phillip Garrido became a religious fanatic, preaching his increasingly bizarre message to whoever would listen. He started standing outside his front gate, preaching to neighbors and holding religious revivalist meetings under a blue tarpaulin in his garden.

According to neighbors, small groups of followers began showing up at the Garrido house, where they were met by Nancy. They were then taken to a makeshift church, where Alyssa, Starlit and Angel would be waiting. Then Phillip Garrido would stroll in with his guitar, and start reading the Bible and singing religious songs.

He tried to convert his printing clients to his self-styled religion, warning it was their only salvation as there was "a huge mind-blowing change" about to happen.

"He started talking about a huge event that was about to happen," said Tim Allen. "He really never talked about specifics, like Christianity or God. He talked in vague terms, in big terms about religion and made broad, sweeping statements."

Allen and his employees would humor him, before sending him on his way.

"What can you say?" Allen explained. "We let him talk about whatever he wanted and listened, and then we thanked him for bringing in our business cards and paid him."

Whenever Deepal Karunaratne arrived at 1554 Walnut Avenue for a business meeting with Alyssa, Phillip Garrido would come out and start talking "strange stuff" about angels.

"He was always trying to preach to me," recalled Karunaratne. "Sometimes I go there in a hurry. [Alyssa] brings my stuff. As I'm trying to leave he jumps in my car and sits down with the Bible. And he's preaching to me and I can't get away. I say, 'Phillip, I have to go. I need to get back to work.'"

One morning Karunaratne was over at the Walnut Avenue house when Phillip Garrido walked in with Angel and Starlit. Then he asked why the girls were not at school.

"Phil said, 'We don't trust our public school system,'" said Karunaratne. "'We teach them at home.'"

As Phillip Garrido devoted more and more time to his new church, Alyssa ran Printing For Less, assisted by her daughters. She now personally dealt with all the customers and was the consummate professional. But unfortunately her e-mails and letters were full of spelling mistakes, as if they'd been written by a child.

On May 7, 2007, Ben Daughdrill had just got off the phone to Alyssa after a business conversation, when she sent him this confirmation e-mail.

"i will take a look at the price sheet and send you over a

copy of the revised brochure tomorrow. as to the pictures sorry . . . but we don't have a digital camera . . . hopefully you can find a way to get me those pictures you want so i can add them to them [sic] brochure. i can get the brochures to you pretty fast within the week of final approval of the brochures. How many are you going to order and do you want them on glossy or matte paper, thick or thin?"

A few months later, she e-mailed Daughdrill again.

"here's the business cards in jpeg format," she wrote, "let me know if you need anything else thank you."

But all the clients liked working with Alyssa, and made allowances as she always got the job done.

"She was always good at getting us what we wanted," said Daughdrill. "You got the feeling she was doing all the work."

Marc Lister said during his many visits to Walnut Avenue over the years, he formed the impression Alyssa enjoyed her work.

"She never had anything bad to say about Phil," he observed.

Cheyvonne Molino of J & M Enterprises said Alyssa did all the designing, worked the computer and e-mailed people.

"In the early days it was fax," recalled Cheyvonne. "Then all of a sudden it was e-mail. She did the work and he delivered."

Maria Christenson often wondered about the charmingly childish designs now popping up on her receipts, envelopes and business card orders.

"She started putting all this little kid's stuff on my stationery," she recalled. "I asked Phil about it and he said, 'Oh Alyssa, one of my kids did it.' But I've never seen her. He didn't let me in the house or let me deal with her at all. He always came to me."

At 9:24 A.M. on May 15, 2007, The Man Who Spoke With His Mind posted an important message on his blog in capital letters. Under the title "Disclaimer," Phillip Garrido told the world of his "ABILITY . . . TO OPEN DOORS THAT WILL HONOR THE CREATOR AND HIS ETERNAL PURPOSE FOR MANKIND."

And he outlined his mission to gain the attention of "SCI-ENTISTS, PHYSICISTS AND EDUCATORS" for a "MA-JOR WAKE UP CALL."

He then quoted Jeremiah 9:24. "LET HIM THAT BOASTS BOAST ABOUT THIS . . . THAT I AM THE LORD, WHO EXERCISES KINDNESS, JUSTICE AND RIGHTEOUSNESS ON EARTH, FOR IN THESE I DE-LIGHT."

A few weeks later, he brought his two daughters along with him when he visited an aunt in Brentwood, California. When asked who they were, he replied he was babysitting the little blonde girls for a neighbor. But his aunt was suspicious, later calling his brother, Ron.

"My aunt told me," Ron recalled, " 'I swear that oldest girl is his daughter. She's got his eyes.' "

That fall, Dilbert Medeiros gave Phillip Garrido almost $18,000 of his life savings to get his church started. Later the sick eighty-one-year-old pensioner, whom Phillip and Nancy had befriended and taken on outings to the zoo, claimed it was only a loan.

A few months later, after he moved into residential care, Medeiros complained that Garrido refused to repay the loan. The police were called, but after a lengthy investigation, Contra County prosecutors found insufficient grounds to charge him.

Later Phillip Garrido would be accused of looting the se-nile old man's bank account for years, getting him to write out numerous checks.

On October 10, Phillip Garrido's parole officer visited his house, informing him that as a registered sex offender, he must undergo a mental health evaluation under the newly passed Jessica's Law. Named in memory of nine-year-old Jessica Lun-sford, who was abducted and murdered in Florida in 2005, "Jessica's Law" was championed by California governor Ar-nold Schwarzenegger, and passed by voters as Proposition 83 on November 7, 2006.

The new law prohibited sex offenders from living within

2,000 feet of schools and parks, and over the next few years a large proportion of offenders would descend on unincorporated Antioch, which provided a perfect cover. Jessica's Law also allowed twenty-four-hour Global Positioning Satellite (GPS) monitoring of parolees for life, which Phillip Garrido would get the following year.

The parole officer duly referred Garrido to the California Department of Corrections and Rehabilitation Outpatient Clinic. It would be the first time the parolee had ever received any mental health treatment from the California parole department, although his original conditions of parole nineteen years earlier included mental health counseling.

With all the new attention he was now receiving from the authorities, Phillip Garrido was becoming increasingly paranoid. One afternoon, a camera-equipped Google mapping car slowly drove past 1554 Walnut Avenue when something strange happened. Soon after it went by the house, photographing the street, an old beat-up van came out of the Garrido driveway and followed it.

The Google camera photographed the van for several blocks, before it suddenly turned down a side street and disappeared.

34

CLOSING IN

On January 29, 2008, Nancy Garrido took over management of her husband's music career, launching her own blog called "Talent Revealed." On it she appealed for financial backers, offering them "a unique music investment opportunity."

"As you know it takes money to produce and promote music," she wrote. "I'm looking for an investor to invest in my husbands [sic] music. The profits from your investment will double, that's how confident I am about his music. He has so much music to share with the world. I'm looking forward to meeting you. Please. If you are an investor please send email to: *nancybgarrido@yahoo.com*."

That would be Nancy's first and only entry on "Talent Revealed."

Three days later, retired police officer turned private investigator Ralph Hernandez arrived at 1554 Walnut Avenue, to meet his new client. For the enterprising Phillip Garrido had decided to patent his black box invention, to finance his God's Desire Church. So he had contacted Antioch-based Aardvark Investigations & Consulting company, which he found in the Yellow Pages. He then hired the sixty-one-year-old ex-cop to interview his clients, who had once witnessed his demonstrations, and prepare a report to be submitted as part of his patent application.

While Phillip Garrido was expounding the unearthly qualities of his black box to the P.I., Nancy and a blonde teenage girl walked in.

"I sat in the living room," recalled Hernandez. "It seemed a typical ranch-style house, nothing unusual for that neighborhood."

Garrido became very "excited," as he showed the private investigator his black box, explaining how it allowed him to talk to angels. The private eye thought him an intelligent man with deep religious convictions, if perhaps a little eccentric.

"He wanted to start a church," said Hernandez, "or ministry."

Garrido volunteered that he was on parole but lied, claiming it was because he had assaulted someone in an argument. Later P.I. Hernandez said he had seen nothing abnormal during his visit.

Over the next few weeks, Hernandez personally interviewed five of the eight Printing For Less clients who had witnessed Garrido's demonstrations.

And on March 15, he submitted his confidential investigation report to his client.

"Each reaffirmed," he wrote, "that they did in person witness Mr. Garrido's presented demonstration, experienced its results and acknowledged playing their individual and honest signatures on their own individual Declarations."

A week earlier Phillip Garrido had called 911, after his ailing eighty-seven-year-old mother had fallen down.

"My mom," stammered a worried Phillip Garrido, after the emergency dispatcher asked what the problem was. "She's not responding . . . her eyes are open and she looks like she's breathing really hard."

The Antioch Fire Department responded to the house to help the aged woman. It would be the first of half a dozen distress calls either Phillip or Nancy would make over the next year, as Pat Franzen's health declined further.

On April 14, the California Department of Corrections and Rehabilitation fitted Phillip Garrido with a GPS ankle bracelet, in line with Jessica's Law. But given his previous assessment as a low-risk sex offender, he was placed on a passive GPS monitoring system. Under the program, Garrido had to obtain prior permission from the parole department before traveling more than twenty-five miles from his home.

Phillip Garrido would breach the "electronic zone," which had been placed around 1554 Walnut Avenue, numerous times without any comeback from his parole officer.

The Concord Parole Department had also programmed the system to send out an alert if he left his house between midnight and 7:00 A.M. And over the next fourteen months, agents received fourteen alerts that he had broken his electronic curfew. But no action was taken on any of them.

Betty Upingco, whose daughter had discovered Garrido was a registered sex offender, says she often saw her neighbor out late at night, prowling around the neighborhood.

"I'd see him walking down the street at eleven o'clock at night," she recalled. "I don't know what he's doing. Sometimes I would see him come back and sometime I never saw him again. Then I started freaking out."

On April 24, Phillip Garrido officially registered his Church of God's Desire as a nonprofit religious organization, with him as company president. The incorporation papers were officially witnessed by Debra Bowen, the Secretary of State of the State of California, and an official state seal was affixed to the certificate.

"God's Desire," wrote Garrido on his blog that day, "is an established incorporation and is protected under the constitutions [*sic*], first amendments rights."

One of the first people he told was his older brother, Ron, boasting that his new church was going to make him rich. He also sent his church's articles of incorporation to his newly assigned parole agent, Juan Castillo, informing him that he would now be working full-time on church business.

"If my family needs me to assist in the printing business," he told the agent, "I will provide deliveries from time to time."

He wrote that he would now be devoting himself to "preparing the body of knowledge" and "the principles behind the creators' desires and qualities to be presented by my church."

Then along with the letter to his parole agent, he enclosed his vehicle registration slip.

He also told Tim Allen he was getting out of the printing business, so he could preach full-time.

"He rambled," said Allen. "It made no sense."

On May 5, Phillip Garrido posted investigator Ralph Hernandez's report, as well as a copy of his clients' affidavits, on the Internet. After pointing out his investigator was not affiliated with his black box project in any way, Garrido warned of possible legal action against anyone who publicly spoke out against it.

"Please consider it slanderous and malicious in nature," he wrote, "to speak against this truth as it would be misleading to the public and a serious violation of our civil rights . . . a person can and will be held liable."

On May 15, California parole agent Juan Castillo paid his first visit to 1554 Walnut Avenue to check on his GPS monitoring strap. Agent Castillo visited again on May 30, when he was told by Nancy that Phillip was out.

When Castillo came again at 7:17 A.M. on June 6, there was no answer when he rang the doorbell, so he left one of his business cards on the front door. The following day he returned at 7:44 A.M.

"[Garrido] was acting very strange," he later wrote in his report, "weird to say the least by ranting on about God and loudly singing songs. Other than that, nothing out of the ordinary."

When Agent Castillo next visited at 8:53 A.M. on June 17, he was surprised to see a young blonde child there. He asked who she was, and Phillip explained it was his brother's daughter, and he was taking care of her.

"[The parolee], wife, 12 year old female niece and mother present," the agent wrote in his report. "[I] conducted a visual cursory search by walking around the entire house with negative results. [I] questioned [parolee] about young girl whom he states is his brother's daughter."

The next time Agent Castillo visited Walnut Avenue, at 6:56 P.M. on July 17, Nancy was armed with a video recorder, and Phillip told him she would be videotaping everything that happened.

"[Parolee's] wife was present," Castillo reported later. "She states she is going to video tape and record me."

The agent then carried out a "brief visual cursory search" of the Garrido house "with negative results."

Four days later, Phillip Garrido came to the parole office in Concord at midday, where he was fingerprinted and his DNA taken.

Agent Castillo's next visit to Garrido's home was at 8:13 A.M. August 5, where he saw Phillip and Nancy Garrido and Pat Franzen. Once again Nancy videotaped him conducting another "visual cursory search," with the same negative results as before.

On August 15, Agent Castillo reported an early morning visit, writing how Phillip Garrido "displays real strange behavior." On his next visit at 9:16 A.M. on September 10, he wrote that Garrido "is really weird acting."

And when the agent arrived at 7:36 A.M. on September 26, he found Garrido outside in his driveway drawing oil out of his car.

"No changes," he later reported, "but displays strange behavior."

That summer Phillip Garrido started taking Angel, now fourteen, and Starlit, almost eleven, with him on his client rounds.

"He brought them in a few times," recalled Tim Allen. "I met them. I shook their hands and everything. They were very, very beautiful . . . with bright blonde hair and striking blue eyes. And their facial expressions and everything were just perfect."

The two girls always wore unfashionably long dresses that fell below their knees.

"They wore clothing that looked homemade," recalled Allen. "Their hair was washed and combed and they didn't look dirty. They were very polite. A little bit shy but not like they were scared."

Whenever they arrived at Allen's showroom, Garrido would park his old gray Dodge van outside in the lot, and then walk in with his daughters. The younger, Starlit, had a birthmark on her forehead she always covered with her blonde bangs. She also stayed close to her father, holding his hand, while Angel stood just behind him.

"They were two well-mannered little girls," said Cheyvonne Molino. "They would come in my office and use my computer, while Dad was on his errands. The little one was very, very talkative. The big one was quiet."

During the hot weather, Garrido started bringing bottles of water for his customers, sending one of the girls to collect them from his van and then leave them on the client's counter.

"All of a sudden he started bringing the water to all his customers," said Cheyvonne. "It was something that he was teaching them. He never went into details."

One day the girls proudly told Cheyvonne that their father had started a church in the basement. She asked how many church members there were.

"There are five of us," replied Angel. "Our dad is the minister."

While Nancy stayed at home with Alyssa, Phillip Garrido began taking his daughters on outings to the San Francisco Aquarium, followed by meals at the Hometown Buffet in Concord. He also took them to the library, the beach, and to see movies at a nearby mall.

And according to Deepal Karunaratne, Alyssa also took her daughters out for day trips while Phillip stayed home, working on church business.

"Sometime when I call Alyssa is not there," he said. "And Phillip answers and says today is the girls' day out. They go out to the movies, shopping and eat out and come back."

Once Deepal received a call from Phillip Garrido, asking for a ride, as his car had broken down in Concord. As the realtor was in Brentwood at the time, he asked Garrido to take a bus and meet him halfway.

"So I picked him up from Pittsburg," recalled Deepal. "And the whole family were there so I gave them a ride."

Angel and Starlit were now often seen shopping with their father at Kmart, a few blocks away from his home.

"The older girl was very clingy with him," recalled Kmart cashier Survitrius Honeycutt. "And neither one would say anything. They didn't have an expression."

Honeycutt also remembered that Garrido occasionally came in alone, buying lubricants and other sex aids.

On several occasions, Deepal Karunaratne and his wife Mala would see Phillip and his daughters shopping in various stores on Deer Valley Road, Antioch.

"And I asked, 'Hey Phillip, are they your kids?' " said Mala. "He said, 'Yeah,' and then he walked away."

On July 10, a special task force, composed of several Costa County law enforcement agencies, did a sweep of known sex offenders in Antioch. Several deputies arrived unannounced at 1554 Walnut Avenue, searching every room of the house. Then they went in the backyard, not venturing past the eight-foot high back fence, as they had no idea the Garrido property line extended back any farther.

The officers later reported finding nothing suspicious at the house, and that Phillip Garrido, who had last registered as a sex offender three months earlier, was in full legal compliance.

On Saturday, July 19, Phillip Garrido staged an hour-long lecture and black box demonstration on the Berkeley campus at People's Park. Two months earlier he had informed parole agent Castillo about the event, claiming he was exercising his constitutional rights to practice his religion.

"This presentation will gain national attention," he told his parole officer, "bringing scientists, physicists, psychologists, educators and religious leaders from around the world, turning their attention toward California."

He boasted that once the media printed his religious message, the state of Nevada would be engulfed in such a "public and political crisis," he would be released from any further parole conditions.

He had invited the FBI and several University of California, Berkeley, departments to attend his Berkeley event, and was disappointed when none turned up. Ultimately it was less than earth-shattering, with Nancy, Alyssa and his two girls handing out pamphlets and bottles of water to the homeless and several curiosity seekers who wandered in.

When he returned home to Antioch, he posted a stirring account of his latest black box demonstration.

"I publicly disclosed new information," announced Garrido on his Voices Revealed blog. "And provided a live demonstration. The lecture was designed to raise the awareness of the general public . . . to undermine the ignorance that prevails concerning voices and begin saving lives."

Two days later, the new president of the God's Desire Church held what he called a "Cultural Trance" for the skeptics who still refused to believe in the powers of his black box.

In his blog, he likened the nonbelievers to people who once believed the earth was flat. He urged them to forget their conditioning and preconceived ideas, so they could hear what they never heard before.

"In the days of Columbus," he wrote, "everyone knew the earth was 'flat.' Today everyone knows it is not possible to produce voices for others to hear as experience clearly marked it as not possible."

He also advised anyone "under the influence of illegal drugs, or if you think you are being led by voices," to seek professional help immediately.

One afternoon Polly White, who shared her back fence with the Garridos, was spraying weeds in her garden when she looked through some broken boards in the fence and saw a little blonde girl, playing by the pool.

When the girl looked up and saw her, Polly said, "Hi, how are you?"

"Fine," replied the girl.

"Are you getting ready to go swimming?" asked the pensioner.

"No," said the girl.

Then Polly asked how old she was, and the girl replied ten.

"I have a little grandson that's your age," Polly told her. "Maybe you'd like to come over and play with him sometime?"

"No," said the girl, shaking her head.

When Polly asked her name, she turned around and ran off.

The next day the fence had been boarded up. The Garrido backyard was no longer visible.

That October, parole agent Eddie Santos was assigned the difficult Phillip Garrido case. He first visited 1554 Walnut Avenue at 3:30 P.M. on November 26, meeting Garrido and his mother, finding "no new info" to report.

Later that day, he prepared a case review of Parolee Garrido. He found that Garrido, who was initially paroled on June 8, 1999, for rape, had a "stable residence," lives with his wife and is unemployed. He advised he be kept at the "current level" of supervision.

From now on Agent Santos would visit Garrido's home twice a month, as well as seeing him occasionally in his office for group meetings and drug testing.

That Halloween, Phillip Garrido dressed up in a gorilla costume and took his daughters trick-or-treating. At Christmas, he visited Deepal and Mala Karunaratne's home with Nancy and Alyssa to exchange holiday gifts. Mala said Alyssa had visited their home on numerous occasions, but always with Nancy or Phillip. Phillip usually sat in the middle of the carpet, and started preaching from his Bible or singing his songs, much to the Karunaratnes' annoyance.

A few months earlier, when their daughter had gotten married, Alyssa had done all the invitations for the shower and the wedding. So that Christmas they wanted to thank her.

"Alyssa had done so much printing for me," recalled Mala, "so I thought I should give her a gift. She's the most sweetest girl that you ever could meet, so I told her to come."

When Mala gave Alyssa her present, she opened it and became very emotional.

"She hugged me," recalled Mala. "She said, 'You don't have to do this.' I said, 'I have to do more than this because your prices are so low.'"

35

THE SECOND COMING

As 2009 dawned, Phillip Garrido became obsessed with the Second Coming of Christ and the pivotal role he would play in it. He started preaching with a new intensity.

"He'd talk about the Second Coming," recalled Lorenzo Love. "He said God's coming back and will save people who do drugs and forgive them for their sins."

Every couple of weeks he would arrive at Love's towing company, and deliver an impromptu sermon.

"He believed that God did not judge you as you are," said Christine Meacham. "He told us he had drugs, gambling and sex problems but through his church he was found and reborn. That the heavenly father was going to save him."

But when no one appeared to be taking his message seriously, he became more and more upset.

"Phil was not getting the reception that he had anticipated," said Marc Lister. "He was getting frustrated because people were just blowing him off. A lot of times he'd talk to me and he'd come to tears, as he kept saying, 'You've got to believe me! You've got to believe me!'"

Lister now believes that all the years of smoking methamphetamine and taking other hard drugs were taking their toll. Although Lister says he has no firsthand knowledge that Garrido was manufacturing meth in his backyard, as later reported, it was easy enough to get in town.

"Every other house has dope in Antioch," he said. "The place is a shithole. I mean you can buy it next door."

One morning that spring, Phillip Garrido arrived at Maria Christenson's recycling plant with his younger daughter, Starlit. He was acting so strangely she was certain he was high on something.

When Maria asked who the little girl was, Garrido snapped, "Oh, this is my daughter. We've got to go."

"She was clinging to him," Christenson remembered, "and she was dressed kind of old-fashioned, like something you'd wear twenty years ago on a farm. That's what caught my eye. She was so pale and her skin wasn't the right color."

During the brief period they were in her office, Starlit seemed interested in Christenson's collection of brass animals in a display case.

"She wanted to look at it," Maria said, "but he wouldn't let her talk to me. I think maybe he was doing drugs, because he was so wired and in a hurry all the time."

On May 3, 2009, Jaycee Dugard turned twenty-nine. It was now almost eighteen years since she was kidnapped by Phillip and Nancy Garrido. Although she had assumed a completely new identity as Alyssa Franzen, she still clung to a vestige of her old life by writing every day in her secret journal. It was her *only* true expression of her real identity, a way of voicing her true feelings of being trapped by a madman in a bizarre netherworld.

Over the years she had grown to love Phillip and Nancy Garrido, but she also knew she could never escape their clutches without risking her daughters' safety.

Living like campers in tents in the hidden backyard for so many years had made Alyssa resourceful. And despite the terrible conditions, she had done her best to create a home for Angel and Starlit. A large welcome sign hung over the concealed entrance, along with several plastic butterflies and other rather pathetic homey touches. There were drawings and artwork all over the various sheds and tents, and the children's five cats were probably more comfortable than their owners.

The ten-foot-by-ten-foot shed, where Alyssa had been held in restraints for her first eighteen months in captivity, now housed the Printing For Less operation, with several computers and printers. There were bookshelves full of magazines and books about cats, as well as several romance novels by Alyssa's favorite author, Danielle Steel. There was also a filthy fish tank and a microwave.

Nearby was a small blue tent where Alyssa, Starlit and Angel's outdated thrift-shop clothes hung on plastic racks. It was stuffed with dressers overflowing with clothing.

Another old faded tent alongside served as their sleeping quarters, with dirty stripped-down couches for beds. In one corner on a small dressing table was a large cosmetic box, full of old makeup, hairbrushes and combs.

And every night, while Alyssa and her daughters made do with the deplorable conditions they had grown used to, Phillip and Nancy Garrido slept soundly inside the house in comfortable beds.

That June, Pat Franzen's already frail health worsened, with her worried son summoning emergency services three times over a three-week period.

On June 5, the California Department of Corrections and Rehabilitation had introduced a new GPS system. And Phillip Garrido had started tampering with his GPS ankle bracelet. Over the next three months, Garrido's signal was lost almost every night for hours at a time. But almost all the electronic alerts to the Concord parole office were ignored.

A month later, on July 6, Phillip Garrido posted a new entry on his "Voices Revealed" blog. Entitled "A Power That Has Been Kept Hidden," it rambled on incomprehensibly about his new religion and saving the world. And it talked about "an intelligently prepared plan that is hidden in the scriptures" that will "inspire all humanity."

He and Alyssa were now working on an ambitious eight-day series of seminars and demonstrations, to be sponsored by their client J & M Enterprises and held in a tent on their premises. Alyssa designed a series of flyers and posters, showing a new sunrise, to publicize the event.

"Don't Miss Out," read the God's Desire Church flier. "Something brand new is taking place."

Alyssa had also designed a stunning new logo for "God's Desire," to accompany its newly stated mission: "To instruct and encourage intellectual, moral, and spiritual improvement."

The event would run Monday through Friday from noon to 4:00 P.M. and on weekends from 10:00 A.M. to 5:00 P.M., with a one-hour break for lunch.

During the eight-day event, Phillip, Nancy, Alyssa and the two girls all manned the God's Desire Church tent that had been set up in Jim and Cheyvonne Molino's front yard. At various times they would all sing together, as Phillip Garrido strummed along on his guitar. And Garrido gave demonstrations of his black box at periodic intervals.

But although all advertising material says the event's sponsor was J & M Enterprises, mentioning its "Large stock of used parts for all model cars and trucks" and twenty-four-hour towing service, Jim and Cheyvonne Molino later distanced themselves from it.

"He said he had a flier stating he was going to have a tent here," explained Cheyvonne. "He was just hanging out at the back of our lawn, okay."

Her husband, Jim, says the God's Desire event was very informal.

"He had a tent out front," he later told a local television station, "that he would sit and talk to people. He'd play music for them and get them interested in the Bible."

A few weeks later, on August 14, Phillip Garrido blogged about the event's great success.

"During the month of July 2009," he wrote, "J & M's Enterprises . . . was the host to a powerful demonstration, the Creator has given me the ability to speak in the tongues of angels in order to provide a wake-up that will in time include the salvation of the whole world."

* * *

Two days after the J & M Enterprises event, Phillip Garrido delivered an order of postcards to East County Glass and Window Inc. It was the third attempt at getting them right, as owner Tim Allen had repeatedly returned them with mistakes.

"We had ordered some postcards," explained Allen, "and they were wrong. So we asked him to make them again and the same had happened. This time they were correct and he brought them in and dropped them off."

Allen thought the printer was even more distracted than ever, and was now contemplating finding a new print company, after almost fifteen years with Printing For Less.

Love's Transport and Tow, Inc., was also having problems with the deteriorating quality of Garrido's work. When Garrido arrived in mid-August with his Bible and several thousand numbered invoices, owner Christine Meacham was appalled at the glaring mistakes.

"They were smeared," she said. "They were crooked. And I'm wondering if he had the young girls do it, because nothing's ever been wrong before."

After she pointed out the mistakes, Garrido agreed to redo them. But suddenly he started talking about an amazing new spiritual development, eerily different from the usual message he preached.

"He said this is a new revelation," recalled Meacham. "It's going to be different once the world knows. The time is going to come."

Phillip Garrido also told Janice Gomes it was almost time to start his God-given mission to save the world.

"Janice, trust me when my story hits, it's going to be worldwide," he told her breathlessly. "You're not going to believe what God healed me of. You're not going to believe the kind of person I was."

Now, Phillip Garrido's sole topic of conversation was an upcoming trip with his daughters to the People's Park on the University of California, Berkeley campus.

"He kept telling me, 'I'm going to Berkeley! I'm going to Berkeley,'" recalled Maria Christenson. "That was all he kept thinking about. He wanted to go to Berkeley so bad."

Janice Gomes believes his Berkeley trip was the culmination of four years of planning.

"He was stepping out," she said. "This is time. He was prepared for this. He believes in what he's doing—as crazy as it is."

A few days later, Marc Lister ran into Garrido at a mutual friend's house. Garrido gave him one of his black boxes, asking if he could take care of it, along with a stack of other church material.

"I think he had come to a crossroads," said Lister. "He was fed up with no one listening to him, and had decided to turn himself in and bring his message to the world."

In hindsight, Lister believes that Garrido had now decided to take his message to a global stage, and deliver Jaycee Lee Dugard back to the world.

"Within days the world's going to know my story," he told Lister, who advised him to get back on his meds.

At 8:10 A.M. on July 29 Agent Santos arrived at Walnut Avenue, for his twice-monthly visit. Garrido said he was unable to supply a urine sample for drug testing at that time. Three hours later, the parole officer returned to collect it.

A few days later, Phillip Garrido attended a funeral of a relative. It would be the last time Ron Garrido would ever see his younger brother, who was acting strangely, pacing to and from his car.

"Crazy, crazy, crazy," Ron would later say.

On Saturday, August 15, Phillip Garrido brought Starlit and Angel to Cheyvonne Molino's daughter's "Sweet Sixteen" birthday party, held at a nearby water park. Previously Garrido had asked if his daughters could attend, as they had become closer to the Molinos during the recent God's Desire religious event on their property.

"Phil wanted to know if he could bring the girls," said Cheyvonne. "I said not a problem."

As it would be a dance party for about 125, she told Phillip that his daughters should wear sundresses and sandals.

The party officially started at 9:00 P.M., but Garrido arrived two hours earlier with the girls, to help decorate the dance floor.

"A girlfriend of mine pointed out how clingy the older girl was to Phillip," said Cheyvonne. "It was almost like she was sending out a message, 'That's my man.' At least that's how it looked to us."

Before the party got into full swing, Garrido left, saying he would pick up his daughters later.

"They were mixing and mingling," said Cheyvonne. "And they didn't stay together because we had a big space. They interacted just like the rest of the kids."

At around 9:15 P.M. a photographer arrived to take pictures of the guests. He took a photograph of Starlit and Angel, wearing matching sky-blue sundresses. Soon afterwards, Garrido returned, saying he was taking the girls home, as they were not used to loud rap music.

"When their dad picked up around 9:30," said Molino, "I walked them to the car and I asked them if they had fun. And they both squealed, 'Oh, yes!'"

Part Three

36

On Monday morning, August 24, Phillip Garrido drove Angel and Starlit forty miles west to the FBI office at 450 Golden Gate Avenue, San Francisco. They walked in the front entrance of the Philip Burton Building, passing through a security machine. Then they took an elevator up to the thirteenth floor, and Garrido walked over to the front desk, with his two daughters following behind.

He then handed a copy of his updated twenty-seven page "Origins of Schizophrenia Revealed" manifesto to an agent, saying it was important that he read it as soon as possible.

After leaving the building, Garrido and his daughters drove across the Bay Bridge to the University of California, Berkeley. They spent a few minutes at Sather Gate, where Angel and Starlit handed out God's Desire leaflets, before walking over to the campus police headquarters at 1 Sproul Hall and going down to the basement.

Garrido walked up to the receptionist, announcing that he wanted to hold a major event on the main campus, showing a stack of pamphlets and manifestos. Then he was directed into the office of the campus police special events manager, Lisa Campbell. As he walked in, he signaled his daughters to wait outside.

When he bounded into her office, Lisa Campbell was working on her computer with her back to him. She turned around to see the tall, thin, balding man with striking blue eyes.

"He came into my office," recalled Campbell. "He was extremely animated. Clearly unstable."

After he had formally introduced himself as Phillip Garrido, president of the God's Desire Church, Campbell asked about his event and what it had to do with the University of California.

"Ah, you're going to love this," replied Garrido. "The FBI are involved. The entire world is going to want to know. It's God's desire. It's God's purpose."

Then, as he passionately rambled on, Campbell looked into her outer office to see two young blonde girls in long dresses staring at her, with the same piercing blue eyes as the man inside.

She asked Garrido whose children they were, and he said he was their father. Then Campbell summoned the girls in, asking how they were. But they just stood there silently like stage mannequins.

"It was as though he had set it up [to] create a distraction," she said. "And they were just there in eye view."

The former Chicago police officer immediately felt something was very wrong.

"I looked at him," remembered Campbell, "and I looked at the girls. He's going on and on and on and he's extremely animated and they're not. They were really poles apart."

So Campbell decided to investigate further. As she had another appointment waiting outside, she asked if he could come back tomorrow, explaining she was busy right now but would love to find out more about his event.

"He didn't expect that reaction," said Campbell, "because he expected to be blown off. And so I said, 'Would you be interested?' He said, 'Absolutely. You're going to really love this. You're going to be so grateful that you did this.'"

Then she made an appointment for Garrido to return with the girls the following afternoon at 2:00 P.M.

"I wanted to get him in as soon as possible," she explained.

After they left, Campbell went next door into campus police officer Allyson Jacobs's office, saying there was something very strange about the guy who just came for an event permit and the two young girls with him.

"Well, let's run him," replied Officer Jacobs, who immediately went to the dispatch office, requesting one of the clerks check a "Phillip Garrido" on the police computer. A few seconds later the computer got a hit.

"She prints out this rap sheet longer than I can imagine," recalled Jacobs. "He was on federal parole for kidnapping and rape, and he was also a sex registrant. And my red flags went up, because [Lisa] had mentioned something about two young kids."

Officer Jacobs then went and told the events manager that the man whom she had just interviewed had a long history of sex crimes. And she offered to sit in at tomorrow's meeting with Phillip Garrido.

"I didn't feel comfortable," said Officer Jacobs, "with her being alone with a convicted rapist."

Several hours later, Phillip Garrido and his girls arrived at Janice Gomes's daughter's house to deliver some business cards on their way back to Antioch. After his trip to Berkeley, Garrido was in great spirits, suddenly bursting into song.

"He starts singing to her," said Gomes, "scares her half to death."

At exactly 2:00 P.M. on Tuesday afternoon, Phillip Garrido arrived back at the Berkeley campus police building with Angel and Starlit. They went straight into Lisa Campbell's office, where she was waiting with Officer Allyson Jacobs.

As soon as he sat down, Garrido opened up an attaché case he had brought with him, drawing out a copy of his "Origins of Schizophrenia Revealed" booklet.

"He hands us this book," recalled Jacobs, "and then he goes off on this tangent about how he can hear voices, and he's got all these people that can attest to that."

While Garrido ranted on and on about a black box, Officer Jacobs looked at the two girls. The eldest, Angel, was standing stiffly by her father with her hands on the front of her legs, looking up at the ceiling, while the younger, Starlit, just stared at her, making her extremely uncomfortable.

As a mother of two young sons, Officer Jacobs was immediately struck by how unnaturally pale and gray the girls were, compared with their father's normal skin tone. Later Jacobs would describe their clothes as something out of *Little House on the Prairie*.

"The younger daughter was staring directly at me . . . with this eerie smile on her face," she recalled, "as if she was looking into my soul."

Then, apologizing for interrupting him midflow, Jacobs asked who the two young ladies were.

"Oh, these are my daughters," he replied. He grabbed hold of Starlit, declaring, "I'm so proud of my girls. They don't know any curse words. We raised them right. They don't know anything bad about the world."

The two campus officers both had a weird, uneasy feeling when he said that. For the two girls looked like brainwashed zombies, fearful of saying anything that might upset their father.

Officer Jacobs asked the girls what they were doing with their father.

"I'm socializing them," Garrido answered for them. "Showing them how it's done."

When Jacobs asked him to explain, Garrido replied, "By interacting with people."

Then, out of nowhere, Phillip Garrido began telling the two officers how he had once been arrested for kidnapping and rape thirty-three years ago.

"And I was kind of, okay," said Jacobs. "I knew that but I just didn't think he would throw that out there—especially in front of these little girls. Then the younger daughter said, 'And we have an older sister that lives with us too. She's twenty-eight.' And the older sibling said, without missing a beat, 'twenty-nine.' And went right back up to her dad, who seemed kind of bothered that that was even mentioned."

When they had first walked in, Officer Jacobs had noticed

Starlit had a large discolored bump over one eye, and wondered if she had been abused.

"So I asked her," said Jacobs, " 'What's wrong with your eye? What happened?'

"And she says, really robotic, 'It's a birth defect. It's inoperable and I'll have it for the rest of my life.' It was rehearsed and it caught me off-guard. I really think my mother's intuition kicked in at that point."

Both officers tried to engage the girls in conversation, to get as much information as they could.

"We'd ask questions," said Jacobs, "and the younger daughter would focus her attention towards us. Give us eye contact. Answer our questions. The older one. Not so much. She was just all over the place. Her eyes were darting up at the ceiling. She was looking at her dad and just in awe . . . as if she was in worship of him. I kind of got the feelings these kids were like robots."

When Lisa Campbell asked what grades they were in at school, they both replied in unison, "We're home-schooled."

Then, after about fifteen minutes, Phillip Garrido suddenly announced they had to leave. And as the two campus police officers had no real evidence to call in social workers, they had no alternative but to let them go.

After they left, Allyson Jacobs decided to call Phillip Garrido's parole officer and tell him how strangely he was acting. For she was concerned that if he was supposed to be on medication, he obviously was not taking it and the two girls might be in danger.

So she telephoned parole agent Eddie Santos at the Concord parole office, and when the call went to voice mail she left a message.

"[Phillip Garrido] came in today with his two young daughters," she told him, "and he was going on this schizophrenic rant. He was clearly unstable and I really think you should do a check on him. Maybe go to his house. Make sure his kids are okay, because they were a little off to me."

It was late afternoon when parole agent Santos returned to his office and listened to Officer Jacobs's voice message. He immediately called her back, but was told that she had left for the day.

So Santos asked his colleague Agent La Grassa to accompany him to 1554 Walnut Avenue, Antioch, to investigate further. When Santos rang the front doorbell at 6:00 P.M., Phillip Garrido answered, and was immediately detained and handcuffed by the front gate.

Then, while La Grassa guarded Garrido outside the house, Santos went in.

"Inside the residence," the agent later wrote in his official report, "were Garrido's wife, Nancy, and his elderly mother Mrs. Franzen."

Santos then searched the entire house, but found no signs of anyone else. He drove Phillip Garrido to the Concord parole office for further questioning.

On the drive over, Garrido kept saying he had done nothing wrong. The two girls, he said, were his brother Ron's daughters, and he had permission to take them with him to the Berkeley campus. After they'd returned to Antioch, he said one of their parents had collected them.

Back at the Concord parole office, Agent Santos reviewed Garrido's file with his supervisor G. Sims. They accepted Garrido's story about the girls being his nieces, never bothering to check it out with his older brother.

The parole officers determined that Garrido had not violated any of his parole conditions. For although he had a "no contact with minors" special condition, it did not apply, as he had no conviction involving underage children.

"Therefore," reported Agent Santos, "we dropped Garrido back to his [residence]."

Garrido was then ordered to report back to the Concord parole office the following morning at 8:00 A.M., to discuss the Berkeley incident further.

37

"MY NAME IS JAYCEE LEE DUGARD"

At 8:00 A.M., on Wednesday, August 26, Officer Allyson Jacobs arrived at work, finding a message from parole agent Eddie Santos to call him as soon as possible. When he came on the line, he asked her to tell him exactly what had happened the day before with Phillip Garrido and the two young girls.

"So I went through the whole story from start to finish," Jacobs recalled. "And when I got to the part of his two daughters, he says, 'He doesn't have any daughters.'"

On hearing this, Jacobs felt her stomach sink, wondering if they had let a dangerous kidnapper go and should have stopped him.

"Well," she told the parole agent, "he had two daughters with him that day. They have his blue eyes. They were calling him Daddy."

Then she told him how one of the girls had mentioned having a twenty-nine-year-old sister at home.

At the other end of the line, Agent Santos could see Phillip Garrido entering the parole office, followed by his wife, Nancy, and three young girls. He told Officer Jacobs he would look into the matter and put down the phone.

He then watched as Garrido signed in at the front lobby, and the four females he was with sat down. When Santos came out of his office and opened the lobby door, Garrido started walking toward him, gesturing for the women to follow.

"I instructed Garrido to stop and wait in the lobby," Agent

Santos later wrote in his report. "I asked the women to continue in and I escorted them to the conference room."

Nancy and the three girls all sat together on one side of the conference table, facing the parole agent.

Then Agent Santos introduced himself and asked for their names.

"The adult female identified herself as Alyssa Franzen," wrote Santos. "I asked the two female juveniles their names and Alyssa responded by saying that the younger child was named Starlit and was eleven years old. Alyssa then stated that the other juvenile was named Angel [and] was fourteen years old."

Agent Santos asked who the girls' parents were, and Alyssa immediately said that she was their mother. When Santos commented that she looked too young to be their mother, Alyssa started laughing, saying she gets that all the time. He then asked how old she was, and Alyssa said she was twenty-nine, giving her real date of birth of May 3, 1980.

He asked for her identification, and Alyssa said she had left it at home.

"When I asked her to spell her full name for me," reported Santos, "she hesitated for a moment and out loud slowly spelled, 'Alyssa Franzen.' It was apparent she was having trouble trying to spell the first name."

He then asked where she lived, and Alyssa replied that she and her daughters lived with various friends, occasionally staying at the Garridos' house. But when Santos said he needed some personal details to confirm their identities, Alyssa became "extremely defensive" and "agitated," demanding to know why she was being "interrogated."

At that point Nancy Garrido broke into the conversation, demanding to know why he was interrogating them when they had done nothing wrong. Santos replied that he was not, but merely investigating an incident that happened with Phillip Garrido and the two girls the previous day on the Berkeley campus.

Alyssa said she knew Phillip Garrido had taken the two girls to the campus, and that she was aware he was a registered sex offender and on parole.

"I asked [her] if she knew what crime he committed," Santos wrote in his report, "and she advised he kidnapped and raped a woman over thirty years ago and that he was a changed man. She felt completely safe with her kids around Garrido.

"She immediately started saying that Garrido was a great person, good with her kids and that he had a gift. The two girls also made comments about how good Garrido was to them."

When Agent Santos started asking Alyssa more questions, she refused to answer, saying she might need a lawyer. Nancy agreed, asking Agent Santos why he was asking so many questions.

Santos assured Alyssa that she was not in any trouble, and he was just conducting an investigation, and everything she said would be kept in the file.

"But she became more agitated," wrote Santos, "and started saying that she didn't do anything wrong. At this point I asked Nancy, [Alyssa] and the two girls to wait downstairs so I could talk to Garrido."

While Nancy Garrido took Alyssa and the two girls outside to wait in their car, Agent Santos brought Phillip Garrido upstairs into his office. After they sat down, facing each other across his desk, Agent Santos asked exactly what Alyssa's relationship was to the girls.

"What do you mean?" asked Garrido anxiously.

Then Santos repeated his question. After a brief hesitation, Garrido replied that they were sisters, saying Alyssa was twenty-nine and the oldest. Then Santos asked who their father was.

"Garrido briefly thought for a while," wrote Santos, "and stated that the father was a relative of his."

Once again Santos asked who the girls' father was, and the parolee cryptically replied that "the father was the son of his mother."

"For clarification," reported Santos, "I stated, 'So that makes him your brother?' Garrido looked at me with astonishment and stated, 'Yes.' He advised that the parents were divorced and that the girls were living between them and other people."

Garrido said that their father's name was Ronald Garrido, saying he knew his brother lived in Oakley, but did not know his exact address or phone number. He said the girls' mother's name was called Janice, and lived somewhere in Brentwood, California. He also did not know her address or phone number.

At that point, Agent Santos stopped the interview, asking Garrido to wait in another office with another parole agent.

At around 9:00 A.M., Santos briefed his colleague Agent Lovan on what was going on. They then walked outside to the car, where Nancy and the three girls were waiting. For Santos had now decided to confront Alyssa about the discrepancies in her and Garrido's stories, believing she was the one who had lied.

First he separated Alyssa from the others, before asking why she had lied to him.

"What do you mean?" she snapped.

Then Santos told her that Phillip Garrido had told him that she was the girls' older sister and not their mother.

"[She] looked confused," Santos later wrote, "and advised that she had custody of the girls, implying that she was not the mother but a guardian with full custody."

He then informed her that if she continued not to cooperate, he would be forced to contact Child Protection Services or the Concord Police Department. Alyssa then changed her story, admitting she was the girls' "biological mother," but did not know what was going on.

Santos said he did not believe her, asking for identification or a relative's phone number who could verify her story. Alyssa replied that she had learned a long time ago never to carry ID, or give out any personal information to anyone.

"When I asked her to explain herself," reported Santos, "she kept on saying that she didn't know what was going on and that she needed a lawyer."

By this time Nancy Garrido had come over to tell Alyssa that she needed a lawyer.

"[Alyssa's] demeanor changed," noted Santos. "She became more concerned about her children. I asked her why Garrido would say that you were all sisters and she said, "He was just trying to protect me.'"

At 9:17 A.M., Eddie Santos dialed 911 on his cell phone, requesting a police officer to come to the Parkside Drive parole office as soon as possible.

While they were waiting for police to arrive, Starlit said she needed to use the restroom immediately. Not wanting to split them up, Agent Santos escorted them all over to Concord Library, which was adjacent to the parole office.

"While walking to the restroom," wrote Santos, "[Alyssa] stated, 'I am sorry that I lied to you.' She then began to say that she was from Minnesota and that she was running and hiding from an abusive husband."

She explained she had been on the run for five years, and was "terrified" her husband would find her and the children. Then she patted the parole agent's shoulder, saying, "You can see why I learned a long time ago never to give out my personal information."

The library was closed and on the way back to the parole office, Agent Santos assured Alyssa that everything she told him would be confidential. But Alyssa replied she could not take that chance, and was not saying another thing.

At 9:30 A.M., Officer Mike Von Savoye of the Concord Police drew up outside the Parkside Drive parole office. Eddie Santos briefed the uniformed officer about the situation, saying he did not believe Alyssa's story about the girls.

Officer Von Savoye then questioned the girl, who said her name was "Alyssa Franzen," refusing to say any more. Then she abruptly changed her story, claiming her real name was "Ally Smith." At this point, Officer Kaiser arrived from the Concord Police Department as backup.

While they were questioning Alyssa, little Starlit said she needed a restroom urgently, so everybody went into the parole office, so she could relieve herself there. Once inside, the Concord police officers separated Alyssa from Nancy Garrido and the two girls, so she could be questioned alone by Officer Kaiser.

In the interview room, Alyssa adamantly stuck to her story, that she was from Minnesota, running away from her abusive husband. So to try and break the deadlock, Phillip Garrido was brought into the room with Alyssa.

"Once Garrido came into the room," Agent Santos later wrote, "it appeared that [Alyssa] kept looking to him for answers. Garrido stated that she should get a lawyer and . . . not cooperate. I asked Garrido to stand up and escorted him back to my office."

Then Agent Santos asked Garrido why Alyssa was protecting him.

"What do you mean?" he asked.

When Santos said she was definitely trying to protect him from something, Garrido said she needed a lawyer.

At that point Sergeant Hoffman of the Concord Police Department came into the office to question Garrido. And Santos left to see if Officer Kaiser had managed to get any more information from Alyssa.

A few minutes later the sergeant came out, saying that Phillip Garrido had now admitted he was the girls' father.

"I reentered the room," wrote Santos, "and asked Garrido why he made us go through all this? He stated something to the effect of not knowing why. I asked him if he didn't tell us because he didn't want his wife Nancy to know, and he said, 'Oh no! She knows and she forgave me a long time ago.' "

Agent Santos said it did not make sense, and there had to be some other reason. Then Garrido became evasive, refusing to answer any more questions. But Agent Santos persisted, asking why he had taken so long to tell them. Finally, he said that he would explain why if Alyssa was brought into the room to hear it too.

"I told him I would not do this," wrote Santos, "but he insisted that if I did, he would basically tell me, but he wanted her to be in the same room."

Santos said he didn't want to "drop a bomb" on Alyssa, and he would only bring her in if Garrido told him first.

Then suddenly, Phillip Garrido broke down and told him the truth.

"A long, long, long time ago," he began, "I kidnapped and raped her."

An astonished Agent Santos then asked where her parents were, and Garrido replied, "Somewhere in Los Angeles."

Leaving Garrido inside the interview room, Santos went out to tell Sergeant Hoffman. Then the sergeant went back in with Alyssa, telling her what Phillip Garrido just admitted.

She then broke down in tears, admitting her real name was Jaycee Lee Dugard, and she had been kidnapped eighteen years ago by Phillip and Nancy Garrido and repeatedly raped over the years.

At 11:30 A.M., Lieutenant James Lardieri walked into the front lobby of the Concord Police Department as several detectives swept past him on the way out. One explained they were going to the Concord parole office, where a man was in custody for a parole violation. There was also a young woman who said she had been kidnapped in Nevada eighteen years ago.

"That's all the information they had at that point," said Lardieri, who heads up the Investigation Unit. "They did not have a name."

Then Lardieri went into his office and punched up the "National Center for Missing & Exploited Children" website, and started searching for any 1991 abduction cases from Nevada. But the information he had been given was wrong, and the kidnapping had actually happened just over the border in South Lake Tahoe, California.

"So I'm waiting and waiting," recalled Lieutenant Lardieri, "and I haven't heard back from anybody at the scene. So I go into the California website, and I came upon the case of Jaycee Lee Dugard."

Lardieri dimly remembered the well-publicized 1991 abduction, as he was already working in law enforcement at the time. And he was looking at Jaycee's missing poster and her photograph when his phone rang.

"It's my sergeant," Lardieri recalled. "He tells me, 'We have Jaycee Lee Dugard here.' The hair on the back of my neck stood up for about an hour. It was just very strange."

* * *

After Jaycee Lee Dugard finally revealed her true identity, she, Nancy and the two girls were taken to the Concord Police Department at 1350 Galindo Street. Phillip Garrido, who was now being held under a parole violation, was transported there separately in handcuffs and placed in a holding cell.

"When Jaycee came in she was crying and was visibly upset," recalled Lieutenant Lardieri, who took charge of the investigation. "The girls were quiet. She looked ten years younger than she was, about nineteen or twenty."

Anxious to put Jaycee and her daughters at ease, the lieutenant brought them into the investigations area, placing them in a comfortable interview room with a couple of officers.

"We didn't want a bunch of people standing around gawking at them," he explained. "So it was very low-key and casual."

Nancy Garrido, who was not under arrest at that point and had willingly come back to the station, was left in the public lobby downstairs, until detectives could question her further.

In the meantime, Lieutenant Lardieri contacted the El Dorado County Sheriff's Department, the lead investigating agency on the 1991 Jaycee Lee Dugard kidnapping case.

"I got hold of one of their investigations lieutenants," he said, "and I told them we had Jaycee Lee Dugard. Well, he was elated."

The department was located in Placerville, California, about three hours drive from Concord, but two cold-case detectives happened to be in Stockton, just forty-five minutes away. So they were immediately dispatched to Concord to take over the investigation.

While they were waiting for the detectives to arrive, Lardieri sent some officers to Antioch to secure Phillip Garrido's house until a search warrant could be signed by a judge.

"Mr. Garrido's elderly mother was still there," said Lardieri, "so we had to make some arrangements to have her taken care of by the Contra Costa Regional Medical Center."

At around 2:00 P.M., El Dorado County detectives R. Straffer and R. Fitzgerald arrived, briefly meeting with Lieutenant Lardieri to draw up a game plan. It was agreed that the Concord

Police Department would assist El Dorado in the preliminary investigations.

"It flowed very well," recalled Lardieri. "We assisted with some interviews of Mrs. Garrido and the two daughters. The El Dorado County detectives interviewed Jaycee and Phillip Garrido."

As the afternoon progressed, Jaycee managed to compose herself enough to give a full statement to the El Dorado detectives.

"She was able to tell her story to them," said Lardieri. "The two younger girls were very talkative. They were talking about what they do at the house and stuff. They probably felt safe being around our people."

A few hours later, Nancy Garrido was arrested, after confessing to helping her husband kidnap Jaycee Lee Dugard. Hearing of their arrests, Jaycee Lee Dugard tearfully begged the investigators to free them, saying that now she had been found everything was all right, and she didn't want the Garridos arrested. But her pleas fell on deaf ears.

At 9:00 P.M., Phillip and Nancy Garrido were transported to the county jail at Martinez, where they were booked. Nancy was held on $4.195 million bail, but as a parolee Phillip was ineligible for bail.

38

"THEY FOUND JAYCEE"

Around 3:00 P.M. on Wednesday afternoon, Tina Dugard was preparing a salad when she received a call from an El Dorado County investigator, asking for her sister Terry's phone number. Tina, forty-two, gave it to him, although he refused to say why he needed it.

A few minutes later, FBI agent Chris Campion called Terry Probyn on her cell phone at Riverside School District, where she worked as a secretary.

"We've got Jaycee," he told her excitedly.

At first Terry thought it a cruel hoax. But then Campion put Jaycee on the phone, so she could hear her long-lost daughter's voice for the first time in eighteen years. After a short, highly emotional conversation, in which Terry asked some family questions that only Jaycee could answer, she was convinced that it really was her daughter.

Then Agent Campion, who had been involved in the investigation from the beginning, came back on the line.

"She's got something else to tell you," he said, handing the phone back to Jaycee.

"I have babies," Jaycee announced.

"How many babies?" asked Terry.

"Two," she replied.

Agent Campion came back and without going into details told her Jaycee had been with some people who were now in police custody.

* * *

After putting down the phone, Terry called her youngest daughter Shayna, now nineteen, with the incredible news. She then drove home, falling into Shayna's arms.

At around 4:00 P.M., Shayna telephoned her father, Carl Probyn, now sixty-one, and put Terry on the line.

His estranged wife first asked if he was sitting down.

"They found Jaycee," she told him, taking a short pause. "She's alive."

"And we both lost it," recalled Carl. "We cried for ten minutes."

Terry told him that she had initially thought it a bad joke, but then asked Jaycee a few questions only she would know the answer to.

"She remembers everything," said Carl. "They talked back and forth and she had the right answers to all my wife's questions about her childhood. [My wife's] in shock. I told her and my daughter to sit down there and think of questions to ask her."

Then Carl asked Terry if they had known the abductors personally, and she replied no. She said the police were taking DNA samples from Jaycee to make certain it was her, but she was convinced it was.

A few minutes later, Tina Dugard received an excited call from her niece Shayna, saying Jaycee had been found.

"I don't know what I felt," Tina later told *The Orange County Register*. "I just said, 'What?' I'm sure I repeated that word several times. . . . We both started crying hysterically."

Then it was agreed that she would meet Terry and Shayna at Ontario Airport the next morning, taking the 6:00 A.M. flight to San Francisco to be reunited with Jaycee and her two daughters.

Late afternoon, a judge signed a search warrant for 1554 Walnut Avenue, Antioch, which had been sealed off with yellow police crime tape. Then FBI agents and officers from the El Dorado County Sheriff's Department moved in to begin the search.

At the end of the backyard, the officers saw an eight-foot

fence, lined by tall trees. There was an old dishwasher, garbage cans and other rubbish backed up against it.

Then an investigator pulled a blue tarpaulin that hung over the fence, and it came apart revealing a narrow entrance. He squeezed through to enter the secret world where Jaycee and her daughters had lived.

A crude hand-painted welcome sign was strung between two branches, and there was the sound of wind chimes. In front of them was a maze of variously sized outbuildings, shacks and tents. There was also an eight-foot-by-four-foot steel cage.

The backyard within a backyard was strewn with rubbish. Broken toys, discarded furniture, appliances, cardboard boxes and yard cuttings were dumped everywhere. There was an open septic hole, and the makeshift outside toilet had not been connected to any septic tank or sewer.

And investigators also found, hidden among rusting vehicle parts, tarps and plastic buckets, Phillip Garrido's old beat-up two-tone sedan that he and Nancy had used to abduct Jaycee so many years ago.

"It was as if you were camping," said El Dorado County sheriff Warren Rupf, who was one of the first officers to enter the backyard. "The structures are no more than six foot high. All the sheds and tents had electricity furnished by electrical cords. Nothing more sophisticated than that. There was a rudimentary outhouse and a rudimentary shower."

A rusting children's playground set with two swings and a slide lay next to a ramshackle old barn. At one corner of the large yard was an empty raised swimming pool, full of dirty leaves. Nearby were two adult canvas chairs, standing next to a child's deck chair. A large hollowed-out Halloween pumpkin rested on a laundry basket.

Then investigators entered one of the larger tents, staring in disbelief at Jaycee and her daughters' appalling living conditions. There was a sofa covered in old pillows, papers and electrical equipment. A pile of dirty women's clothes and underwear had been thrown in one corner, and old mattresses, cushions and toys covered moth-eaten old carpets. A teddy bear lay on the floor next to four naked Barbie dolls and an open container for lice treatment.

There was a large collection of cat books, puzzles and figurines and a box of Special Kitty pet food.

They then ventured into the ten-foot-by-ten-foot shed, which had been soundproofed and could only be opened from the outside. Inside they found Phillip Garrido's guitars and recording equipment as well as restraints.

By the side of it was a derelict tent, held together by broken wood and pieces of tarpaulin. All the windows were boarded up and the doors nailed shut.

But Jaycee and the girls were not the only residents of this virtual prison, which would later be compared to a concentration camp. A Labrador mix and a Rottweiler roamed around the backyard, happily coexisting with five pet cats. There was also a pigeon, three cockatiels and a mouse, which was kept in a cage. Investigators immediately called in the Contra Costa County Animal Control, which collected the animals to take care of them.

By nightfall, investigators had started removing bags of evidence from the backyard. But it would take several weeks to complete the search.

By this time, reporters had started arriving at Concord Police Station after a tip-off that there had been a major development in the famous Jaycee Lee Dugard kidnapping case. But police officers had been ordered not to comment to the media, who were already camped outside the Galindo Street police headquarters.

"Our big concern was that we wanted to protect their privacy," said Lieutenant Jim Lardieri. "Because we knew once this case got to the press it was going to be huge."

Later that night, Carl Probyn broke the dramatic news that his stepdaughter had been found alive after eighteen years. In telephone interview with the Channel 10 Sacramento News from his home, he was overcome by emotion.

"It's an absolute miracle," he declared. "Can you imagine this after eighteen years?"

Probyn told how the FBI had called his wife, Terry, and given her the news, before putting Jaycee on the line. He said he knew few details about where Jaycee had been living all this time, except "she was with some people and . . . they are in custody."

"I told my wife I want those responsible to be taken down," said Probyn. "No deals at all."

Berkeley campus police officer Allyson Jacobs was driving home from work when her cell phone rang. And she answered to find a highly excited parole agent Eddie Santos.

He informed her that Phillip Garrido was a kidnapper and the other daughter at home was Jaycee Lee Dugard, whom he had abducted eighteen years ago. Then he congratulated her for solving the case, calling her a hero.

"And I said, 'Cool, that's great,'" she recalled. "I'm glad that I helped this family."

It was getting dark as Jaycee, Angel and Starlit were taken to a nearby motel by witness victim advocates, until they could be reunited with their real family the following day. It would be Jaycee Lee Dugard's first night of freedom since June 10, 1991—6,574 days after she was snatched off the street in South Lake Tahoe by Phillip and Nancy Garrido.

That night Jaycee finally told her daughters the terrible truth, of how Phillip Garrido had kidnapped her when she was the same age as Starlit. And that she was their biological mother and not their older sister, as they always believed.

On hearing this, and that Phillip and Nancy Garrido, whom they had thought of as their parents, were now in jail, the girls began crying uncontrollably. They deeply loved and worshipped their father and hated to think of him and Nancy imprisoned.

Over the last eighteen years, Jaycee had bonded with Phillip Garrido, seeing herself as his wife. It would take many months of professional counseling and help to free them all from the mental prison Phillip Garrido had so carefully constructed.

39

"A GENETIC CONNECTION"

At 6:00 A.M. on Thursday, August 27, Terry, Shayna and Tina caught a flight to San Francisco to be reunited with Jaycee. Although Terry was overjoyed to be seeing Jaycee again after so many years, she had some trepidation about meeting her two grandchildren for the first time.

Tina Dugard had been up all night, with all the excitement of learning her beloved niece had returned. She had finally managed to grab an hour's sleep and then overslept, almost missing the flight from Ontario Airport.

At San Francisco International Airport, they were met by FBI agent Chris Campion, who drove them to the motel where Jaycee and her daughters were waiting. When they arrived, a witness advocate informed them that Jaycee, Angel and Starlit were all in a room, and that they should go in separately.

Terry went in first, then Shayna. When Tina's turn came she walked into the room and Jaycee threw her arms around her.

"Auntie Tina," she sobbed.

Both women looked at each other for the first time in eighteen years, and just burst into tears, hugging as tightly as they could.

"I looked at her and I knew right away," Tina would later tell *The Orange County Register*. "After eighteen years you have a sense of, 'Could this possibly be true?' She absolutely knew who I was. She remembered me right away . . . it was one of the happiest moments of my life.

"There was an instant connection. It was almost a genetic connection. An instant sense of family, for all of us."

Tina described the reunion as "surreal" and "fabulous," saying she, Angel and Starlit discovered an instant rapport and soon bonded.

"I'm a teacher," she said. "I know kids. And I can tell you that they are a normal eleven and fifteen-year-old."

The amazing family reunion was also attended by FBI agent Campion, who had become personally involved in the case since first being assigned to it in 1991.

"It was a very emotional scene," he recalled in an FBI podcast. "So Terry, right now, is understandably just ecstatic. Both of them were just overjoyed to be with each other again. The two daughters are probably as happy as Jaycee to be part of this family."

For the next five days, all six members of the family would remain at the secret location on the outskirts of San Francisco, getting to know each other, assisted by a team of therapists and counselors.

A few hours earlier, detectives from the El Dorado County Sheriff's Office had collected Phillip and Nancy Garrido from the Contra Costa County Jail, transporting them to the Placerville Jail to await their arraignment.

Then Lieutenant Bryan Golmitz of the El Dorado County Sheriff's Department issued a press release over the Internet, announcing Jaycee Dugard had been found and there would be a 3:00 P.M. press conference at Placerville Fairgrounds with more details.

Headlined "Kidnapping Victim Located After 18 Years," it read, "1991 kidnap victim Jaycee Dugard has been located in good health in the greater Bay Area of California. Jaycee Dugard was abducted on June 10, 1991 from South Lake Tahoe, CA. At the time of the incident, it was reported that a vehicle occupied by two individuals drove up to Jaycee Dugard and abducted her in view of her stepfather.

"Since the date of the occurrence the investigation has been ongoing and today's events could bring it to resolution."

* * *

At 3:00 P.M., El Dorado County undersheriff Fred Kollar addressed the media at a press conference at the Placerville Fairgrounds. It was being carried live by all local television stations and streamed over the Internet.

Standing by an American flag, the bald-headed, bespectacled undersheriff looked genuinely moved by the occasion. Standing alongside him on the podium were El Dorado County district attorney Vern Pierson, who would prosecute the case, and supervisory special agent of the FBI Deidre Fike.

"Good afternoon, everyone," began Undersheriff Kollar, clearing his throat. "I'm very happy to be in front of you under these circumstances. Jaycee Dugard was found alive in Antioch.

"Just to remind you just a little bit. She was kidnapped in June of 1991. She was taken off the street in front of her house. As you all know there was nothing then, nor is there anything now, to indicate that this was anything other than a stranger abduction of an eleven-year-old.

"On August twenty-fifth—Tuesday—the UC Berkeley Police encountered a suspect, Phillip Garrido, seeking access to the UC Berkeley campus. This alert Berkeley police officer took notice of Phillip Garrido and two young women who were in his custody. Police officers looked into Garrido's background and found that he was on federal parole overseen by the California Department of Corrections and Rehabilitation."

Undersheriff Kollar then told the reporters how Garrido had been convicted of rape and kidnapping in 1976. After discovering his record, the campus officer had then contacted his parole officer, who had summoned Garrido to his office.

"Garrido brought along with him two minors," said Kollar, "as well as Nancy Garrido and a female named Alyssa."

Kollar explained that as the parole officer had never seen Alyssa and the two young children during his visits to Garrido's home, he was suspicious and contacted the Concord Police Department.

"Ultimately," said Kollar, "the female named Alyssa was identified as Jaycee Dugard. Subsequent interviews with Jaycee and the Garridos provided information that only the victim and kidnappers could know. DNA confirmation is being sought to confirm Jaycee's identity.

"The Garridos—Nancy and the male—were taken into custody, and an investigation led to their residence in Antioch. The two minor children turned out to be children of Jaycee and the male suspect Garrido. They along with Nancy Garrido were living together at the residence in Antioch since the original kidnapping.

"A search of the residence revealed a hidden backyard within the backyard. The hidden backyard had sheds, tents and outbuildings, where Jaycee and the girls spent most of their lives. There was a vehicle hidden in the backyard that matched the vehicle originally described at the time of the abductions. The tents and outbuildings in the backyard were placed in a strategic arrangement to inhibit outside viewing and to isolate the victims from outside contact."

The undersheriff said that "family reunification" was already underway, but it will be "a long and ongoing process," involving witness victim advocates, the FBI and the National Center for Missing and Exploited Children.

"Both suspects are now currently in custody in the El Dorado County jail," he said. "Photos of both suspects are on our website and we would welcome any additional information linking them to this or any other criminal activity."

FBI special agent Deidre Fike then spoke about the role the bureau had played in the eighteen-year investigation into Jaycee Dugard's abduction.

"In 1991 the FBI opened a kidnapping investigation [into] the disappearance of Jaycee Dugard," she said, "and has been working it jointly with the El Dorado County Sheriff's Office. On the day that she arrived at the parole officer's office with the subjects, the Concord Police Department contacted the FBI in San Francisco to advise them that Jaycee Lee Dugard was alive."

She said she contacted Agent Chris Campion, who is based in Sacramento and had been assigned to the Jaycee Dugard case since the beginning.

"He immediately responded," she said, "and we continue to

work jointly with the El Dorado County Sheriff's Office in furtherance of this investigation."

Undersheriff Kollar then took reporters' questions, saying his officers were still interviewing Jaycee and her daughters and Phillip and Nancy Garrido.

One reporter asked about Jaycee's condition when she had been found.

"She was in good health," replied Kollar, "but living in a backyard for the past eighteen years does take its toll."

Another reporter asked if Jaycee had asked for help.

"I don't know that," said Kollar, "but in discussion with detectives, she was relatively cooperative, relatively forthcoming. She wasn't particularly evasive at all."

Then he was asked if Jaycee and her daughters had been living in sheds.

"It's hard to describe," he replied, "but there was a secondary backyard that's screened from view from literally all around. The only access to it is a very small and narrow tarp. Her and the two children were living in a series of sheds. There was one shed entirely soundproofed. It could only be opened from the outside. Another shed had more access to the public and then two tents."

A television reporter asked about Jaycee's two children.

"None of the children had ever gone to school," he said. "They've never been to a doctor. They were kept in complete isolation in this compound at the rear of the house. From what they have both said he fathered both of those children with Jaycee. They are with Jaycee and whatever group is assisting in the reunification."

The undersheriff then revealed that Nancy had been with Phillip Garrido during Jaycee's kidnapping, and matched Carl Probyn's description of the female in the car.

"My understanding," he said, "is that they went directly to that property from the kidnapping. Jaycee has been there ever since and the children were born there and lived there. They were in relatively good physical condition. They weren't obviously abused. They weren't malnourished. No obvious indicators."

District Attorney Vern Pierson refused to comment on specific charges, saying his office would be filing a criminal complaint tomorrow at noon in El Dorado Superior Court.

"Beyond that," he said, "I don't think I should comment."

Immediately after the press conference, the sheriff's office released mug shots of both the Garridos. Phillip looked in a trance, staring straight at the camera. There are two large scabs on the left side of his nose, and his short receding hair is uncombed. Nancy looks drawn and haggard, her unwashed dark hair tangled around her shoulders. She looks helplessly at the camera, as if not quite sure where she is.

Carl Probyn watched the televised press conference with an Associated Press reporter and photographer at his home in Orange, California. And during the dramatic revelations about the deplorable conditions Jaycee had been living in, he grimaced—being photographed, holding his hands up to his face in horror.

Asked his reaction after the press conference, Jaycee's now graying stepfather said he was just "overwhelmed" by what had happened in the last twenty-four hours.

"It broke my marriage up," he said tearfully. "I've gone through hell. I'm a suspect until yesterday."

Later that afternoon he held his own press conference at his home, for local television news stations.

"My name is William Carl Probyn," he said. "I'm Canadian. I go by Carl."

He said he was still in "total shock" since Terry had called him the previous afternoon with the amazing news.

"I had given up hope of having her alive," he said, as he laid out old photographs of Jaycee on a table. "I was in the process of wanting to recover her body basically. And now to get her back alive is like winning the lottery. She sounds like she's okay up to a point. She's probably still mentally eleven years old. She's gone through so much."

He said he was also struggling to understand why Jaycee had not come forward earlier.

"I don't know if she was brainwashed," he said. "I don't

know if she was walking around on the street. I don't know if she was locked up under key for eighteen years. I have a million questions."

About an hour later, Terry called with an update on Jaycee and the girls, as Carl was being interviewed by Paloma Esquivel of the *Los Angeles Times*. And on learning new details about Jaycee's early days of captivity, when she was locked in a shed in Phillip Garrido's secret backyard, he burst into tears and begged her to stop.

"I don't want to hear any more," he told her.

Then, after putting down the phone, he voiced his disgust at what Jaycee had endured at the hands of Phillip and Nancy Garrido.

"No schooling, no nothing—I was hoping it wasn't that scenario," he told Esquivel. "This is pretty horrific stuff, to be treated like an animal. These people. I'll never forgive them. It's already devastated our lives."

Later Probyn would be asked what it was like living for so long under a cloud of suspicion, that he was somehow involved in Jaycee's disappearance.

"I'm free now," he said. "They caught him and it's solved."

But he was still angry with several in-laws, who had hired an investigator to find evidence against him.

"I don't want these people back in my life," he said. "They actually raised money . . . to put me in jail."

Straight after the press conference, the world's media descended on Antioch, California. The sleepy backwater San Francisco suburb was suddenly overflowing with television news crews and scores of reporters, hungry for any information on Phillip and Nancy Garrido. Over the next few weeks, newspapers as far away as England, Australia and China would cover this almost unprecedented story, making Jaycee Lee Dugard something of an international superstar.

By late afternoon, as a helicopter circled overhead, taking aerial photographs of 1554 Walnut Avenue and its secret back garden, reporters were knocking on the Garrido neighbors' doors for interviews.

"If you didn't look into this guy's eyes and see straight evil," neighbor Sam Kovistl told a reporter, "you'd be blind. You're not even looking in the eyes of a human. I could tell he had something to hide."

Before long, reporters found Phillip Garrido's Voices Revealed blog, and began tracking down his printing clients, listed in his black box affidavits. And it soon became clear that Jaycee, Angel and Starlit were well known to many of them.

Realtor Deepal Karunaratne told reporters that he had known Jaycee as Phillip Garrido's oldest daughter, Alyssa, often seeing her on a day-to-day business basis.

"She does all my work and does all the designing," he told the *Reno Gazette-Journal.* "Every time she comes she's very well-dressed and she seemed to be very healthy and happy."

Tim Allen, president of East County Glass & Window, Inc., said he used Phillip Garrido's printing business for more than a decade, describing him as an "out there" religious fanatic.

"He was always talking about this new religion thing, rambling," said Allen. "He seemed like a simple guy with a mental problem."

Allen told reporters that over the last several years, Garrido had started bringing two "cute little blonde girls" into his showroom, saying they were his daughters.

"They looked normal," he said. "They spoke really well and one even shook my hand."

Cheyvonne Molino of J & M Enterprises said she knew Angel and Starlit well, and they had even attended her daughter's Sweet Sixteen birthday party, just a couple of weeks earlier.

"We didn't realize anything was wrong," she said, "except they didn't go to school with other kids."

Molino described Angel as very "clingy" to her father, saying they were both "very shy." Sometimes he brought them over to visit her teenage daughter, so they would have someone their own age to talk to.

In Walnut Avenue, neighbors told reporters that it was common knowledge that Phillip Garrido was a sex offender. The neighborhood children called him "Creepy Phil," and always kept their distance.

Damon Robinson, who had lived next door to the Garridos for the last three years, explained how in 2006 his former girl-friend had seen little children living in the backyard in tents.

"I told her to call the police," he said. "I told her to call right away."

40

At 4:45 P.M. that Thursday afternoon, KCRA-TV anchor Walt Gray was about to go on air for his five o'clock newscast when his boss told him he had a phone call from Phillip Garrido. At first the veteran newsman thought it a joke, but when he realized it really was Garrido, calling from Placerville Jail, he took a deep breath and went into an audio booth, turned on a tape recorder and picked up the phone.

"This is going to be a powerful, heartwarming story," Garrido drawled in an eerie whisper. "You are going to be really impressed. It's going to take world news."

Garrido told the anchorman he had tried to contact him earlier that day, but had not been able to.

"Go to the Federal Bureau of Investigation," he said, "fifteenth floor in San Francisco and ask for a copy of the documents I left with them three days ago. This is for you—the mass media."

Garrido said the documents he'd left with the FBI were "something powerful," urging him to read them before they had an exclusive face-to-face interview.

"Because what you're going to have in your hand," said Garrido, "will take world news immediately."

Walt Gray then asked why he had selected Jaycee Lee Dugard to abduct back in 1991.

"I'm so sorry," he replied, explaining he would have to wait until he could sit down and do it correctly. "I have no desire to hold back these things. There's a powerful, heartwarming story if you would just cooperate with me. I'm so sorry because I don't want to disappoint you right now; I know I just have to do this in an orderly fashion."

Then, after informing Garrido he was taping their conversation, Gray asked what he thought his situation was right now.

"Well, I am in a very serious condition," Garrido replied, "but I can't speak with you about this. I have to wait. I guarantee you as time goes on you will get the pieces of the story. You are going to fall over."

Once again he told Gray to get the documents from the FBI, as they would play a big part in his "major trial."

"Phillip," asked Gray, "what do you hope happens once the documents are out, once the trial begins or is over?"

"Well, let me tell you this," Garrido replied, "when I went to the San Francisco Bureau . . . I was accompanied by two children that are Jaycee Lee Dugard's two children that we had. And then they accompanied me to Berkeley. To really start this off please get those documents. They will not disappoint you . . . you are going to be in control of something that is going to take the world's attention."

"Right, so, Phillip," said Gray, "I know that you served some time in the nineties. . . . What have you been doing all this time in terms of employment? What keeps you busy?"

"The last several years," answered Garrido, "I completely turned my life around, and you're going to find it the most powerful story coming from the witness—from the victim. . . . If you take this a step at a time you're going to fall over backwards, and in the end you're going to find the most powerful, heartwarming story revealing of something that needs to be understood. And that is as far as I can go. I really want to help you but I have to make sure the media is protected correctly."

Gray then asked if Jaycee would be contributing most to this story.

"Jaycee will also handle that with her lawyer," he replied. "We're going to coordinate this. . . . Wait till you hear the story of what took place at this house and you are going to be absolutely impressed. It's a disgusting thing that took place from the end to the beginning, but I turned my life completely around.

"I'm so sorry, Mr. Gray. I want to help you further, but I also need to protect the sheriff's office . . . the government, and I need to protect the rights of Jaycee Lee Dugard."

Then Gray asked what he meant by "heartwarming story," if it was a love story or about children.

At this point Phillip Garrido began to cry.

"It is a constructive story about turning a person's life around and having those children, those two girls. They slept in my arms every single night. I never touched them . . . I can't go any further because if I do you know I'll go too far."

Gray then asked if Jaycee and the two children were okay.

"Absolutely," said Garrido, composing himself, "the youngest one was born and from that moment on everything turned around. These people are going to testify to these things."

And he forecast that as soon as his trial began, "many hundreds of thousands of people" would come forward to testify about his powers.

Finally, the newsman said there was concern that Jaycee and her daughters had never received any medical attention.

"We just didn't have the finances," he explained, "and we were very concerned."

Walt Gray then ended the fifteen-minute interview, thanking Garrido for his call.

"I am not going to play with the media," Garrido replied. "I am going to leave this with you, because you are the first person here I was able to talk to. And I'm going to stop right there. Thank you, sir."

"Have a good day," said Gray, putting down the phone.

That night Jaycee Lee Dugard slept under the same roof as her mother and younger sister for the first time in eighteen years. They had now been moved to a suite in a Concord hotel, and a witness protection officer had gone shopping to buy Jaycee, Angel and Starlit new clothes. They only had the clothes they were wearing when they had left the previous morning with Phillip and Nancy Garrido.

Tina Dugard, who is a third-grade teacher, played a key role in the early reunification. But it was not easy, and there was a great deal of tension, as Jaycee felt guilty she had bonded with her kidnapper. And Angel and Starlit were also devastated that their father had been arrested, and they would probably never see him again.

When Terry called her estranged husband Carl to give a further update, her mother-in-law Wilma Probyn answered the phone, as he was busy with a television crew.

"She said Jaycee was doing good," recalled Wilma, "that she's got a lot of guilt, that she bonded with this guy. I think that's the only reason she's alive, because she did bond with him. Terry says . . . she looks like she did when she was taken at eleven, and she's twenty-nine. She looks healthy."

Over the next couple of days, Jaycee, Angel and Starlit started receiving intense counseling, from a psychologist provided by the National Center for Missing and Exploited Children. It would be the beginning of many months of work to deprogram them, after all the years of brainwashing by the Garridos.

"Jaycee had to explain to them," said Carl Probyn, "that she had been kidnapped. They didn't even know that. They are upset about this because that's their father and he's in jail."

The first steps included rigorous interviews by a special psychological recovery team of experts, to help Jaycee reclaim the identity that was stolen from her as a child. Terry, Shayna and Tina would have to accept that she was no longer the little girl she had been before the abduction. The fact that Phillip Garrido had fathered her two children made things far more difficult.

As Nancy and Phillip Garrido were the only parents Angel and Starlit had ever known, it would take months of intense therapy and love before they fully accepted Jaycee as their mother and their new family.

Forensic psychiatrist Dr. Keith Ablow, who is not treating Jaycee Dugard or her two daughters, said that helping them recover would be like "walking a psychological tightrope." But their prognosis was good.

"Jaycee Dugard's road back depends upon the mind's agility," said Dr. Ablow, a Fox News contributor, "because now she must see that she was in danger from predators who posed as her saviors. She must somehow find her original sense of self, revisit the horror it must have been to cede all control to her assailant and take the journey from viewing herself as a helpless victim to seeing herself as a survivor."

As for treating the children, Dr. Ablow suggested that Jaycee might tell them that "their father is a sick man, but now they are safe and very well cared for. They know nothing but the life they have lived and will need teams of healing professionals to encourage them to share their thoughts and feelings in order to have any hope of escaping severe mental disorders."

Like everyone else, Katie Callaway had been following the dramatic discovery of Jaycee Lee Dugard on the news. And on Thursday evening, she was walking by her television to feed her Maltese dog when she heard the newscaster say, "Phillip Garrido, Contra Costa."

Katie froze, wondering if it could possibly be the man who had kidnapped and raped her thirty-three years earlier.

Then she looked at the screen, seeing his picture and the spelling of his name. The youthful face she remembered had aged over the years, and they were pronouncing his name wrong, but she instantly recognized the man who had ruined her life.

"I started screaming," recalled Katie, now fifty-seven. "I thought, 'Oh my God, that's the man who kidnapped me.' I was shocked. I was stunned. I started shaking and I couldn't stop for about four hours."

Since she disappeared in 1988, after her last encounter with Garrido at Caesar's Casino, she had moved to an anonymous town in central California, becoming a realtor. But she was no longer the trusting young woman who had unwittingly allowed Phillip Garrido into her car.

She took strict precautions and never let clients into her car. If she felt uncomfortable with them, she would insist they leave their ID at her office.

Even after going underground, she was also convinced that Phillip Garrido was still pursuing her, as every few weeks a strange woman would call her office, pretending to be an old friend. Now Katie is convinced it was Nancy Garrido.

In 1995, Katie moved to Las Vegas, working as a dealer at Bally's Casino, still living in fear of Phillip Garrido turning up one day.

On July 19, 2002, she met her husband, Jim Hall, at the Laughlin River Run, where he was playing saxophone with a local band. They married in March 2003, and she took her husband's surname of Hall, dropping her own maiden name to make it harder for Garrido to ever find her.

Soon after they met, Katie told Jim about how Phillip Garrido had kidnapped and raped her. And that Thursday night he was upstairs in their Las Vegas home when he heard her loud, piercing screams.

He first thought, from Katie's screams, that his father must have had another heart attack. But he ran downstairs to find her trembling in front of the television.

"That's the guy," she said, pointing at the television.

41

MEA CULPA

On Friday, August 28, the Jaycee Lee Dugard story made front-page headlines across the world. "Captive For 18 Years—Nightmare of Woman Snatched as a Child," screamed the *New York Post*; "U.S. Sex Monster Boasts of 'Heartwarming' Kidnap Story," trumpeted the London *Daily Star*; and "Horrific Tale of American Kidnap Girl Laid Bare," splashed the *Sydney Morning Herald*.

Phillip Garrido's father Manuel and older brother Ron, who live next door to each other in separate houses in Brentwood, California, were now both talking to the press. And both agreed this had come as no surprise.

"He's a fruitcake," Ron, now sixty-five, told the *San Francisco Chronicle*. "It just seems so bizarre, but I can believe it. I know my brother."

Ron compared his younger brother to infamous 1960s cult leader Charles Manson, in the way he controlled Nancy, whom he described as "a robot."

Manuel Garrido explained to reporters that his son had received serious head injuries as a teen in a motorcycle accident.

"They had to do surgery," said the eighty-eight-year-old. "After that he was a different boy. Tell those . . . cops to treat him like a crazy person, because he's out of his mind."

Phillip Garrido's first wife, Christine Murphy, also re-emerged to tell *The Sacramento Bee* that he was "a monster." She described him as a drug abuser and said that she had divorced him after he went to jail for kidnapping and rape. The last thing she had heard was that he had found God and married a Jehovah's Witness in Leavenworth.

On Friday, Carl Probyn was interviewed on all three network morning shows. He told CBS's *Early Show* he was getting regular updates on Jaycee and the girls' progress from his estranged wife Terry.

"She told me that Jaycee feels really guilty for bonding with this guy," he said. "She has a real guilt trip."

A few minutes later, he told NBC's *Today* show how Jaycee's "mellow" personality had probably saved her life.

"She just bonded with this guy," he said, "and she didn't try to get away. If she had been really spunky and fought and tried to escape, maybe [she] would have been killed."

He then appeared on ABC's *Good Morning America*, explaining the abduction had broken up his marriage and "ruined" so many lives.

"My wife says that Jaycee looks good," he said. "She looks almost like when she was kidnapped. She looks very young. She doesn't look twenty-nine at all."

Then Ernie Allen, president of the National Center for Missing and Exploited Children, explained the enormous significance that the story had for hundreds of American families whose children have disappeared without a trace.

"The Jaycee Dugard case is huge," he said. "There are some people who assume that when a child disappears there is no hope. This provides hope for so many searching families."

By Friday morning, many questions were being asked about how Phillip and Nancy Garrido could possibly have gotten away with it for so long. How was it possible in this day and age to have kidnapped an eleven-year-old girl and fathered two children with her, while they spent their entire lives in his backyard?

That morning, under the Freedom of Information Act, *The Sacramento Bee* officially requested California parole records for Garrido, who had been under its supervision since 1999. The paper also demanded his parole officer Eddie Santos's field notes, listing his visits to the Garrido home and Phillip Garrido's office appointments.

And the California inspector general David Shaw had also quietly launched his own official investigation into the matter. Governor Arnold Schwarzenegger's appointee wanted to find out if there had been "any misconduct" by any of Garrido's parole officers over the years, and whether any changes were required in the state parole system.

California Department of Corrections and Rehabilitation Department spokesman Gordon Hinkle said Phillip Garrido's parole agent Eddie Santos, whose name he refused to divulge, should be congratulated.

"Most of America, including myself," he told the *Los Angeles Times*, "has been trying to figure out how somebody can go to this house and not see any evidence of people there. We're dealing with a criminal, and he and his wife were being very elusive. They were very deceptive and very stealthy in how they were keeping these individuals hidden."

Hinkle said his department was proud of the crucial role it had played in breaking the case, calling it "inappropriate to be pointing fingers at any law enforcement agency."

He then issued a press release praising Garrido's parole agent for his "diligent questioning and follow-up."

That morning it was also revealed that the Antioch Police Department had missed several chances over the years to discover Jaycee and her daughters. The *San Francisco Chronicle* reported that in July 2008, Antioch police officers had searched 1554 Walnut Avenue in a multiagency task force exercise to check on sex offenders.

"There were zero signs of kids living there," Antioch Police sergeant Diane Aguinago told the *Chronicle*.

Far more embarrassing was an interview with former Garrido neighbor Erika Pratt, who said she had dialed 911 after seeing little children living in tents in the backyard. But although a deputy from the Contra Costa County Sheriff's Office had come and questioned Phillip Garrido, he left without searching the house, as he did not have a warrant.

The story also reported Contra Costa County Sheriff's Department spokesman Jimmy Lee confirming his department was aware of Phillip Garrido and had had contact with him in the past.

"We need to investigate further," Lee said, "to determine what that contact was."

At around noon, Contra Costa County sheriff Warren Rupf hastily called a press conference at his Pine Street, Martinez office, apologizing to Jaycee Lee Dugard for not rescuing her earlier.

"On November the thirtieth 2006," he began, "we missed an opportunity to bring earlier closure to this situation. A caller to our 911 dispatch offered that there were tents in the neighbor's backyard, that people were living in them and that there were young children.

"The caller also said that Garrido was psychotic and had a sexual addiction. We made contact with Mr. Garrido in the front yard of his home. The responding deputy determined that there was not any criminal misbehavior, but warned Mr. Garrido that there were code restrictions with regards to living outside in a residential neighborhood. He did not enter, nor request to enter, the backyard.

"This is not an acceptable outcome. Organizationally we should have been more inquisitive, more curious and turned over a rock or two. Our work product should have resulted in a better outcome. We missed an opportunity to have intervened earlier.

"No one knows that we could have found Jaycee or the other children on that day in November 2006, and I cannot change the course of events. But we are beating ourselves up over this and will continue to do so. I am first in line to offer organizational criticism. Offer my apologies to the victims and have accepted responsibility for having missed an earlier opportunity to rescue Jaycee."

At 1:00 P.M., Phillip and Nancy Garrido, their wrists shackled in front of their waists, were brought into El Dorado Superior

Court for arraignment in front of Judge Douglas Phimister. The Placerville courtroom was packed with more than a dozen TV and newspaper photographers.

Dressed in bright red jail-issued jumpsuits, the Garridos, both holding copies of the sixteen-page charges, each sat in the jury box by their respective newly court-appointed lawyers. Throughout the four-minute hearing, Nancy wept through black-rimmed glasses. Her long black hair hung over her face, and she constantly put her head in her hands, shielding herself from photographs. Phillip looked frail and morose, sitting with his public defender, Susan Gellman, staring into space and totally unresponsive.

Neither of the defendants spoke as each of the twenty-nine charges were read out loud, with Jaycee Lee Dugard referred to only as "Jane Doe."

The Garridos were both charged with multiple felony counts of rape, forcible lewd acts on a child and kidnapping for sexual purposes. They were also each charged with over a dozen special allegations that could bring the death penalty if they were to be convicted.

Through their attorneys, Phillip and Nancy Garrido pled not guilty to each and every charge.

Before the hearing, El Dorado County deputy district attorney Trish Kelliher had filed a motion in court revealing that a stun gun had been used to "subdue the victim" during the 1991 abduction. It also stated that Jaycee had reported being sexually assaulted on "multiple" occasions.

"I believe Phillip Garrido is a clear danger to the public and children in particular," stated the motion. "Defendant has no apparent ties to El Dorado County and given the severity of the charges, he is a flight risk."

Judge Phimister then denied the Garridos bail, remanding them in custody until September 14.

After the hearing, Chief Assistant District Attorney William Clark refused to comment on whether Nancy had also raped Jaycee Dugard or detail any evidence against them.

"She is legally charged with rape," said Clark, "on the theory she participated in it. We don't have to prove she physically did a rape. All we have to prove is that she aided and abetted with the knowledge of the crime."

He told reporters that the twenty-nine felony counts were divided into the various time periods through which Jaycee was held by the Garridos. And they directly related to evidence law enforcement had gathered since Jaycee was found. The periods covered in the charges include the month following Jaycee's abduction on June 10, 1991, although it did not specify when the first rape happened.

Outside the court, Nancy Garrido's new lawyer, Gilbert Maines, told reporters that he had only met his new client a few minutes before the hearing, and had not yet reviewed the charges against her.

"You saw her," he said. "She's sitting in the jury box crying."

While Phillip and Nancy Garrido were in court, Pittsburg police began digging up their Walnut Avenue backyard. They were searching for any evidence to connect the Garridos to a string of ten murders of prostitutes in Pittsburg in the early 1990s.

After obtaining a search warrant, teams of Pittsburg investigators moved in with special digging equipment as reporters and news crews watched their every move from the street.

For the last couple of days, investigators had been sifting through the Garrido home and its backyard, looking for evidence in the Jaycee Lee Dugard case. But on Friday evening, they were joined by new teams of forensic science investigators with trained sniffer dogs, searching for evidence that Phillip Garrido was also a serial killer.

A Contra Costa police source told the *San Francisco Chronicle* that one of the dead women had been discovered in a Pittsburg dismantling yard where Phillip Garrido had once worked and occasionally preached.

Pittsburg police investigator John Conaty, who had worked the prostitute serial killings and is still in law enforcement, immediately reopened the investigation after Garrido's arrest.

"Every law enforcement agent in sight is looking at this

guy," an unnamed investigator told the *San Francisco Chronicle*. "It's safe to say that the closer you get to where he is or was, the more interest there is."

Captain Dan Terry of the Contra Costa County Sheriff's Department confirmed that Phillip Garrido had already been interviewed about the prostitute killings.

"Pittsburg police," said Capt. Terry, "for whatever reason decided that he was a person of interest."

The spate of vicious murders had begun in November 1998, when the body of fifteen-year-old Lisa Norrell, who was not a prostitute, was found in the Pittsburg industrial park that Garrido was reported to have worked in at the time. Over the next three months, the bodies of Valerie Dawn Schultz, Rachael Cruise and Jessica Frederick were found strangled and stabbed around the same rural area. Another woman who had been discovered barely alive was believed to have been attacked by the killer.

Pittsburg police also named Phillip Garrido as a person of interest in the 1992 unsolved murders of two other prostitutes, Sharon Mattos and Andrea Ingersoll.

And as darkness fell, investigators from the Pittsburg and Antioch police departments, as well as the Contra Costa County Sheriff's Department, started moving heavy digging equipment into the Garrido backyard in readiness to begin the grim search for bodies.

42

THE SEARCH

On Saturday morning, as temperatures soared past a hundred degrees, a dozen investigators carried out another search of 1554 Walnut Avenue and its almost one-acre backyard. Investigators also focused on the house next door, which Phillip Garrido had taken care of for three years, sealing it off with yellow crime tape.

"This morning," announced Contra Costa Country Sheriff's Department captain Daniel Terry at a press briefing, "Pittsburg police have sealed off the house in Antioch to investigate potential connection between a series of murders of prostitutes in the Bay Area in the early 1990s."

Investigators also revealed that they were searching for evidence linking Phillip Garrido to three missing girls who had disappeared between 1988 and 1991 in circumstances similar to Jaycee Dugard's. Michaela Garecht, Ilene Misheloff and Amanda Campbell had all been abducted within an hour's drive from Antioch. Michaela, who was nine when she was snatched in front of a friend at a supermarket in Hayward, California, bore an uncanny resemblance to Jaycee, with her blonde hair and blue eyes.

"If Jaycee can be alive, Michaela can be alive," her mother, Sharon Murch, told reporters. "It really has my hopes up."

Investigators spent the day searching Phillip Garrido's backyard, methodically going through the various sheds and tents where Jaycee Dugard and her daughters had lived. An officer used a metal detector to scan the backyard, while another cleared branches with a chainsaw. Other officers dug holes with shovels before raking through the ground.

Outside the Garrido house, television trucks were parked on both sides of the street. About twenty journalists, many having flown in from England, were pacing up and down in front of the house as photographers with high-power zoom lenses photographed the investigators working in the garden.

The previous night, resourceful Los Angeles–based English freelance photographer Nick Stern had managed to climb over the police barrier, getting into the backyard. He then spent almost an hour photographing the inside and outside of the various tents and shacks.

His seven high-definition color photographs showed the welcome sign at the hidden entrance, as well as the beds and dressers used by Jaycee and her daughters. He also shot the strange collection of books in one of the tents, composed solely of cat books and true crime. There were also pictures of a dirty aquarium with rotting algae and a rack full of clothes, makeup, hairbrushes and various broken toys. One photo showed a yellow stuffed bird toy, lying in the dust outside a tent.

But the pictures did not represent how the backyard looked when police had first arrived. For since then, teams of investigators had been through, literally tearing everything apart in their search for evidence.

On Sunday, Stern's sensational photographs, for which he is rumored to have received $1 million plus, started appearing in newspapers and magazines all over the world.

Later the Contra Costa County Sheriff's Office spokesman Jimmy Lee described the photos as "unfortunate," but said Stern would not be prosecuted.

Late Saturday night, Shayna Probyn posted a short message about her newfound sister Jaycee and the family reunion on her MySpace page.

"As of this moment," she wrote, "we are just reuniting and everything is going well. She's only 29. She has the rest of her life to live and I have a lot of love to share with my sister and new nieces. In due time my mom will make statements and so will I if needed, but you have to understand this time is critical."

On Sunday morning, August 30, police erected a chain-link fence at the front of the Garrido house, boarding up all the windows to prevent any more photographers entering. And after Contra Costa building inspectors had declared the house unsafe because of its "junkyard conditions," police warned anyone found on the property would be arrested.

At around midday, a team of FBI investigators arrived with cadaver-sniffing dogs. They spent the afternoon roaming around the backyard next door in the scorching three-digit temperatures.

Later two bags of evidence were carried out of the backyard by officers in hazmat suits, and it was eventually confirmed that investigators had uncovered a bone fragment in the backyard of the house next door.

Contra Costa County Sheriff's Office spokesman Jimmy Lee told reporters outside clamoring for information, "We are taking that bone back for further testing and analysis so we can make a determination if it is animal or human."

He emphasized that Damon Robinson, who lived in the house next door, was not a suspect.

"We know Phillip Garrido had access to the property," said Lee. "It looks like he lived in a shed on that property. Right now we're looking at specific areas."

That afternoon, Manuel Garrido told the *New York Post* he believed his son was a serial killer.

"He was a sex addict," declared his father. "I believe my son killed the prostitutes."

He also speculated that Phillip had wanted children so badly, he had persuaded Nancy to help him kidnap Jaycee Dugard to bear them.

"I believe with all my heart," he told the *Post*, "that he decided that if [Nancy] couldn't conceive, he'd find someone who could. So the pair of them hatched the deal and went out to someone who could give them babies. Jaycee was at the wrong place at the wrong time, and Nancy grabbed her."

Garrido thought his son had deliberately selected a young girl who was easier to control.

"I know the sort of guy he is," he explained. "He would be able to intimidate and bully [her] into accepting everything they said."

He also criticized his ex-wife, Pat, for not stopping Phillip Garrido's madness.

"[She] must have known about Jaycee," he told the *Post*. "She lived there all the time. She could have done something, but didn't."

This would be the last interview Manuel Garrido would give for free. From then on he demanded money up front.

But his father was not the only one convinced that Phillip was a serial killer. After learning of his friend's arrest, Marc Lister went up to his attic and retrieved the three compact discs that Garrido had given him of his music, a few years earlier. When he listened to the lyrics for the first time, he was horrified.

"I was absolutely sick to my stomach," he recalled. "I said, 'Oh shit, I don't believe this.' "

According to Lister, besides the creepy love songs Garrido had written about Jaycee Dugard, there were also others about murders, including details of where victims were buried.

"I could take the CDs and play them through," Lister explained, "and say, 'Okay, dig here. You're going to find a body.' "

Lister painstakingly transcribed all twenty songs, before taking them to his attorney for safekeeping.

"[In one] he's burying some bodies," he said. "He talks about 'going through the mountain in the early morning.' That would be up at Lake Tahoe, where you go through a rock which is in the mountains. And when you come out the sun always shines on the other side. Then he talks about seeing a man standing on the hill, holding a skull."

Lister also believes that Phillip Garrido abducted other girls besides Jaycee and did unspeakable things to them.

"I believe in Phil's schizophrenic state of mind," he said, "that if he was angry at Jaycee, and he didn't want to hurt her, that he'd go and take it out on other young females."

And Garrido's onetime Rock Creek bandmate Eddie Loebs was also listening to his old song lyrics, since reading about his arrest.

"You see where the guy really was at with women," said Loebs. "Now I hear his song 'Insanity,' and it takes on a new meaning."

That Sunday, Carl Probyn was in New York for a whirlwind media tour. He appeared on several morning and cable shows, giving updates on how Jaycee and the girls were adapting to their new freedom. And with the insatiable media interest worldwide in the Jaycee Lee Dugard story, he had hardly slept since Wednesday, when it first broke.

"We're basically on the same level as [Ted] Kennedy's funeral today," he told the *Reno Gazette-Journal* by telephone from a suite in the Trump World Tower in Manhattan. "I mean it's that big of a news [story]. I've probably done fifty interviews today. My wife's really appreciative that I'm doing these interviews and being the spokesman."

And again he told the *Gazette-Journal* that Jaycee had "strong feelings" for Phillip Garrido.

"She really feels it's almost like a marriage," he said.

Probyn also hinted that the reunion had not gone entirely smoothly, and there was still much work to do.

"They are doing fine," he said, "not fine, but fine for the situation. My wife says that Jaycee is an excellent mother, and they are bonding, playing little games like checkers. They are doing okay for the situation."

While in New York, Probyn had breakfast with Diane Sawyer, as well as being interviewed by Geraldo Rivera, who had first covered the Jaycee Lee Dugard story in 1993.

"Carl, shake my hand," said an emotional Rivera on his

program for the Fox News Channel. "I've got to give you a hug. Congratulations."

Carl told him it was the first time he had felt happy since his stepdaughter's kidnapping in 1991.

"My heart is feeling good," he said. "I mean I couldn't ask for a better scenario. I never expected this."

Then Rivera asked how Jaycee was doing.

"She's fragile," said Probyn. "She's a real mellow girl. Did you see how beautiful she was? And it paid off. I mean she survived eighteen years. I think if she would have been feisty and tried to climb the fence every day or whatever, she probably wouldn't be here right now."

After filming the studio segment Geraldo Rivera took Carl Probyn out on his sailboat around New York Harbor.

43

ANTIOCH 94509

On Monday, August 31, the *Los Angeles Times* revealed Antioch was a haven for sex offenders, with one of the highest levels in America. The devastating front-page story reported that more than one hundred registered sex offenders lived within Phillip Garrido's 94509 ZIP code.

"It's a small, scruffy unincorporated island," read the story, "largely surrounded by the hard-knock city of Antioch."

Antioch had been particularly hard-hit by the recession, reported the *Times,* with the median price of homes falling 40 percent in the last year. Foreclosures were rampant, with 699 new ones being filed in July 2009.

But perhaps the main reason for attracting so many sex offenders was Jessica's Law, which had been passed in November 2006. From then on, sex offenders released from prison could not live within two thousand feet of schools, churches or parks, where children regularly gather. And this had turned the unincorporated part of Antioch into a magnet for them, as it had none of these amenities.

Captain Daniel Terry, who heads the investigative division at the Contra Costa County Sheriff's Department, told the *Los Angeles Times* that the county had a staggering 1,700 registered sex offenders. And there was just one detective assigned to the 350 his station was responsible for monitoring.

"These people are walking among us everywhere," he said ominously. "This is reality."

Resident Dawn Cordy lived a few blocks away from Phillip Garrido and at least three other registered sex offenders. She told the *Times* that these people moved to Antioch because they can with few questions asked.

"We're mostly an older bunch," explained Cordy, fifty-two, "and we don't pay them much attention. This is Boonieville."

Antioch mayor Jim Davis attempted to distance his city from Phillip Garrido, maintaining the unincorporated area was not really part of his town, although he said he would like to annex it, so it could be policed properly.

"There's a lot of building out there violating code," he said. "If the city were out there, all the sheds and tents out there would not have been tolerated."

On Monday morning, investigators resumed searching the backyard next to the Garridos' where the bone fragment had been found. Five cadaver dogs were brought in to walk the large area as reporters waited outside on Walnut Avenue, closely watching every move.

Around 6:00 P.M., investigators finished their four-day search and began packing up their gear. As they removed the crime scene tape from around both houses, they refused to comment on whether there had been any further discoveries.

Betty Upingco, who lived opposite the Garrido home, said all the police activity was upsetting everyone on Walnut Avenue.

"It freaked me out," she said. "Then the more and more you hear of it, you're thinking, 'Oh my God! This guy lived three doors down from us.'"

That night Katie Callaway Hall, as she was now calling herself, and her husband, Jim, appeared on CNN's *Larry King Live*. Over the weekend, the *Reno Gazette-Journal* had put Phillip Garrido's entire 1976 trial transcript on its website, as well as the police report. The 304-page trial transcript graphically detailed exactly what Garrido had done to Katie during the eight hours he was with her. It also revealed Garrido's bizarre sexual obsessions, including how he used to masturbate in front of seven-year-old girls.

Katie and Jim Hall had flown to New York for a series of television interviews, telling their family and friends to tune to CNN at nine o'clock without explaining why. And when Katie told her harrowing story to viewers, it was the first time many of their family and closest friends had heard about it.

"My heart goes out to Jaycee," she told Larry King. "I can't imagine what Jaycee is going through. He had me for eight hours, he had her for eighteen years."

Katie said she was sickened that Phillip Garrido had been freed from prison so early, and no one had bothered to listen to her.

"I want to scream from the depths of my soul," she told King. "Scream because my fears turned out to be justified. He struck again."

The next morning, Lieutenant Brian Addington of the Pittsburg Police issued a press statement, saying no evidence had been found during the four-day search to link Phillip Garrido to the ten unsolved prostitute killings.

"The search lasted four days," it said, "and covered the entire house and backyard, including all of the structures and tents. We also checked an adjacent neighbor's backyard.

"Aside from a few items that will require further forensic examination before they can be completely excluded, we did not locate any evidence to connect Phillip and Nancy Garrido to Pittsburg's unsolved cases."

Late one night, a convoy of unmarked police cars drew up outside 1554 Walnut Avenue. By this time most of the reporters had left, and no one noticed the plainclothed detectives lead Jaycee Lee Dugard into the backyard. It was the first time she had been back since the morning of Phillip and Nancy Garrido's arrest.

Investigators needed Jaycee to show them around the ramshackle backyard she had been imprisoned in for so long. There was a psychologist at her side the entire time to help her cope with all the emotions of returning to the place where she had been imprisoned for so long.

Then for the next several hours, police with flashlights led her around every shed and tent, asking her to describe in detail exactly where she had been imprisoned and what had happened where.

Several times Jaycee broke down in tears, revisiting the scenes of her nightmare. But with the experts' gentle guidance, she showed investigators where Garrido had locked her up after the abduction, and where he had first raped her a month later. She also showed them where she had given birth to Angel and Starlit.

"Jaycee literally had to fight for breath," a source inside the investigation told the *National Enquirer*, "as she looked at the makeshift toilet, stained sofa beds, battered chests of drawers and plastic storage units that she used as she struggled to make a normal life for her kids."

Then she bravely mapped out for investigators how she and her daughters had lived in squalor, providing valuable ammunition for the prosecution in the case against Phillip and Nancy Garrido.

Soon afterward, Jaycee and her daughters moved into an FBI safe house in San Francisco with Terry Probyn and Shayna. And the long task of deprogramming Jaycee and the girls began in earnest, as prosecutors continued their questioning.

Their investigation included Jaycee's secret journal, which she kept the entire time she was with the Garridos. The heart-wrenching diary provides a compelling look into her twisted relationship with her captors, and the mental cruelty they wielded over her.

A source inside the investigation revealed to the *National Enquirer* that Jaycee still had feelings for the Garridos and loved them. After the couple's arrest, Jaycee begged prosecutors to drop all charges against them, saying she was now safely back with her family.

For years, Phillip Garrido had instructed Jaycee on what to do if police ever arrested him. He told her to immediately find an attorney, so she would be able to communicate with him via their respective lawyers and under the radar of law enforcement.

Inside the safe house, the highly specialized team of psychologists were actually trying to re-create their day-to-day lives in the backyard to ease them back into the world. A senior police source told the London *Sun* that although Angel and Starlit were both highly intelligent, they had little understanding of the world.

"They have never watched TV," said the police source, "and have no concept of math, geography or history. They have never heard of the president of the USA or anything about the wider world."

Psychologists had determined that Jaycee and the girls should initially maintain the same routine they had had with the Garridos. So the television sets had been removed, as the girls had never seen one. It was also to protect them from exposure to the media coverage of the case.

"They are being given TV microwave dinners and their favorite meatloaf meals," reported *The Sun*. "They have never had soda drinks, so they get cooled water, which is what they are used to."

Jaycee and her daughters all slept in the same room, as they had done in their backyard tent. And on a positive note, psychologists noted that Angel was now coming out of herself, although Starlit remained painfully shy.

44

"SHE LOVED JAYCEE VERY MUCH"

On Wednesday, September 2, Nancy Garrido's defense attorney, Gilbert Maines, appeared on all three network morning TV shows. The veteran lawyer, who has practiced in California for more than forty years, boasts on his website that he has earned the respect of both judge and jury, as well as his peers.

"Compromise and obtaining a settlement," says his home page, "is a skill just as important as winning in the courtroom. Mr. Maines is a counselor who wants to take his client where the client wants to go and do it in the most expedient manner possible."

So far Maines had spent just two hours with Nancy Garrido, who remained in deep shock one week after her arrest.

"She's distraught, she's scared," Maines told Meredith Vieira on NBC's *Today* show. "She seems to be a little lost at the moment."

He said that although Nancy understood why she was in jail, she loved Jaycee and the girls and considered them family.

"There came a time when she felt they were like a family," said Maines. "She loves the girls very much and she loved Jaycee very much. And that seems a little strange given the circumstances, but that's what she had said to me."

When Vieira asked if Nancy had explained how Jaycee had first come to Walnut Avenue, Maines refused to answer, saying it violated attorney-client privilege. However, he would be exploring Nancy's mental condition at the time of the abduction.

"I would be derelict in my duty," he said, "if I didn't pursue every avenue that was available, and one of them certainly is to look into her state of mind at the time and prior. And I can't say right now that she is incompetent to stand trial. I think my plan is sometime in the near future to have her evaluated. To have an expert talk to her and spend some time with her."

The attorney also revealed that he had received threats since taking the case and planned to hire a bodyguard.

"I just try and ignore those," he said.

A few hours later, Tina Dugard gave an exclusive interview to the *Orange County Register* about the first five days she had spent with her niece Jaycee and her two daughters. With all the sensational stories out there, Jaycee's family had decided it was time to take the media initiative.

"There's a sense of comfort and optimism, a sense of happiness," the forty-two-year-old teacher told reporter Greg Hardesty in her living room. "Jaycee and her girls are happy."

Tina said after the emotional family reunion, everyone had bonded and reconnected, as police investigators and counselors hovered in the background.

"People probably want to think that it's been this horrible, scary thing for all of us," she said. "[But] the horrible, scary thing happened eighteen years ago and continued to happen for the last eighteen years. The darkness and despair [have lifted]."

Tina, who is thirteen years older than her niece Jaycee, then described how all six of them soon started acting like a normal, ordinary family.

"[There was] laughing and crying and sitting and holding hands," she said. "All three are very tight."

She said during their downtime, when they were not being interviewed by investigators or seeing counselors, Jaycee reads mystery novels while her daughters play computer games.

One night Tina and Jaycee watched a DVD of the Disney movie *Enchanted*, starring Julie Andrews. Then they discussed their favorite films and what they had seen recently. Jaycee told her aunt she wanted to see Sandra Bullock's new movie, *The Proposal*.

She said Angel and Starlit loved playing their favorite game, *Super Mario Smash Brothers,* on Nintendo DS and drawing pictures.

One day, Tina said, she took Angel and Starlit outside the safe house for a nature walk. And as they all lay on the grass watching the clouds float by, the girls told their great-aunt how they loved animals and climbing trees.

"It was a beautiful day," recalled Tina.

In the media battle for the Jaycee Lee Dugard story, the TV tabloid show *Inside Edition* appeared to be winning. Over the next several weeks the show broke a number of exclusives, including the first and only TV interview with Phillip Garrido's first wife, Christine Murphy.

"He's a monster," said Murphy. "I was always looking for a way to get away."

She said she was in love with him when they eloped in 1973, after being high school sweethearts. But when they moved to South Lake Tahoe, Phillip started becoming more and more controlling and violent. He spent all day taking LSD or smoking dope, and was always trying to get her to participate in orgies with "multiple partners," but she refused.

She also accused her ex-husband of stabbing her in the face with a safety pin after another man flirted with her. And she showed the still visible scar to the cameras.

Chris said she had had no idea her ex-husband had been released from prison until hearing he'd been arrested for kidnapping and raping Jaycee Lee Dugard.

"It made me sick to my stomach," she said.

Garrido's first wife also blamed Nancy for allowing it to happen under her roof.

"She knew what she was doing," said Murphy, "and she knew what was going on. She must have been really in love with him or so infatuated with him that she was willing to do anything."

A week later, Jaycee's biological father, Ken Slayton, now sixty-four, was interviewed on *Inside Edition* with his daughters—and Jaycee's half-sisters—Sarah, twenty-four, and Brittany, twenty-one.

"I'd skin them," said Slayton, when asked what he would do to the Garridos. "I think they should live as long as they possibly can, and someone should torment them as much as they did Jaycee and those little girls."

Slayton said he had "mixed emotions," but would like to be a part of his daughter's life.

"My girls are asking if [Jaycee] is their sister," he said. "If Jaycee wants to meet us, we're here."

But *the* biggest interview of all would be the first one with Jaycee Lee Dugard. And Oprah Winfrey had reportedly sent a personal letter to Jaycee, inviting her on her show to tell her story for the first time. Also said to be in heated competition for the coveted first interview were Barbara Walters and Diane Sawyer.

On Thursday, September 3, Tina Dugard called a press conference at the FBI's Los Angeles office, reading a prepared statement. She was introduced by the Dugard family's newly appointed spokeswoman, Erika Price Schulte.

"The smile on my sister's face is as wide as the sea," declared Tina joyously. "Her oldest daughter is home."

Tina refused to discuss how Jaycee and her daughters were treated by the Garridos, or what their life was like in captivity. But she did say that Angel and Starlit knew exactly what was going on, although they had not read any newspaper coverage of the story or watched television.

"Right now it's about reconnecting," she explained. "Not only have we laughed and cried together, but we've spent time sitting quietly, taking pleasure in each other's company."

Dugard said that while in captivity, Jaycee had taught her daughters how to read and write, doing a great job with what little she had available.

"[They] are educated and bright," she said. "It's clear they've been on the Internet and know a lot of things. Jaycee did a great job with the limited resources she had and her limited education, and we are so proud of her."

After reading her statement, Dugard refused to take any questions from the media. Then Schulte handed out three new preabduction pictures of Jaycee, saying there would be no further comment from the family for now.

That afternoon, Lieutenant Leonard Orman of the Antioch Police Department also called a press conference, revealing that when Phillip Garrido was twenty-one, he had been arrested for raping an underage girl. He explained that the victim, who wished to remain anonymous, had contacted investigators after recognizing Garrido's photograph on television. She wanted to be certain that law enforcement knew of Garrido's April 1972 arrest, but was not interested in pressing the case now.

Lieutenant Orman said that the police did not intend to charge Garrido after all that time, as it was past the statute of limitations. And although the 1972 case file no longer existed, police had records confirming Garrido's arrest.

"After numerous inquiries from the press," said Lieutenant Orman, "regarding the 1972 incident, it became apparent to us the press were pursuing these details and also the identity of this victim. We are now speaking about this case in hopes that it will satisfy the press's curiosity."

Lieutenant Orman said the girl and a friend had gotten into a car with Garrido and another man outside Antioch Library. After driving around Antioch, Garrido had taken her to a seedy motel on East 18th Street and given her barbiturates. Her worried parents had later tracked her down at the motel, finding her in bed with Garrido.

The parents then summoned the police and Garrido was charged with rape, contributing to the delinquency of a minor and providing drugs to a minor. Later at the preliminary hearing the girl refused to testify, after threats that the defense attorney would paint her as a "whore" and a "slut," if she took the stand against Garrido. This left the Antioch Police Department no alternative but to dismiss the case and let him go free.

Lieutenant Orman was then asked if he thought there were other young victims of Phillip Garrido out there, still too scared to go to the police.

"Other victims," said Lieutenant Orman. "I think there's a good chance of that. Yes."

* * *

A few miles away, Marc Lister was playing a selection of Phillip Garrido's music for reporters from the *San Francisco Chronicle,* the *Contra Costa Times* and KTVU-TV. He had invited them to his attorney's Walnut Creek office to listen to samples from the three CDs Phillip Garrido had once given him.

After the listening session, Lister announced he planned to turn the CDs over to investigators, and then use the music to raise money for abused women and children. But he first wanted to sit down with Jaycee to discuss it, ensuring that it would not "impair or slow down" her recovery.

"I think there's some sort of message here," Lister told the *Times*. "I think it's disturbing. It's a bit twisted. It's not right."

Lister said that when Garrido had given him the disks in 2006, he told him that some day his songs would "be heard around the world."

Lister and his attorney gave reporters transcribed song lyrics and played them short extracts. They also showed one of Garrido's Printing For Less business cards, claiming the beautiful blonde girl on it was Jaycee. They refused to allow it to be photographed.

That night, the London *Sun* newspaper posted a story on its website quoting a senior investigator on the case speculating that Jaycee may have had more children, whom Phillip Garrido then killed because they were male.

"She was raped continually," said the detective, "and you would think there would be more babies. Garrido is a self-confessed pedophile and experts have told us he would only want daughters with her, and he would see any sons as a potential threat."

The detective said this was one of several lines of inquiry, and Jaycee would be asked whether she had given birth to any more babies.

"Is he that much of a sicko that he could dispose of any male babies?" asked the detective, adding that investigators were also talking to Angel and Starlit about whether their father had sexually molested them. But to date no evidence to support these speculations has ever been produced.

On Labor Day, there was a Pink Ribbon Parade through South Lake Tahoe, to celebrate the discovery of Jaycee Lee Dugard. And Jaycee's stepfather Carl Probyn returned to the town for an interview with the Australian version of *60 Minutes.* Later he joined two thousand people in the grand parade, holding a thousand pink balloons and chanting Jaycee's name.

"I wanted to come back to support these people," Probyn told a reporter, adding that he hoped to be reunited with Jaycee within the next several weeks. "They supported us."

The joyful parade, organized by Soroptimist International, reversed the route of the previous one in 2001, on the tenth anniversary of the abduction, to symbolize Jaycee's return. The marchers, many of whom openly wept, included Jaycee's classmates, friends and teachers. And it brought the town to a halt, stopping traffic as motorists spontaneously got out of the cars to applaud Jaycee.

And all over the town were hundreds of Jaycee's "missing" posters, with a line drawn through the word "missing."

Two days later, the Contra Costa Sheriff's Department announced that the bone fragment found in the backyard next door to the Garrido house was "probably human." Spokesman Jimmy Lee said it would now be analyzed by the state laboratory to see if a DNA profile could be developed.

"It should be noted," he said, "that it is not uncommon to find Native American remains in Contra Costa County."

With the Jaycee Dugard story still making front-page headlines two weeks after it broke, Oprah Winfrey now publicly requested an interview with her.

"This is the one I want," the talk show queen emphatically told *The Insider,* a gossip TV show. "I want that interview."

And she revealed that for the first time ever she had called one of her producers, making sure they were working on a story.

Later there would be reports that Oprah had offered to pay $1 million for the exclusive sit-down interview.

Nancy Garrido was having a tough time inside the Pacerville Jail, where she was being kept in isolation for her own protection. Her attorney Gilbert Maines described her as "very lonely," and there were rumors that other inmates had threatened to rape and kill her.

There were also reports that the Garridos, who were being housed in the same jail, were both under suicide watch.

El Dorado County Sheriff's Department lieutenant Pam Lane said the high-profile prisoners received three meals a day and were able to shower every other day. They were allowed outside their cell one hour a day for exercise.

Both had access to television and newspapers, and were reported to be following coverage of their case. And Phillip Garrido had undergone surgery to remove three suspected cancerous growths at the bridge of his nose.

At 8:00 A.M., Monday, September 14, Phillip and Nancy Garrido were back inside El Dorado Superior Court for a brief ten-minute bail hearing. That morning, London's *Daily Mirror* reported that Jaycee Dugard had agreed to appear on *Oprah* for $1 million.

Scores of journalists jostled for position inside the courtroom, as photographers stood to the side photographing the Garridos.

As before, Nancy used her long hair to shield her face from photographers' lenses, while Phillip, wearing a bandage over his nose and a gray beard, sat expressionless throughout the proceedings.

Judge Douglas Phimister, now assigned to the Garrido case, fixed Phillip's bail at $30 million and granted a request from Gilbert Maines that his client Nancy, who was being held without bail, undergo psychological evaluation.

Susan Gellman then told the judge her client had been pressured by several police departments that want to interview him about other cases.

"He does not consent to be questioned for any purpose," she said.

The only time the Garridos spoke was when the judge asked if they waived their right for a preliminary hearing within sixty days, answering "Yes, sir."

Later, outside the court building, El Dorado district attorney Vern Pierson pleaded with reporters to respect Jaycee and her family's privacy.

"I've heard comments referring to this family as a piece of property to be had," he declared. "I think they needed to be left alone. As Abraham Lincoln said, let us all rise to the better angels of our nature and leave this family alone during this time of reunification."

He also said that investigators were continuing to pursue other leads in the case.

"As of today," he said, "there are no additional charges. That's not to say there won't be."

The district attorney also applauded the actions of Phillip Garrido's parole agent Eddie Santos, describing them as "within the finest standards of law enforcement and public service.

"This parole agent successfully broke through the elaborate, well-planned cover story that was nineteen years in the making. We all owe him a debt of gratitude."

One reporter then asked if Jaycee Dugard had been approached about testifying against the Garridos.

"Let me just generally say," he replied. "Typically, in every criminal case because of the United States Constitution and the confrontation clause—ultimately a witness would have to come into court and testify when a case goes to trial. So beyond that I don't think I can comment."

A few hours after the hearing, the Dugard family spokeswoman Erika Price Schulte labeled the reports that Jaycee would appear on *Oprah* as "completely false."

Sometime in September, Jaycee and her family moved into a horse ranch, donated by a millionaire to help speed their recovery. Now that the police interviews were over, the family was receiving continuing private and group therapy sessions.

A key part of the treatment for Jaycee and her daughters had been horse therapy, especially designed to help them establish familiarity and trust with Terry and Shayna. Everyday the whole family rode together through the large ranch, together experiencing the freedom of fresh air and nature, in stark contrast from their imprisonment with the Garridos.

"Jaycee has a horse, Oreo, that she has bonded with," a friend, who had visited them on the ranch told *Hello!* magazine. "[It's] something important to her recovery."

The Dugard family spokeswoman Erika Price Shulte said that as there was no precedent for what Jaycee and her family had gone through, they were taking an "individualized approach" to treatment.

"Horse therapy is part of the reunification therapy they're going through," she said. "Jaycee and the girls really love riding horses."

Angel and Starlit were now being home-schooled in math and English. Tests recently carried out had shown both girls to be highly intelligent and academically equal to school-educated children of the same age.

During their free time, Jaycee and her daughters loved reading and watching DVD movies. Jaycee was also a talented cook, preparing family Mexican meals of rice, beans and salsa.

They had also been reunited with their five cats, although the pigeon, pet mouse and three cockatiels had been adopted by other members of the family. The Contra Costa Animal Shelter was still trying to find a home for the two dogs.

"They are adjusting amazingly well," a source close to the family told *Hello!* "They are smart, playful, funny girls. But they are also very caring and protective of each other—maybe a reflection of how it was for them in captivity."

Jaycee's stepgrandmother Joan Curry told *People* magazine that no one was underestimating the difficulties lying ahead. And that Jaycee would have to come to terms with being repeatedly raped by Phillip Garrido, and her daughters would have to deal with him being their father.

"Jaycee's realistic," said Curry. "She knows this is not going to be the easiest road that she's ever traveled, but she is just very upbeat."

45

NO STONE UNTURNED

On Tuesday, September 15, officers from the Hayward and Dublin police departments descended on 1554 Walnut Avenue, Antioch, and the house next door. They were searching for any evidence tying the Garridos to the disappearances of nine-year-old Michaela Garecht and thirteen-year-old Ilene Micheloff in the late 1980s. Prior to their arrival, both police departments had obtained search warrants on the grounds that the two young girls' kidnappings were so similar to Jaycee Dugard's several years later. Michaela also bore a striking resemblance to Jaycee, with her blonde hair and blue eyes.

The search was expected to take several days and would also involve the FBI and the Alameda and Contra Costa County sheriff's departments.

Police and sheriff's deputies arrived early in the morning, closing off Walnut Avenue to traffic. Then sixty officers entered, wearing face masks, latex gloves and kneepads. Half a dozen large, specially adapted camper-style vehicles also parked in front of the Garrido house to headquarter the operation.

As the morning progressed, TV news crews and reporters returned to Walnut Avenue with a growing anticipation of what might be buried in the backyard. An investigator said that the idea of razing the Garrido house to see if any human remains were buried underneath was now under active consideration.

Dublin police lieutenant Kurt Von Savoye likened the search to "looking for evidence in a landfill."

The searchers spent the day combing the two properties, stacking piles of debris up in the Garrido backyard. Later an ancient green van was towed out of the backyard.

At one point Phillip and Nancy Garrido's two defense attorneys arrived at the house, to carry out their own site inspection, and were turned away.

"[We] were surprised to find police and media at the residence of Phillip and Nancy Garrido," said Gilbert Maines. "[We] had no prior knowledge of the serving of any other warrants by any other agencies."

That afternoon, Michaela Garecht's mother, Sharon Murch, arrived to see firsthand how the search was going. And on her way out she spoke to reporters about the emotional rollercoaster ride she had been on since Jaycee's reappearance.

"I hope this will lead to a resolution," said the mother of four. "If Jaycee can be found alive and come home after eighteen years, then my daughter can be found alive and come home after eighteen years."

She then sent an emotional message to Michaela, just as Terry Dugard had once done to Jaycee.

"Michaela," she said, welling up with emotion, "if you're out there somewhere within the sound of my voice, I just want you to know that we love you, we miss you . . . and we want you to come home."

At 4:30 P.M. the search finished for the day, with nothing significant discovered.

"This is one of the strongest leads [for Michaela] we have pursued thus far," Hayward police lieutenant Christine Orrey told reporters. "We don't walk away from here, thinking we left anything undone that would help us solve these cases. We just want to bring closure for these families, as to what happened to these missing children."

Lieutenant Orrey said neither police department had yet questioned the Garridos. Jaycee had been interviewed by the FBI, but had not mentioned anything about Michaela or Ilene.

On Wednesday morning the search resumed, with forensic investigators bringing in ground-penetrating radar equipment, able to detect human remains up to twenty-five feet beneath the surface. An aerial photo expert was also recruited to analyze a series of aerial images of the Garrido backyard dating back to the 1980s and see what changes had been made.

Braving temperatures in the nineties, investigators spent the day searching the two backyards. Later they removed three truckloads of trash, weeds and debris for closer examination. They also tore down a carport and a shed in the Garrido backyard to see what was underneath.

When the search wound up for the day in the late afternoon, Lieutenant Orrey came out for an impromptu press conference. And what she would say would hit the front pages of newspapers across America the next day.

"We have located what appears to be bones on both properties," she declared, adding that they were already on their way to a police laboratory for analysis.

She said the joint task force now planned to completely clear out the Garridos' back garden, bringing in state-of-the-art radar equipment, for an even more intense subterranean search.

On Thursday, the third day of the search, investigators brought in a six-dog team of cadaver dogs, specially trained to sniff out human remains. Ten more truckloads of debris were removed from the Garrido property, as Hayward and Dublin police investigators dismantled sheds and tents in the backyard, before moving inside the Garrido house for the first time.

That morning Sharon Murch returned and was given a tour of the Garrido backyard. On her way out she told a reporter that she had seen Phillip Garrido's soundproofed shed, and wondered what atrocities he must have committed in there.

"Until someone shows me search positive that my daughter is not alive," she said, "I'm just going to continue to believe she is."

Later, at an afternoon press conference, Sergeant J. D. Nelson of the Alameda County Sheriff's Office said one of the cadaver dogs had picked up a scent, which was later confirmed by a second dog. But he refused to elaborate where on the property that had occured.

On Friday the searchers returned, pulling up a huge concrete slab in the backyard and removing more truckloads of debris. The police also brought in a professional archaeologist to run radar equipment in a grid pattern around the backyard. And he picked up signs of soil that may have been disturbed by a previous digging.

"We're removing concrete slabs that inhibited dogs and machinery to get a look at that area," said Lieutenant Kurt von Savoye. "[We] removed sheds that the dogs and machinery couldn't go to before."

Then the search was put on hold until Monday, so investigators could take the weekend off and be fresh to resume on Monday.

While Phillip Garrido's property was being torn apart for clues, the *National Enquirer* published what it claimed was the first photograph of the grown-up Jaycee Dugard. In what was billed as "a world exclusive" was the photograph of the blonde model on Garrido's old Printing For Less business cards.

The magazine reportedly paid Garrido client Wayne Thompson five thousand dollars for the card.

"Phil gave me the card and said the photo on it was his daughter," the barber told the *Enquirer*. "I know it was her because I met her."

Later, family spokesman Erika Price Schulte told *People* magazine that the *Enquirer*'s picture was definitely not Jaycee.

"Not even close," she said.

Jaycee Lee Dugard and her daughters were all pining for their pets, now being cared for by Contra Costa Animal Control. Lieutenant Nancy Anderson said Jaycee had been in touch through a third party, requesting their five cats, two dogs, three cockatiels, pigeon and mouse be returned to them.

"We're just hoping we can arrange to get them back to Jaycee and the kids," said Lieutenant Anderson, "as soon as possible."

* * *

On Sunday, Carl Probyn attended a fundraising benefit concert for Jaycee at a casino in Stateline, launching a blistering attack on law enforcement for not finding her sooner.

Comparing the Contra Costa County Sheriff's Department to the "Keystone Kops," Probyn said its officers should feel guilty about accepting paychecks.

"It's just mind-boggling," he said. "It makes me sick to think what Jaycee went through."

A reporter then asked Probyn why he had not yet seen Jaycee, almost a month after her discovery. He replied that he was in no hurry.

"I know she's safe," he said. "I know she's alive."

Jimmy Lee of the Contra Costa County Sheriff's Office said the department had already taken responsibility for its mistakes with Phillip Garrido.

"We understand how he feels," said Lee. "Sheriff has . . . taken the blame for what had happened."

On Monday morning the search resumed with a fresh new team of police dogs, especially trained to locate bones. Over the weekend the Garrido backyard had been doused with thirty-six hundred gallons of water, making it easier for the dogs to detect human remains. And before long they located more bone fragments.

On the other side of the backyard, the archaeologist ran his ground-penetrating radar machine, and a septic tank was also inspected.

At the end of the day, Lieutenant Chris Orrey said nothing major had been found, describing the newly found bones as "very, very old," and probably animal.

"Thus far in the operation," she told reporters, "we have not found a piece of physical evidence that tells us conclusively that Phillip Garrido is involved in the Michaela Garecht abduction."

At eleven o'clock the next morning, the weeklong search officially finished, as searchers began gathering up their tools and taking down tents. Later that afternoon, Lieutenant Orrey confirmed the search was over, with no evidence found to link the Garridos to the two missing girls.

"We will walk away from these properties knowing that we left no stone unturned," she told reporters. "We will never have to wonder if we could have or should have, because we know that we did."

Lieutenant Orrey said investigators would continue to examine several "items of interest" removed from the backyard, vowing that the investigation into Michaela's disappearance would continue.

On Wednesday, September 23, Jaycee Dugard's family announced they would now be represented by Sacramento lawyer McGregor Scott, who had come on board pro bono, as he was so moved by her story. Then Scott released a statement from Terry Probyn.

"All of us are doing very well under the circumstances," she said. "We especially appreciate everyone recognizing that what we need most right now is to be allowed to become a family again, within a zone of privacy and security. We hope that our story focuses attention on all of the children still missing, and on their need to be found. We must keep looking for them. As Jaycee shows, miracles can happen.

"Jaycee, her daughters and I are grateful for everyone's generosity, kindness and good wishes these past few weeks. Thank you."

A few hours later, high-profile attorney Gloria Allred called a press conference in her Los Angeles office, announcing she was now representing Jaycee's natural father, Kenneth Slayton. Allred, who appeared with Slayton, his wife and two daughters, told reporters that her client wanted a private meeting with his daughter or a family representative, as well as a paternity test. Allred warned that if the family refused, her client might take legal action.

Then the emotional sixty-four-year-old Vietnam vet, who had brought two photos of himself and Terry during their affair, read out a prepared statement, begging to be reunited with his daughter and two granddaughters.

"Our hearts are open," he said, "and we long to be a loving, supportive family to her and the children."

Allred then told reporters of Slayton's brief affair with Terry Dugard, whom he knew by her middle name of "Susan." It had happened during a camping vacation in August 1979, and she had become pregnant.

"Ken and Susan lost contact," Allred explained, "and about one year later, a friend told Ken that Susan had given birth to the baby, and that the baby looked like Ken."

Allred said her client wanted nothing from Jaycee, except to love her.

After the press conference, Dugard family representative McGregor Scott was asked about Jaycee taking a paternity test.

"The concept of a paternity test is not even on our radar," he replied, adding that Jaycee and her daughters were instead focusing on a "long list of very real and definite issues."

Scott had now met with the family twice, and was working to get Angel and Starlit birth certificates, as well as establishing a trust fund and a possible book contract for Jaycee.

On Thursday, Scott did the rounds of the network morning shows, saying Jaycee was cooperating with law enforcement and receiving counseling with her daughters. They had also visited a dentist for the first time.

"They are very much functioning," he told ABC's *Good Morning America*. "They are very much a family. Watching the dynamic between the sisters [Angel and Starlit] and their grandmother . . . was just a very, very encouraging scene to observe."

Later, Scott told NBC's *Today* show that Jaycee still had mixed feelings for the Garridos, although she fully understood they had done some "bad and terrible things" to her.

In a further interview with CBS News, Scott said Jaycee would almost certainly testify at the Garridos' upcoming trial, baring the "very, very sordid tale."

"Jaycee will, in all likelihood," he said, "be a witness for the prosecution. She's aware of that and understands that."

* * *

On Tuesday, September 29, Phillip Garrido wrote a letter to KCRA-TV news anchor Walt Gray, complaining Jaycee and her daughters' civil rights had been violated. The handwritten letter, written in pencil, had been mailed to Gray from an El Dorado County jail, where Garrido was still being held.

To whom it may concern my first contact: Walt Gray

J.C. Dugard's free speach [sic] rights are being violated, also she has been repeatedly denied access to have an attorney present during questioning. Over & over she clearly expressed this request from the beginning to the conclusion of questioning.

Her civil rights have been clearly violated. Please consider this request to contact her at your earliest possible date.

Take this to a privet [sic] attorney who will look this matter over for her best interest.

Her two children were witnessing the same treatment for them as well.

Contact J.C. by attorney mail only. Protect her and the children's rights, use wise judgment in this matter please!

Thank you.

On Wednesday, after receiving Phillip Garrido's letter, Walt Gray visited the El Dorado County jail to see Garrido and have him explain the letter. But Garrido refused to see him without his attorney, Susan Gellman, present.

When Gellman saw her client's letter, she said she had already warned him not to contact the media, and would do so again, in even stronger terms.

"There are some very sensitive issues in this case," Gellman told Gray, "and those need to be explored, and those are going to take some time. We are really very early in the case, and at this point, it's just not a good idea for anybody to speak with him."

Since Phillip and Nancy Garrido's arrest, 1554 Walnut Avenue had become a tourist attraction. Throughout the day, cars would pull up alongside the boarded-up house so people could pose for photographs outside it. And angry neighbors had called the police numerous times to clear out the ghouls.

"We have had a lot of people coming through the neighborhood with all this hoopla," complained neighbor Betty Upingco. "They're hanging signs on his house like 'No Mercy for Molesters!' What point is that?"

46

"I'M SO HAPPY TO BE BACK"

On Tuesday, October 13, Oprah Winfrey devoted a show to the Jaycee Lee Dugard story. But instead of bagging the first-ever interview with Jaycee, Oprah had to make do with the two Berkeley campus police heroes, Allyson Jacobs and Lisa Campbell.

The Dugard family had recently signed with high-profile agent Frank Weimann of The Literary Group to globally market books by Terry and Jaycee, as well as the first photographs of Jaycee and her family. Also involved in putting the package together was David Schumacher, a Los Angeles–based tabloid reporter, photographer and private eye who was once married to Tamara Rotolo, the mother of Prince Albert of Monaco's acknowledged illegitimate baby Jazmin Grace. Schumacher is well known in Fleet Street for his high-profile scoops over the years, including tracking down Divine Brown, the prostitute at the center of the Hugh Grant scandal.

The Literary Group soon signed lucrative deals with *People* magazine for North America, *Hello!* for England, and the top-selling French publication *Paris Match* for France.

The previous week, Schumacher spent time on the secret ranch, photographing Jaycee with her mother and sister Shayna and the horses that had become such an important part of their therapy.

The powerful photographs of the twenty-nine-year-old Jaycee were unmistakably her. Although her hair is now brown, her radiant iconic smile remains unchanged. Only one picture shows Jaycee with her daughters, but Angel and Starlit face away from the camera, to protect their identities.

Neither Jaycee nor her mother were interviewed for any of the three magazine photo layouts, which all used separate sets of photographs. But the *People* article said Terry had started writing a book about her experiences.

Then in a carefully orchestrated media strategy, at precisely 7:30 A.M. on Wednesday, October 14, a selection of the first photographs of Jaycee were posted on the *People* website. Simultaneously, Dugard family spokeswoman Erika Price Shulte appeared on all three network morning shows, along with several top *People* executives.

First off was NBC's *Today* show, where Ann Curry asked why Jaycee and her family had finally agreed to the photographs.

"First of all her reunification," said Schulte. "This joyous reunion with her family is going very, very well and they really want to share that joy with the world."

Schulte said the family understood the "intense interest" in the "ordeal" Jaycee had come through.

"This is her way," she said, "of thanking everyone for their support and really letting them know that she's doing okay."

Curry then asked if Jaycee was prepared to testify against the Garridos when it eventually came to trial.

"She's well aware that for that prosecution to move forward," said Schulte, "she needs to cooperate and she's fully prepared to do that. She is cooperating fully and they are very pleased with that cooperation."

Then *People* managing editor Larry Hackett was interviewed by Matt Lauer.

"We've covered this story literally from the very beginning," said Hackett. "We were there in 1991 when Jaycee went missing. Since she's been found we've been in contact with the family, and all those around the family, to talk about this."

Lauer then asked why a *People* magazine staff photographer had not taken the photographs.

"They wanted to have control of their own lives," he explained. "Obviously there are people around them who'd love to have this photograph. They thought, 'We want to control this situation. Let's do it now.' "

Lauer then asked if Jaycee and the family had been paid for the photographs.

"We have bought photographs in the past," Hackett replied cryptically, "like all news organizations. I won't get into the details, but we're very comfortable with the situation and that's the way we did it."

That night Shayna Probyn posted a message on Facebook, with a happy mood.

"For all of you asking," she wrote, "yes the picture on people magazine is really Jaycee. She is so beautiful. I'm really proud of her!"

The following day, the *People* magazine cover, showing a smiling Jaycee accompanied by the quote "I'm Happy to Be Back," was on front pages of newspapers throughout the world. And it went on to become one of *People's* biggest-selling editions of the year, with sales of two million.

Two days after *People* magazine hit the newsstands, Phillip Garrido's defense attorney, Susan Gellman, filed a motion in El Dorado Superior Court, asking the prosecution to detail exactly what kind of evidence it had against her client. The six-page request demanded a list of the witnesses the prosecution intended to call at trial, as well as witness statements, police reports, photographs and records of samples of bodily fluids, hair and other items taken during the investigation.

In late October, Carl Probyn was finally reunited with Jaycee, the first time he had seen her since witnessing her abduction in 1991. In a secret meeting at the secluded ranch, Carl also met Jaycee's daughters Angel and Starlit.

"Jaycee is the one who is helping us all through this ordeal," Probyn told the *National Enquirer*. "She was an amazing little girl, and now she's an amazing young woman and mother."

*   *   *

On Thursday, October 29, Katie Callaway Hall and her husband Jim drove five hundred miles to Placerville, California, to attend an 8:30 A.M. routine hearing at El Dorado Superior Court. They arrived early to get a front row seat, as Katie was determined to get a good view of Phillip Garrido, making certain he saw her too. Also waiting in the public gallery was Ken Slayton, who came with his attorney, Gloria Allred.

Tension mounted with the hearing being delayed for forty-five minutes, as attorneys from both sides met Judge Phimister in his chambers. Finally, at 9:15 A.M., the judge called the court to order, instructing the bailiffs to bring in the two defendants.

As Phillip and Nancy Garrido entered the courtroom in shackles, Katie glared at the man who had been her living nightmare for so many years.

"The same old fears came back," said Katie. "I almost broke down. I was surprised. I did not expect to feel so emotional."

The hearing was over in just two minutes, after Judge Phimister postponed it until December 11, when other concerns raised before him in chambers would then be discussed.

The Garridos were then led out of court and taken back to jail.

Outside the courthouse, Katie told reporters she had made eye contact with Phillip Garrido during the brief time they faced each other in court.

"He looked right at me, and I just glared back," she said. "I wanted to let him know I was there. Maybe I wanted to face my attacker for the first time in all these years."

She then vowed to be a "watchdog," attending as many future hearings as possible, with a mission to ensure Phillip Garrido goes away forever.

"I'm not going to shut up and go away like the parole board told me to twenty-one years ago," she said. "I have my own personal reasons for wanting to see him put away."

When asked if she had any message for Jaycee, Katie thought for a second before saying, "Be strong, and remember that he did something horribly wrong."

A few yards away, Ken Slayton was telling reporters how seeing Phillip Garrido for the first time had angered him.

"I just wanted to rip his face off," said the Vietnam vet. "I'm old school. I'm here in case Jaycee Lee Dugard needs a father."

His attorney, Gloria Allred, told reporters Terry Probyn had not attempted to dispute that her client was Jaycee's father but had still not allowed him to contact her.

The following day, Nancy Garrido's attorney, Gilbert Maines, and his wife, Ann, lunched at the select Cold Springs Golf & Country Club, where they were members. The corpulent lawyer ordered salad and iced tea in the restaurant, before retiring to the Grille Room bar. There he lingered over two Jack Daniel's cocktails as he chatted to a couple of other club members.

Later, it would be claimed that the avuncular sixty-eight-year-old attorney had gotten drunk and started discussing the sensational Garrido case, boasting about writing a book and getting a movie deal after the trial.

On Tuesday, November 3, after receiving a tip-off from two people in the bar claiming to have overheard the attorney's conversation, Judge Douglas Phimister summoned them to his chambers for a closed hearing.

Two days later, the judge summoned Maines to Superior Court for a midday unscheduled hearing, without telling him why. At the secret hearing, Judge Phimister dramatically confronted the attorney with the allegations against him—described in courtroom notes as "confidential evidence"—giving him a few minutes to review them.

Then Judge Phimister removed him as Nancy Garrido's attorney, postponing his order to allow Maines to appeal the decision. The judge then sealed all records of the hearing.

Nancy Garrido, who was present at the hearing, later said she had not understood what was going on.

47

"MISSED CLUES AND OPPORTUNITIES"

At 11:30 A.M., Wednesday, November 4, reporters and TV news crews from around the world assembled in room 1190 of the California State Capitol building in Sacramento. California's inspector general, David Shaw, was holding a press conference about the results of his independent two-month investigation into exactly what had gone wrong with Phillip Garrido's parole supervision.

In his scathing forty-page report, the inspector general found the state parole division, who had supervised Garrido for the past decade, could have found Jaycee Dugard and her two girls years earlier.

"During the ten-year period that California supervised Phillip Garrido," Shaw told the press, "the department often failed to follow its own procedures established to supervise dangerous sex offenders. Furthermore, the department failed to utilize available tools, technology and information that could have potentially led to the discovery of Jaycee Dugard and her children."

The inspector general said it was impossible to know for certain if Jaycee and her daughters could have been discovered earlier, if the parole agents had done their job perfectly.

"However," he said, "our investigation revealed that there were missed clues and opportunities to discover their existence sooner than they did."

Among the litany of mistakes he cited was the California

Parole Department improperly classifying Phillip Garrido as minimum risk in June 1999, when they took over his case from the federal authorities and the state of Nevada.

"It's apparent that this initial mistake," said the inspector general, "set the tone for many mistakes to come."

One major error had been the state department's failure to read Garrido's federal parole file. If agents had done so, they would have learned that a federal parole officer had actually searched the hidden backyard, where Jaycee had been held prisoner.

Shaw said Garrido's federal parole report contained "a wealth of information" about his hidden backyard, including a diagram that documented the real size of the property. On it were also several outbuildings, in the so-called backyard within a backyard.

"In fact we discovered," said Shaw, "that a federal parole agent had actually toured one of the buildings that was behind the fence that concealed the area that Jaycee and her daughters were eventually discovered."

California parole agents also never investigated visible utility lines, leading from the house to the secret compound, which were in place when Jaycee was abducted. And Shaw criticized a parole agent for not attempting to check the identity of a young girl he had seen at the house in June 2008. Instead he had believed Phillip Garrido's claim that she was his niece.

The inspector general said that these mistakes had resulted "in the continued confinement and victimization of Jaycee and her two daughters."

Shaw also revealed that the state parole department only properly supervised Phillip Garrido twelve out of 123 months, a stunning 90 percent failure rate. During one thirteen-month period, parole officers never visited Garrido's home a single time.

The parole department also failed to use the available information gathered from the ankle bracelet, which had been fitted on Garrido in April 2008 and updated the following year.

"In the GPS monitoring system that the department used until June of 2009," said Shaw, "parole agents established a time zone surrounding Garrido's house and programmed it to send an alert if Garrido left his residence at night between midnight and 7:00 A.M. System records show that between April 2008 and June 2009, parole agents received fourteen alerts that Garrido had left his residence after the curfew. Disappointingly parole agents ignored each of these alerts."

The inspector general also criticized the department for ignoring other alerts in the thirty-two-day period that the new GPS system was in use until Garrido's arrest on August 26, 2009.

"System records show," said Shaw, "that the parole agents acknowledged the first three, but took no action on any of them. Parole agents also failed to establish a restricted travel zone as required as a condition of his parole, which would have alerted them that within a thirty-two-day period Garrido went outside of his twenty-five-mile zone seven different times."

He said if the parole agents had been doing their job properly, the GPS signals would have told them that Garrido was spending a lot of time in the secret backyard compound. And between April 2008 and June 2009, there were 335 instances of the GPS monitor losing signal.

"Parole agents could have also used this information to find out where he spent his time," said Shaw, "as it can be keyed to time of day. That was almost a nightly occurrence. System records show that parole agents ignored 276 of these alerts altogether. Parole agents acknowledged fifty-nine of the alerts, but apparently took no action.

"Additionally, we identified that there were more significant abnormalities in his GPS information between July twenty-third of 2009 and August twenty-third of 2009. Almost every night Garrido's GPS signal was lost for significant periods of time—typically nine hours. And agents took no action."

The inspector general also blamed parole agent Eddie Santos, whom he did not name, for the way he handled the case after being contacted by Berkeley campus police.

"The parole agent was told that the two girls," stated the

inspector general's report, "were calling Garrido 'daddy' at UC Berkeley, a statement that the parole agent knew to be untrue. However, the parole agent apparently accepted Garrido's story that the two children belonged to his brother."

The inspector general's report also questioned why Santos had then driven Garrido home and released him, rather than contacting his brother to verify if the girls were his.

"Given Garrido's violent past," the report continued, "and his increasingly bizarre behavior as documented by the parole agent and observed by the UC Berkeley police officer, it is not unreasonable to fear that the parole agent's failure to further investigate that night may have placed Garrido's three captives in greater danger or prompted Garrido to flee."

Then Mathew Cate, the secretary of the California Department of Corrections and Rehabilitation, took the podium.

"We agree that serious errors were made over the last ten years," he said. "We obviously deeply regret any error that could have possibly resulted in the victims living under these conditions for even one additional day."

Secretary Cate said that Governor Schwarzenegger's proposed bill of parole reform, to become law on January 1, 2010, would prevent many of these mistakes ever happening again.

"At the end of the day," Cate said, "[we] have a responsibility to protect the public from this kind of abject evil."

As the inspector general's damning report was being released on his official website, the Dugard family's attorney McGregor Scott issued a short statement.

"Ms. Dugard is fully committed to working with law enforcement to ensure Mr. Garrido is held accountable for his crimes."

Two weeks later, parole agent Eddie Santos was transferred from Concord to another parole office after threats were made to him and his family. California Corrections Department spokesman Gordon Hinkle said Santos's children had been taken out of school for their own safety.

"He had received serious threats to his personal safety," Hinkle told the *Contra Costa Times*. "There were threats of several kinds."

A spokesman for the parole agents' union emphasized that the transfer, to an unnamed office, was not disciplinary.

On November 10, El Dorado Superior Court received a letter from Gilbert Maines marked "Confidential Eyes Only Hon. Judge D. Phimister." The following day the judge appointed defense attorney Stephen Tapson as Nancy Garrido's interim attorney, until Maines's appeal could be heard. In the meantime he gave Tapson permission to read transcripts of the allegations against his predecessor, although he could not make copies.

He also ordered El Dorado County jail to allow Tapson access to Nancy Garrido.

"[This] is the most bizarre case I've been involved in umpteen years," Tapson told *The Sacramento Bee*. "Technically, I guess, she has two lawyers."

A few weeks later the *National Enquirer* ran a front-page story entitled "Jaycee Suicide Shock! The Battle to Save Her Life." Inside the magazine, the largely speculative story claimed that behind her "cheery public smile" Jaycee Lee Dugard had the potential to become suicidal.

"While her family insists she's doing well after 18 years of sexual slavery," it stated, "experts warn Jaycee is facing severe psychological problems that could drive her to drug and alcohol abuse, or even suicide."

Quoting experts, the story warned that depression, paranoia and terrifying flashbacks to her time with "the monster" Phillip Garrido could stop her ever being happy in a loving relationship.

Dr. Frederick Bemak, a professor at George Mason University and an expert in child and sexual trafficking, told the *Enquirer* that Jaycee and her family were experiencing a "typical honeymoon period" after her liberation from the Garridos. He warned that when the euphoria passed, Jaycee would have to confront the cruel reality of what had happened to her and her daughters.

"Now that reality is setting in," said Dr. Bemak, "suicide and depression are absolutely reasonable."

A few days later, Shayna Probyn posted the family's reaction to the article on her MySpace page.

"Disgusted by the news articles lately. We are just trying to lay low and enjoy being a family. Looking 4ward 2 the most thankful Thanksgiving of all! MMMM. Mood hungry ☺"

48

"A MASTER MANIPULATOR"

On Thursday, November 12, Walt Gray of KCRA-TV received a bizarre letter of apology from Phillip Garrido, handwritten on yellow legal paper.

"First off," wrote Garrido, "I would like to apologize to every human being for what has taken place. People all over the world are hearing testimony that through the spirit of Christ a mental process took place ending a sexual problem believed to be impossible."

After taking legal advice, KCRA-TV decided not to release any more of his letter at that time.

Defense attorney Susan Gellman said the letter called into question her client's mental competency.

"Mr. Garrido is expressing genuine remorse," she told KCRA-TV. "He would like people to consider the fact that he's a changed man and his story is best told all at one time, instead of in pieces."

The public defender also revealed that she was in the process of establishing whether Phillip Garrido was mentally fit to stand trial.

"He presents obvious issues," she said, "concerning whether or not he is competent to be a defendant, and we are looking into that."

Prosecutor Vern Pierson strongly disagreed, calling Garrido "a master manipulator." This new letter, he said, was just his latest attempt to manipulate the system, as he had done so many times in the past. And Pierson vowed to see that Garrido was punished to the fullest extent of the law.

"We see this as another example of his attempt to control the situation around him and his prior victims," said the district attorney. "These recent statements are eerily similar to what Mr. Garrido told the judge who sentenced him in 1977, and to the parole board when he duped them into releasing him from prison, after only serving eleven years of a fifty-year federal sentence and five-to-life Nevada State sentence."

Five days later, a low-budget adult filmmaker named Shane Ryan announced plans for a movie about the Jaycee Dugard story, to start shooting in December. Its working title was *Abducted Girl: An American Sex Slave*, but the director of straight-to-DVD movies such as *Amateur Porn Star Killer, Sex Kids Party* and "*Warning!!! Pedophile Released*" denied that his film would be exploitive.

"We want to capture how sad this story is," Ryan explained. "But also how interesting. We're trying to figure out a way to do it so it's not exploitive."

Angrily reacting in a statement, the Dugard family's new high-powered public relations spokeswoman Nancy Seltzer branded the plan "exploitive, hurtful and breathtakingly unkind."

Seltzer, whose other clients include Whitney Houston and Garth Brooks, said Jaycee and her family should decide if and when a movie will be made about her life.

November 19, 2009, marked the twenty-first anniversary of Michaela Garecht's abduction. And to mark the sad occasion, a crowd of family, friends and supporters gathered outside the Hayward supermarket where she had been snatched.

Sharon Murch, who had started writing letters to her lost daughter on her blog after Jaycee Dugard was found, addressed the large crowd.

"I don't believe in coincidences," she said. "All this must be for some purpose."

Sharon said everything had changed for her after Jaycee's

reappearance, giving her and so many other parents of abducted children fresh hope.

"As more and more information came out," she said, "I started to understand how [Michaela] might be somewhere and have the ability to free herself . . . that she's with someone she cares to protect, that she doesn't want to reveal herself."

A few days before the poignant anniversary, Murch posted this message for her daughter on her blog, thewonderingheart. blogspot.com.

"You can write to me without telling me where you are or who you are with. If you did, I would want to trace your e-mail address and run to where you are, throw my arms around you and take you home with me. But if it would mean the difference between hearing from you and not, I would refrain from doing that. I long to hold you in my arms. But at the very least if you are reading my words, talk to me please."

One week later, Terry and Shayna Probyn sat down with Jaycee for their first Thanksgiving together in eighteen years. It was a dream come true for Terry, as she played with her granddaughters Angel and Starlit, giving thanks for their true miracle.

As they were waiting to eat a turkey meal with all the trimmings, Shayna posted a mood hungry ☺ message on her MySpace page: "Apparently 22 lb turkeys take a really long time to cook. Dinner pushed to 3 instead of noon so we are all sitting around laughing & eating the pies first. YUMM!"

The night before Thanksgiving, the Third District Court of Appeals in Sacramento blocked Judge Phimister's order removing Gilbert Maines as Nancy Garrido's attorney. Late Wednesday evening, the appeals court ordered Judge Phimister to make available transcripts of the secret testimony accusing Maines of misconduct.

Judge Phimister had already scheduled a hearing the following Monday when he would decide whether to execute his previous order to remove Maines, but the appeals court now said it would take the final decision.

The defense attorney, who had strenuously denied ever discussing the Jaycee Dugard case over drinks at his golf club, now had two sworn declarations to back him up. Bartender Eduardo Bartolome, who had poured the drinks that Friday afternoon, wrote that Maines had never appeared drunk and the alleged conversation had never taken place.

In a separate declaration, club member Sam Cooper claimed he and Maines had discussed their golf games in the bar, and he had never become "intoxicated, loud, or obnoxious." Cooper said that if other club members ever asked about the Garrido case, the attorney refused to discuss it.

"There are some members who are quite vocal," wrote Cooper, "about the fact that they don't think people like these defendants deserve to be represented and that anyone taking on their defense are of questionable ethical or moral standards. When these statements are made directly to Gil he sometimes responds. Sometimes with a rather pointed and crude reply, concerning their lack of understanding of the Constitution or the law or something regarding the location of their heads. He comes to the club to get away from all this," he said.

In a new filing, Maines denied ever seeking the rights to Nancy Garrido's story, or discussing book opportunities or any "other exploitation" of her life story with anyone. And he accused Judge Phimister of summoning him to a private meeting and then ambushing with transcripts of the alleged accusations, made two days before in a secret hearing.

The defense attorney maintained that there was absolutely no "actual or potential conflict of interest" with him defending Nancy Garrido, and his removal would "seriously impair her defense."

He also included a sworn declaration by Nancy Garrido, saying she "did not really understand what was going on" at the hearing where Judge Phimister removed Maines as her lawyer.

"I have a relationship with Mr. Maines," she wrote in a declaration, "and I know and trust him."

Nancy added that after meeting with her interim attorney,

Stephen Tapson, she wanted Maines to remain her attorney, regardless of whether he had or had not a conflict of interest.

At the next El Dorado Superior Court hearing on Friday, December 11, Nancy Garrido was represented by the two defense attorneys, Gilbert Maines and Stephen Tapson. Also adding to the drama were Katie Callaway Hall and Ken Slayton, with his attorney, Gloria Allred, who all sat in the public gallery.

When Phillip Garrido was brought into court in a red jailhouse jumpsuit and shackles, there was an audible gasp. He now had a crew cut and had visibly lost weight since his last appearance. Nancy also appeared much thinner, sitting in the jury box with Tapson, while Maines hovered close by.

When Judge Phimister asked who was representing Nancy Garrido, both defense lawyers replied that they were. The judge then said he had received two new sets of allegations against Maines, which he ordered sealed.

"I don't want anything to prejudice this case, potentially," the judge explained.

He then scheduled the next hearing for January 21, by which time the appeals court would have decided whether Maines should defend Nancy Garrido.

Outside the courtroom, a reporter asked Maines whether the allegations about him discussing the case were true.

"That's enough of that," snapped the lawyer. "I never get drunk or obnoxious and I never discuss the case when I'm drinking."

Once again, TV crews and reporters descended on Katie Callaway Hall and Ken Slayton.

"I just want to make my presence known," she declared as her husband Jim stood next to her. "Any day I see that man in shackles is a good day for me."

And Jaycee's natural father, Ken Slayton, wearing a black leather jacket over a sweater with an American flag, repeated that he wanted to meet Jaycee as soon as possible.

"I don't know what's going on," he said, "but I see there's no man out there, and I think they need a man. And I'm a good man."

* * *

Four days later, the Third District Court of Appeals ordered Judge Phimister to reinstate Gilbert Maines as Nancy Garrido's lawyer, or explain exactly why he had been removed.

"We have carefully examined the record," wrote Presiding Justice Arthur G. Scotland in his ruling, "including the sealed transcripts of two proceedings and other material placed under seal."

Justice Scotland then ruled that the evidence Judge Phimister had used to remove Maines from the case did not support the removal. And he ordered the judge to reinstate Maines as Nancy Garrido's attorney by December 24, or file additional papers by January 5 to remove him.

"It's an early Christmas present," Maines told *The Sacramento Bee*. "I had high hopes of prevailing in this matter. I have a lot of respect for Judge Phimister. I don't know what drove this. I believe he overreacted to chatter."

As Christmas approached, Jaycee Lee Dugard was named one of *People* magazine's twenty-five most intriguing people of 2009. And her iconic childhood picture shared the front page with Barack and Michelle Obama, Brad Pitt and Angelina Jolie and Sarah Palin.

Jaycee had also now received her official California identification card, and Angel and Starlit their birth certificates. On them, the girls surnames are listed as "Dugard," with Angel's birth date listed as August 1994 and Starlit—who has been renamed "Gabriella"—as November 1997. The girls' father is listed as "Phillip Garrido" and mother "Jaycee Lee Dugard," with their place of birth "Walnut Avenue, Antioch."

On Christmas Day, Jaycee, her mother Terry and half-sister Shayna celebrated their first Yuletide together in eighteen years. They all decorated Christmas cookies, breaking out into fits of laughter. Jaycee clowned around in a Santa hat with Shayna, while the two sisters listened as their mother told them the cookie recipe she used. When Jaycee made a mistake with her cookie, everyone burst into laughter.

"I've never gotten to decorate a cookie before," said Jaycee.

Later that night, the three gathered by a roaring fireplace, beneath their Christmas stockings.

"It's a dream come true for me to have both my girls be here with me," said Terry in a family home movie shot that day. "I'm so thankful for the precious moments that we have together. It seems like I've waited an eternity for this."

49

"MR. GARRIDO DOES NOT HARBOR
ANY ILL WILL"

On Thursday, January 7, Gilbert Maines was finally removed from the case, after the Third District Court of Appeals ruled against him. The court had considered five new sealed pieces of evidence against him, including further testimony from a police officer and other new witnesses.

"This comes as a complete surprise to me," the attorney said, after learning he would no longer be representing Nancy Garrido. "They generally said I was talking out of school . . . first off there's not a gag order. And even assuming I did talk—and I don't admit I did—if there's something wrong with that, it's up to my client to say."

Two weeks later, Maines filed his fourth appeal to be reinstated, this time on the grounds that a judge should not remove an appointed counsel against the wishes of a defendant.

"I don't have a choice," he told *Sacramento Bee* reporter Stan Stanton. "Can the court remove appointed counsel at any time it wants to for any reason it wants? My client says she doesn't see that I've done anything wrong, and she wants her lawyer back."

At the next El Dorado Superior Court hearing on January 21, Judge Douglas Phimister formally removed Gilbert Maines, replacing him with Stephen Tapson. The judge noted Nancy Garrido's affidavit asking that Maines remain her lawyer, saying that he could remove an attorney if he considered it in the defendant's best interest.

"This case has been sidetracked by the issues of counsel," declared the judge. "And that could adversely affect the rights of the defendants."

Phillip and Nancy Garrido both attended the short hearing, and Tapson immediately asked for his client to be granted bail. Judge Phimister agreed, fixing Nancy's bail at $20 million, saying he considered her a danger to the community and a flight risk.

After the court hearing, Tapson told reporters that Nancy wanted to send a message through the media to Jaycee and her daughters.

"Mrs. Garrido asked me to tell Jaycee and the kids," said Tapson, "she really misses them. She would obviously love to see them. I'm assuming the forces of evil won't allow that to happen. I've an old briefcase with tears on it."

McGregor Scott, who attended the hearing on Jaycee's behalf, refused to comment about Nancy Garrido's message.

And Gilbert Maines told reporters that he planned to appeal the latest ruling against him. The following morning, twenty agents from the state Franchise Tax Board arrived at Maines's home with a search warrant, seeking evidence of nonpayment of state taxes. They then searched his home, removing computer files and his laptop, while he stood in his bathrobe outside in the rain.

"I've been doing my taxes the same for thirty-five years," he told a TV reporter. "Sometimes I skip a few years and then pay them all at once."

A few days later, he was fired by El Dorado County from his $80,000-a-year position defending clients who can't get a public defender.

"God has a plan," he said. "And his timing is perfect."

At the end of January, the Dugard family quietly took the first steps to sue the state of California for "various lapses" the state parole agents had made with Phillip Garrido. Jaycee, Terry and the two girls each filed claim forms against the California Department of Corrections and Rehabilitation for "psychological and emotional injury."

Family spokeswoman Nancy Seltzer said the family had not decided whether or not they would formally file a lawsuit.

"We are simply preserving Jaycee Dugard's right to file a lawsuit at a later date," she explained, "if that is something she decides is in her family's best interest."

Under the law, victims have six months to file for personal injury against the state, from the time of the incident. The forms filed by the family did not specify an exact dollar amount, except that it exceeded $25,000.

On Thursday, February 4, Phillip Garrido's attorney, Susan Gellman, filed two motions—one to allow him visitation rights with Nancy, and the other to find out where Jaycee and his daughters were now living. The first motion described Phillip as the patriarch of a close-knit all-American family.

"The children were raised as the children of Nancy and Phillip Garrido," it read, "and all five held themselves out to be a family. They took vacations together; they went to the library together; they ran a family business together. The children were home schooled. They kept pets and had a garden. They took care of an ailing family member together. They had special names for each other.

"All of this ended on the day that Phillip and Nancy Garrido was [sic] arrested."

The defense motion asked Judge Phimister to grant the Garridos visitation rights at the Placerville Jail, as they needed to make numerous "family decisions" to prepare their defenses.

"[These] will strongly impact the people they have known and treated as family for the last eleven years," read the motion. "While the underlying accusations are serious, troubling and sad, there can be no doubt that Mr. and Mrs. Garrido acted as parents to two children and raised them for many years, and the decisions they make regarding their course of action in this case will affect those children for many years to come."

Nancy Garrido's new attorney, Stephen Tapson, told Fox News that El Dorado County jail officials had refused to allow the married couple to meet, even though they were being housed in the same facility.

"If one of them were out on bail," he explained, "they could visit each other in jail, just to say hello."

He also revealed that Phillip's attorney had now filed papers demanding prosecutors reveal to the defense where Jaycee was then living. Gellman also wanted to know if Jaycee has her own lawyer the defense attorneys can communicate with, to help them prepare his case.

"We would love to talk to her, obviously," said Tapson, "and they are not telling us where she is and she doesn't have a lawyer that we know of."

The following morning, it was reported that Jaycee Dugard and her family had secretly moved to a safe house, not far from Walnut Avenue, Antioch. Associate Pastor Mari Hanes of the East Bay Fellowship in Danville, California—which has a history of helping victims of human trafficking—claimed her church had set up a fund, paying the $2,500-per-month rent on the new house.

In an interview with the *Contra Costa Times,* Haines said that the money the family had so far received from media interviews and photographs was not enough to pay for their housing and long-term counseling.

"People think that once your name is out there," said the pastor, "you get paid. But unless you have attorneys to broker a deal for you, that's not really the case."

Haines said a church member, who had been counseling the Dugard family, first brought their financial plight to her attention.

"[He] just said, 'Let's be praying for them,'" said Haines, "'It's as bad a situation as we've seen.'"

Then the church had started a fund, so far raising about $13,000 of cash and donated jewelry, now being sold on behalf of the family.

"We're happy to help out for such a good cause," said jewelry store owner Mark Kahn. "You can't help but feel for these girls and what they have gone through."

The next day, after the story appeared in the *Contra Costa*

Times, a Dugard family representative called Pastor Haines, asking her to stop talking to the press. The pastor then immediately refuted the story, claiming to have been misquoted.

"I never told anyone Jaycee and her daughters lived in a safe house near Antioch," she told a local television station. "All I've been told is law enforcement found her a safe home somewhere in central California. The church has been financially assisting Jaycee with rent by putting money into the 'Jaycee Dugard Trust Fund.' Everyone's hearts were touched and we wanted to give our support."

Later Jaycee's mother would speak out, denying any relationship with the East Bay Fellowship Church.

"I feel like I need to set the record straight," said Terry Probyn. "We did accept financial support from an undisclosed benefactor and have no affiliation to any church."

On February 11, El Dorado district attorney Vern Pierson filed the first of two motions, revealing that since his arrest Phillip Garrido had been trying to contact Jaycee Dugard (referred to as Jane Doe) and regain his control over her.

"Defendant Phillip Garrido's control over Jane Doe was well planned and powerful," read the motion. "He is still attempting to exert that control. It is time for the court to put an end to those attempts to manipulate and control his victims and the court system."

In one motion, Pierson revealed that Jaycee had kept a journal during her captivity, quoting three short passages from it, showing the terrible mental power her captor had over her.

"How can I ever tell him that I want to be free," read one passage, written when she was twenty-three. "Free to come and go as I please. Free to say I have a family. FREE."

Pierson also revealed that Jaycee had told prosecutors that Garrido, whom he called "a master manipulator," had instructed Jaycee that if he was ever arrested, she should maintain contact with him through attorneys. The DA pointed out how Phillip Garrido's last words to her at the parole office, before she had revealed her true identity, were to get a lawyer.

"After Defendant Phillip Garrido is arrested," stated the motion, "he attempts numerous times to communicate with the media. In one letter sent in September 2009, [he] attempts to assert Jane Doe's right to an attorney. In another letter, he apologized to 'every human being for what has taken place.'"

Pierson then noted how the wily defendant had mentioned contacting Jaycee in the September 2009 letter "by attorney mail only."

"It is clear, once again," stated the motion, "that Defendant Phillip Garrido is very familiar with the legal system and wants to use the attorney-client privilege to conceal his attempted communications to the victim in this case."

The motion also revealed that on January 28, Phillip Garrido had actually sent Jaycee a letter through his defense attorney.

"Mr. Garrido has asked me to convey," it read, "that he does not harbor any ill will toward [Jaycee] or the children and loves them very much."

When Jaycee Dugard saw the letter, she immediately interpreted the phrase "no ill will" to mean that she wasn't following the prearranged plan.

"[Jaycee] explained," said the motion, "'the plan' dictated that should Mr. Garrido ever be arrested, they were to 'keep in communication through lawyers.' [Jaycee] further indicated her belief that the referral by her former captor and rapist to not harbor ill will, was 'another way of manipulating' her.

"It is clear that the defendant is attempting to use the media and his own attorneys to continue to control [her]."

Pierson wrote that Jaycee had "emphatically stated" that she did not want any contact with the Garridos or their attorneys.

"[She] has further stated," said Pierson, "that she wants our office to enforce her constitutional rights and protect her privacy."

Then he asked Judge Phimister to issue a protective order to prevent any contact with Phillip and Nancy Garrido whatsoever.

A week later, DA Vern Pierson filed a second motion, arguing against Phillip and Nancy Garrido's demands to visit each other. He wrote that longstanding county jail regulations did not allow personal visitations between inmates, particularly if they are co-defendants in a pending criminal case.

"The only justification offered by the Garrido defendants for their extraordinary request to visit with each other," stated the motion, "is that they need to make 'family decisions.' The pseudo-family the Garridos want to discuss was created by the kidnap, false imprisonment and multiple rapes of a young girl, producing two children.

"While it may be argued that a restoration of family values would improve the quality of American life in general, the assertion of family rights in a case where the 'family' was the product of 29 alleged felonies is astonishing."

On Wednesday, February 24—two days before the next scheduled El Dorado Superior Court hearing—public defender Susan Gellman filed a rebuttal motion, claiming her client was suffering from serious mental illness. She claimed that by labeling Phillip Garrido as a "master manipulator," the DA was making the same mistakes that the parole authorities had.

"It appears that Phillip Garrido has been hearing the voices of angels for years," she wrote. "[Jaycee Dugard] spoke to investigators about his self described ability to understand the voices of angels, after Mr. Garrido was arrested. One of the children disclosed this as well, describing how the voices would keep him up at night, and how the angels lived underground and spoke to him from this location."

Gellman cited Garrido's "Origin of Schizophrenia Revealed" manifesto, and his giving it to the FBI two days before his arrest, as proof of his "serious mental illness."

The defense motion appeared to set the stage for a mental health defense by Garrido, as he had done more than thirty years earlier in Nevada.

"Mr. Garrido believes he has a story of transformation to be told," said Gellman. "Mr. Garrido wrongly believes that [Jaycee] is part of his transformation and his disclosure. Mr. Garrido believes that he and [Jaycee] once had a plan to launch a website wherein Mr. Garrido's ability to speak to angels would be revealed to mankind. He remains confused as to why this has not happened. These are not factors indicating manipulation but something else entirely. They indicate thinking that is delusional, but very real to Mr. Garrido.

"They are not acts of harassment or intimidation or attempt [*sic*] to dissuade a witness. They are demonstrations of mental illness."

At a hearing on February 26, Judge Douglas Phimister agreed to allow Nancy Garrido to place two five-minute telephone calls to her husband over the next two weeks. His ruling came over the objection of DA Vern Pierson and El Dorado County undersheriff Fred Kollar, who vehemently opposed any contact. Both the Garridos attended the hearing.

"These are two people who are potentially facing the rest of their lives in prison," said the judge. "To allow them ten minutes to talk to each other is not unreasonable."

He then scheduled another hearing on April 15, to decide what further communication between the co-defendants to allow. And he also authorized the monitoring and recording of their telephone calls, although he would only make it available to the prosecution if the Garridos did anything illegal.

"We may expand the rights of the defendants," he said. "But if there's a problem with the first phone call, then that will be that."

Judge Phimister also refused to reveal Jaycee Dugard's address or phone number to the defense. But he appointed two new attorneys to represent her daughters, saying they would probably be witnesses at the trial and should have a say about being contacted by the Garridos' attorneys.

"It's been a while," said the judge, "but having had three teenage children, I know they don't always follow the lead of their mother."

Once again sitting in the public gallery was Katie Callaway Hall, who later told a reporter that she might be called as a witness at Phillip Garrido's trial, under a victims' rights law that allows past victims to testify.

After the hearing, Nancy Garrido's attorney, Stephen Tapson, said his client was delighted when she learned she could talk to her husband for the first time since their arrest almost six months earlier.

"She loves him," said Tapson. "She almost burst into tears."

Epilogue

On Friday, March 5, Jaycee Lee Dugard spoke for the first time publicly, in a home movie sold to ABC-TV. In an exclusive deal—reported to have been worth as much as $200,000 to the Dugard family—the ABC network heavily featured snippets of the video on that day's *Good Morning America*, *20/20*, and *Nightline*.

The moving home video portrayed a family healing together. Jaycee, Terry and Shayna were shown celebrating Christmas, baking cookies and laughing. In another scene they rode horses on a ranch, as part of their therapy.

"Hi, I'm Jaycee," she said with a big smile. "I want to thank you for your support. It's been a long haul but I'm getting there."

Now a brunette, Jaycee was filmed on a swing, wearing a pink baseball cap, jeans and a black shirt, feeding her two spaniels. But her two daughters were not featured at all in the video, which also contained a personal plea by Terry Probyn for privacy.

"It is my desire to share our miracle with the world," Terry said. "But it has to be done on our terms. Please give us the time we need to heal as a family, without the prying eyes of the photographers and the press. We released this video so you can see that we're happy and well, and when we have more to share we will. As a mother I am pleading for our privacy in this very public story."

On July 1, 2010, California Governor Arnold Schwarzenegger approved a $20 million settlement to Jaycee Dugard and her family. The huge payment was recommended by the state Department of Justice. Although noting in an analysis that the California Corrections Department had denied the allegations against it and that California has legal immunity against such claims, Jaycee's case, they acknowledged, "had a unique and tragic character."

A week later, it was revealed that after her discovery Jaycee had told investigators that parole agents had actually spoken to her and her daughter Angel during their captivity. The agents failed, however, to investigate their exact relationship to Phillip Garrido.

Author's Note

At the time this book went to press, the 29-count criminal complaint against Phillip and Nancy Garrido remains pending and unresolved. Although both defendants deny all charges, there is speculation of a possible insanity defense by Phillip. Separately represented, the details of Nancy's legal defense are not yet known.

In the intense media frenzy that accompanied Jaycee's release from her 18-year captivity, there have been many unsubstantiated media claims. So far there is nothing to support speculation as to either of Jaycee's daughters ever being sexually abused anywhere, and Jaycee has always denied it. Additionally, there is no evidence to connect Jaycee or her children to orgies or sex parties, allegedly observed by some neighbors on the Garrido property.